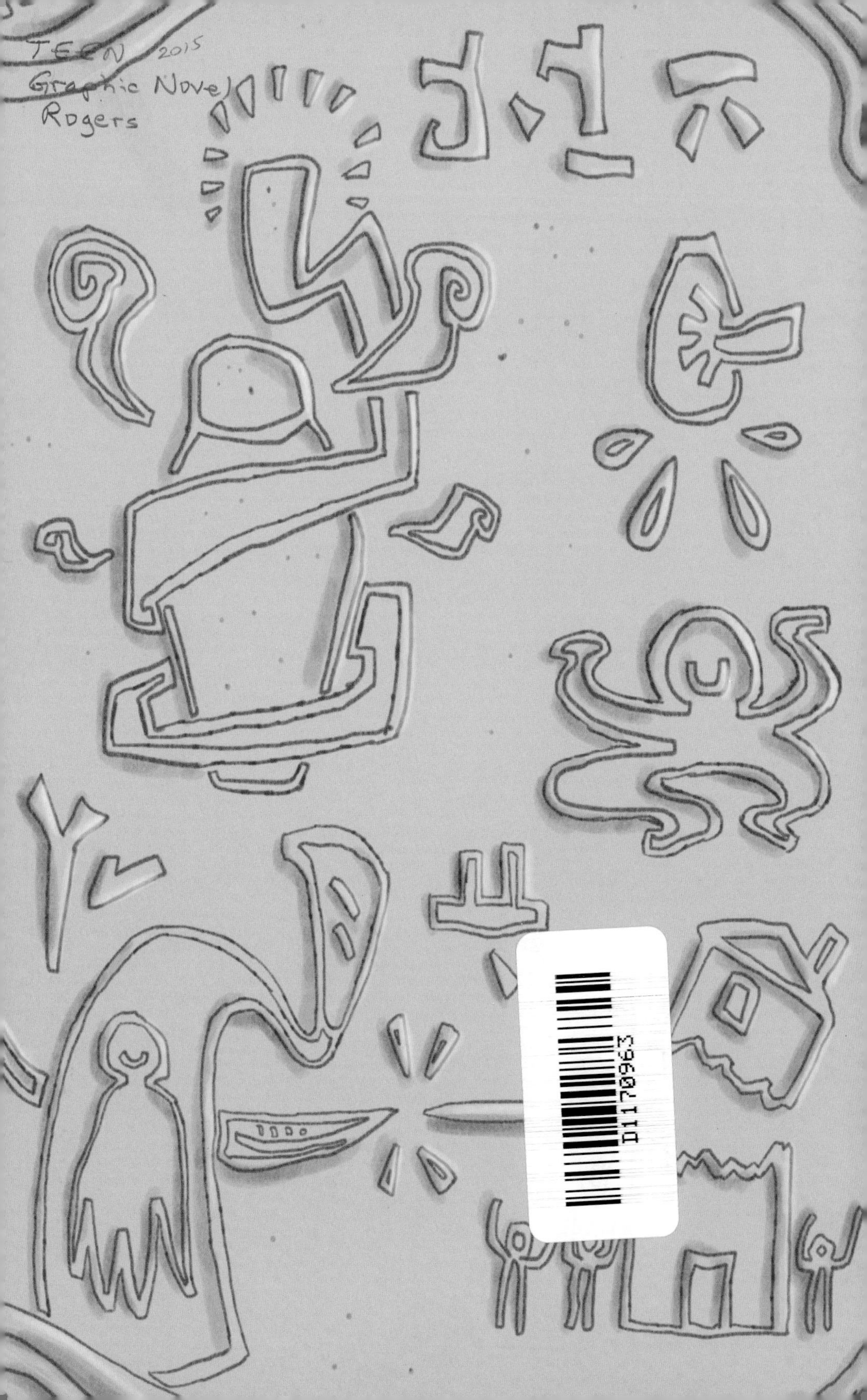

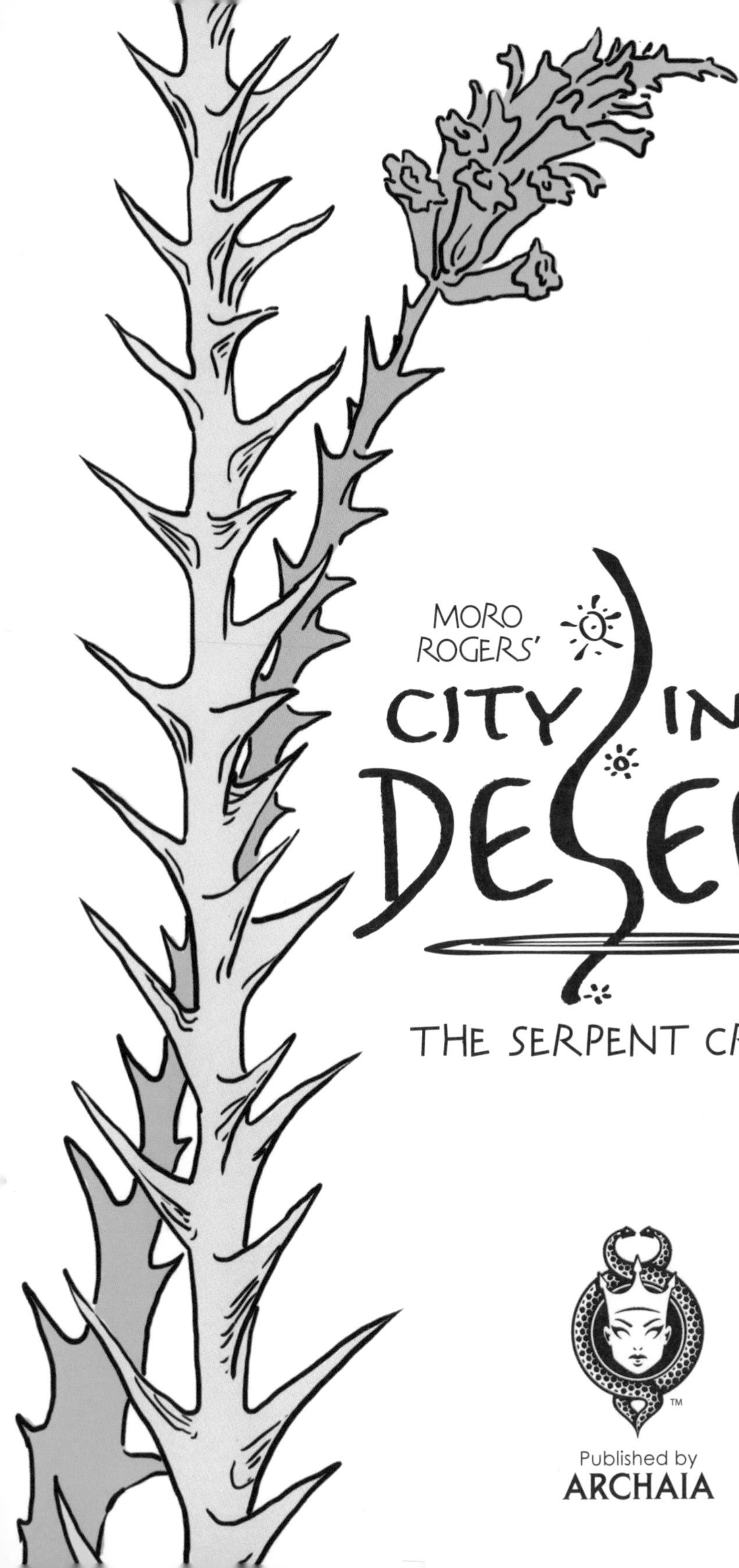

MORO ROGERS'

# CITY IN THE DESERT™

## THE SERPENT CROWN


Published by
ARCHAIA

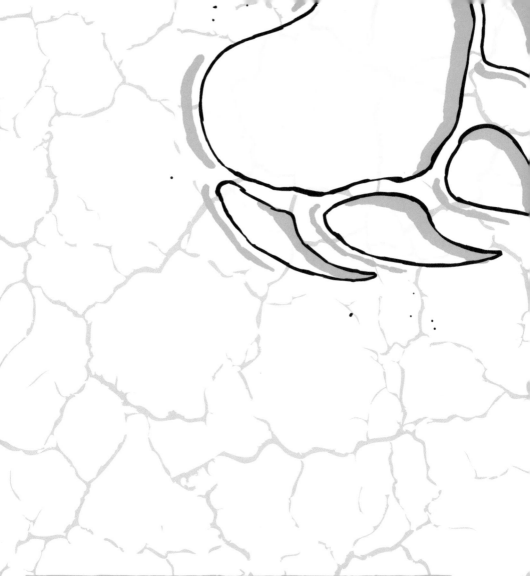

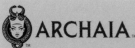

Published by **Archaia**
A Division of **Boom Entertainment, Inc.**
WWW.**ARCHAIA**.COM

BOOM! Studios
5670 Wilshire Boulevard, Suite 450
Los Angeles, California 90036-5679

**ROSS RICHIE** CEO & Founder • **JACK CUMMINS** President • **MARK SMYLIE** Chief Creative Officer • **MATT GAGNON** Editor-in-Chief
**FILIP SABLIK** VP of Publishing & Marketing • **STEPHEN CHRISTY** VP of Development • **LANCE KREITER** VP of Licensing & Merchandising
**PHIL BARBARO** VP of Finance • **BRYCE CARLSON** Managing Editor • **MEL CAYLO** Marketing Manager • **SCOTT NEWMAN** Production Design Manager
**IRENE BRADISH** Operations Manager • **DAFNA PLEBAN** Editor • **SHANNON WATTERS** Editor • **ERIC HARBURN** Editor • **REBECCA TAYLOR** Editor
**CHRIS ROSA** Assistant Editor • **ALEX GALER** Assistant Editor • **WHITNEY LEOPARD** Assistant Editor • **JASMINE AMIRI** Assistant Editor
**CAMERON CHITTOCK** Assistant Editor • **HANNAH NANCE PARTLOW** Production Designer • **DEVIN FUNCHES** E-Commerce & Inventory Coordinator
**BRIANNA HART** Executive Assistant • **AARON FERRARA** Operations Assistant • **JOSÉ MEZA** Sales Assistant • **ELIZABETH LOUGHRIDGE** Accounting Assistant

**CITY IN THE DESERT: THE SERPENT CROWN**, Original Graphic Novel Hardcover, March 2014.

FIRST PRINTING    10 9 8 7 6 5 4 3 2 1    ISBN-13: 978-1-60886-408-9    eISBN: 978-1-61398-262-4

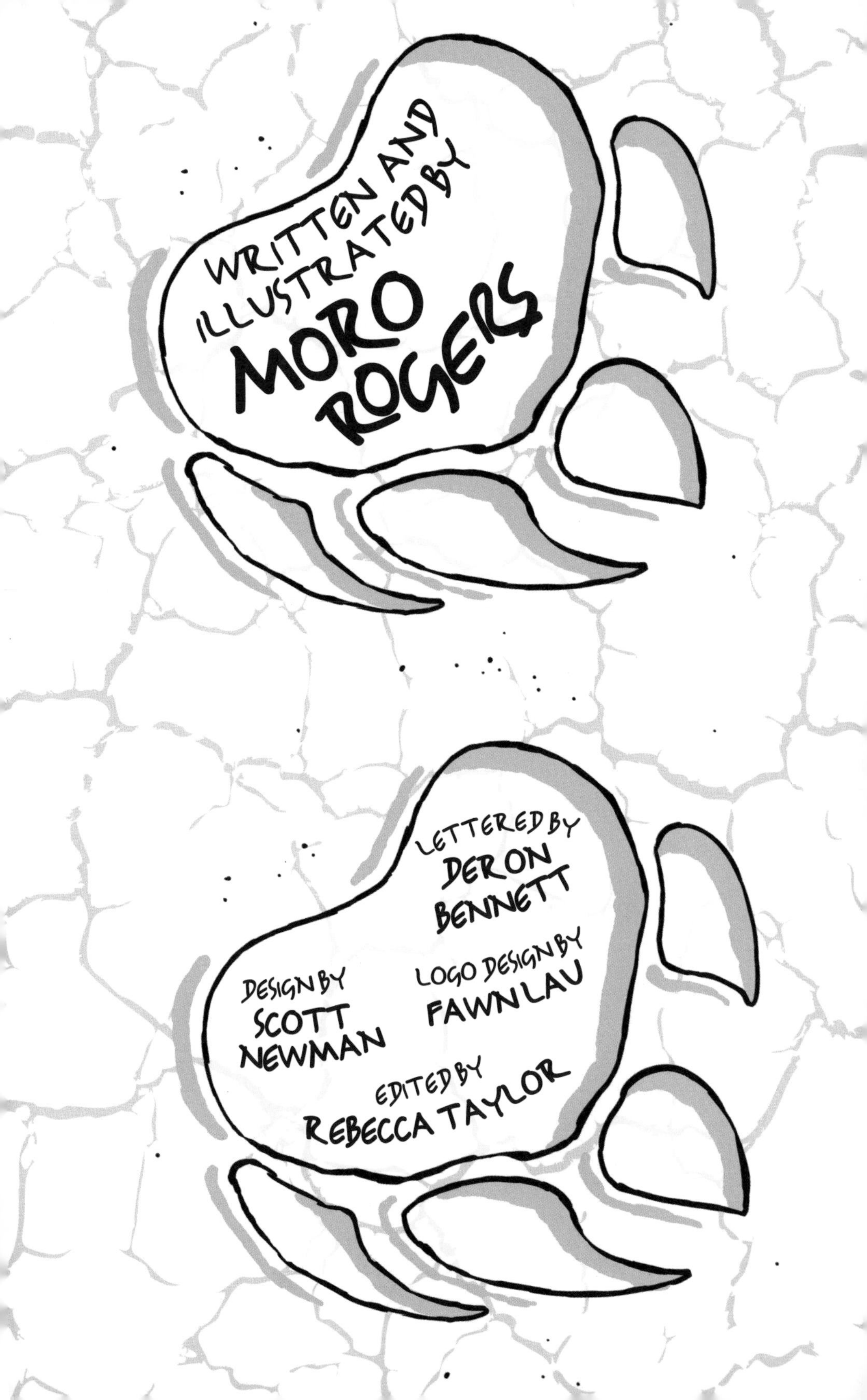
WRITTEN AND
ILLUSTRATED BY
MORO ROGERS
LETTERED BY
DERON BENNETT
DESIGN BY
SCOTT NEWMAN
LOGO DESIGN BY
FAWN LAU
EDITED BY
REBECCA TAYLOR

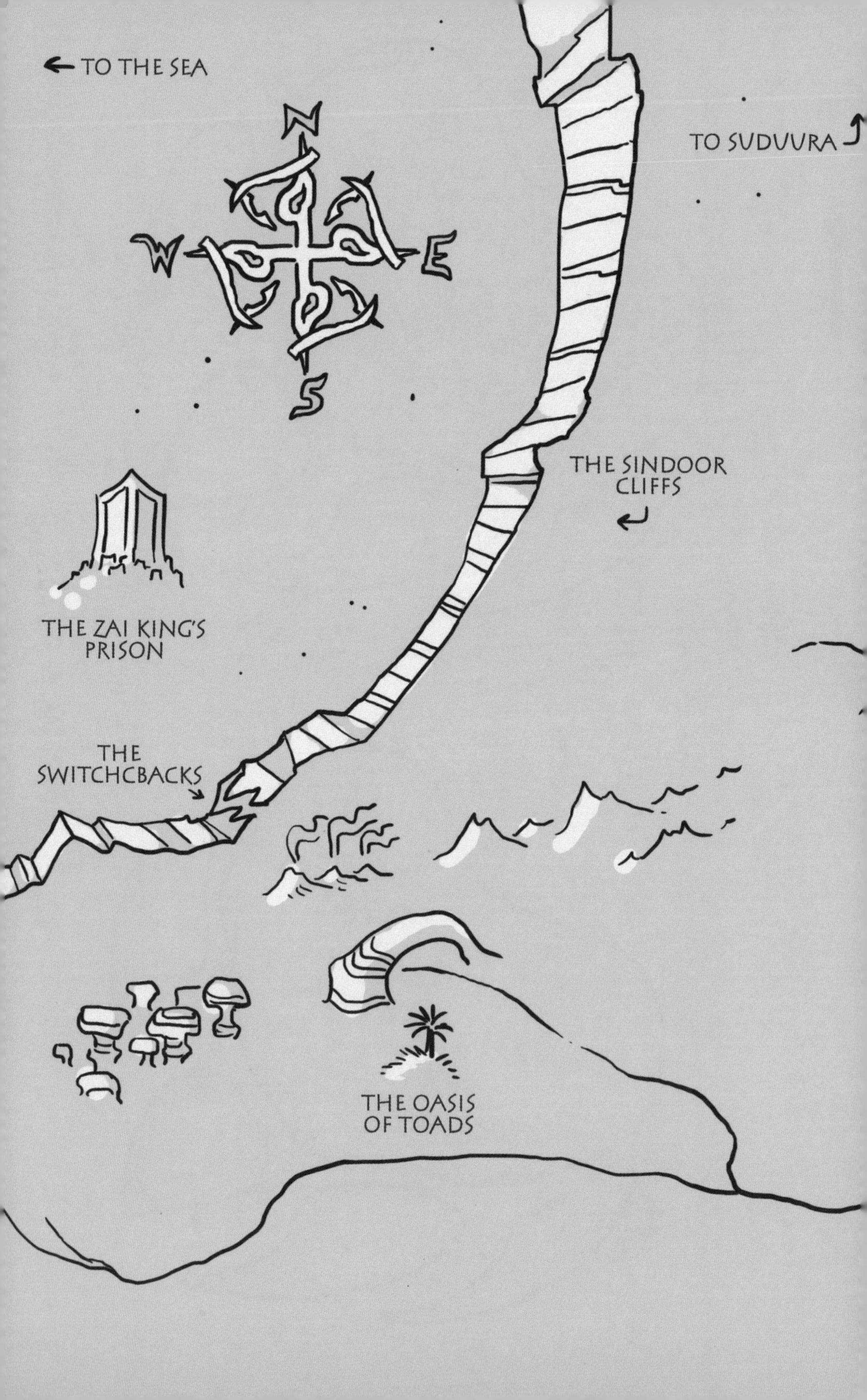

← TO THE SEA
N
W
E
S
TO SUDUURA
THE SINDOOR CLIFFS
THE ZAI KING'S PRISON
THE SWITCHCBACKS
THE OASIS OF TOADS

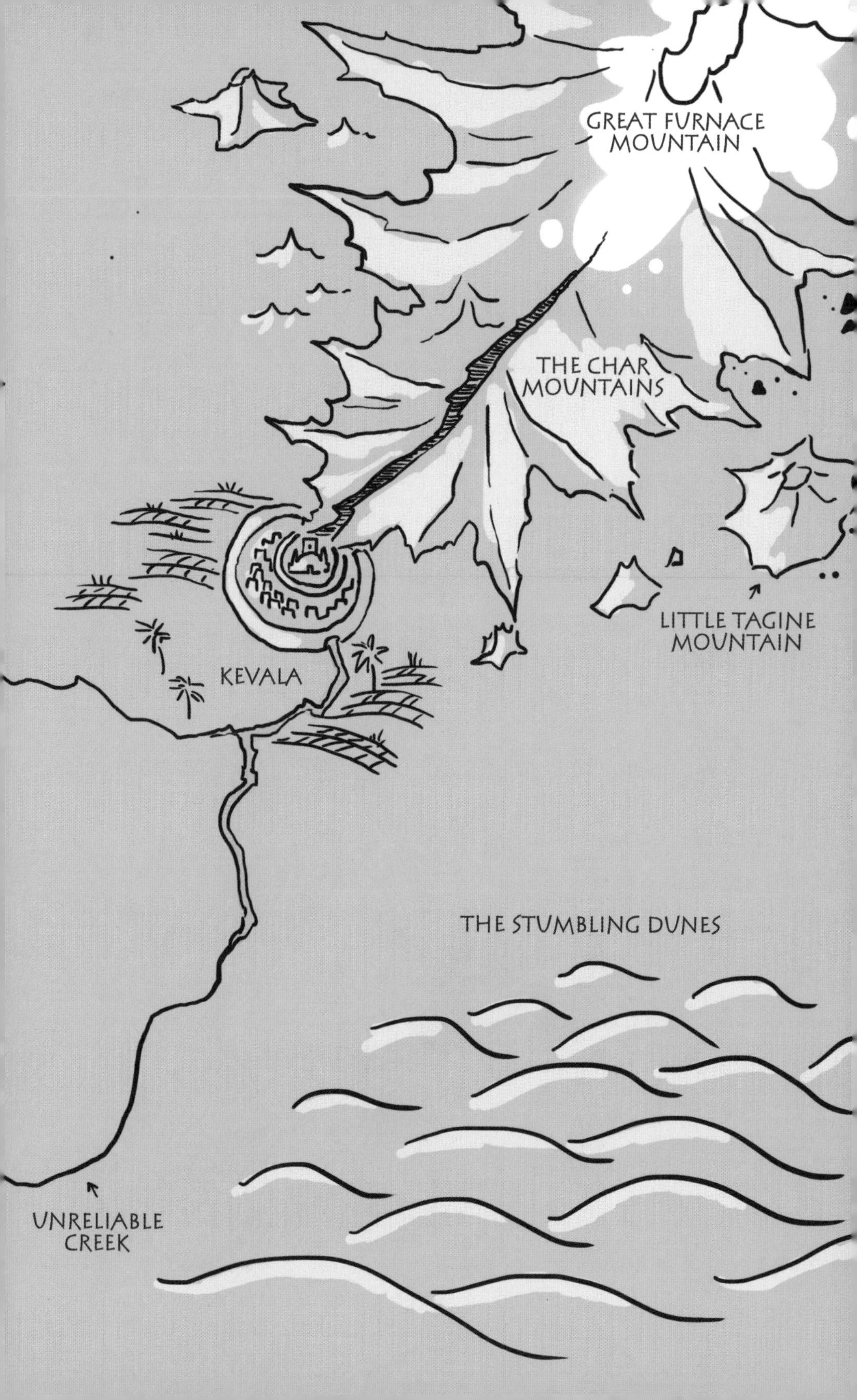
GREAT FURNACE MOUNTAIN
THE CHAR MOUNTAINS
LITTLE TAGINE MOUNTAIN
KEVALA
THE STUMBLING DUNES
UNRELIABLE CREEK

FOR MY MOTHER,
WHO TOLD ME ABOUT
THE FORMS.

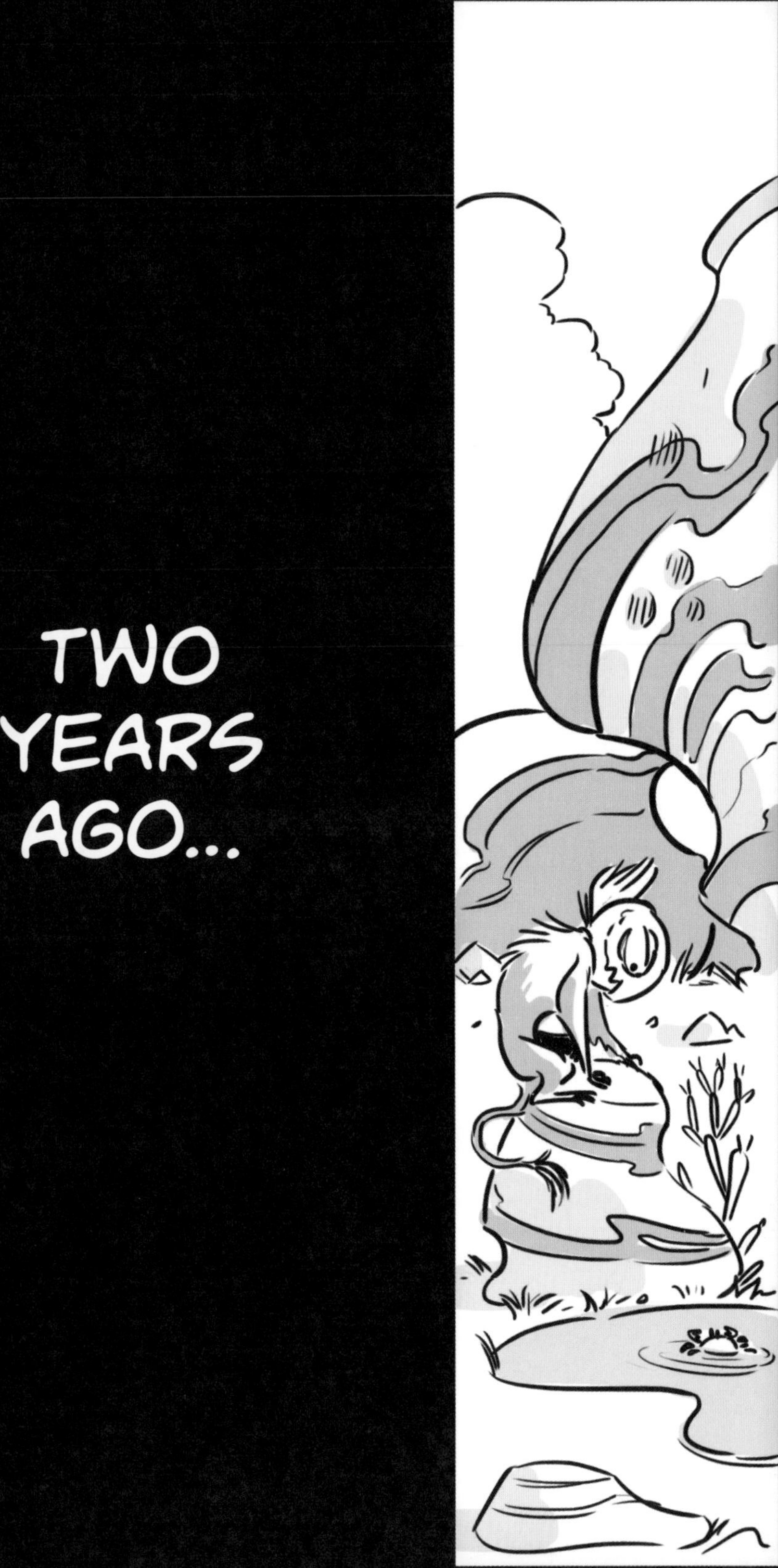
TWO YEARS AGO...

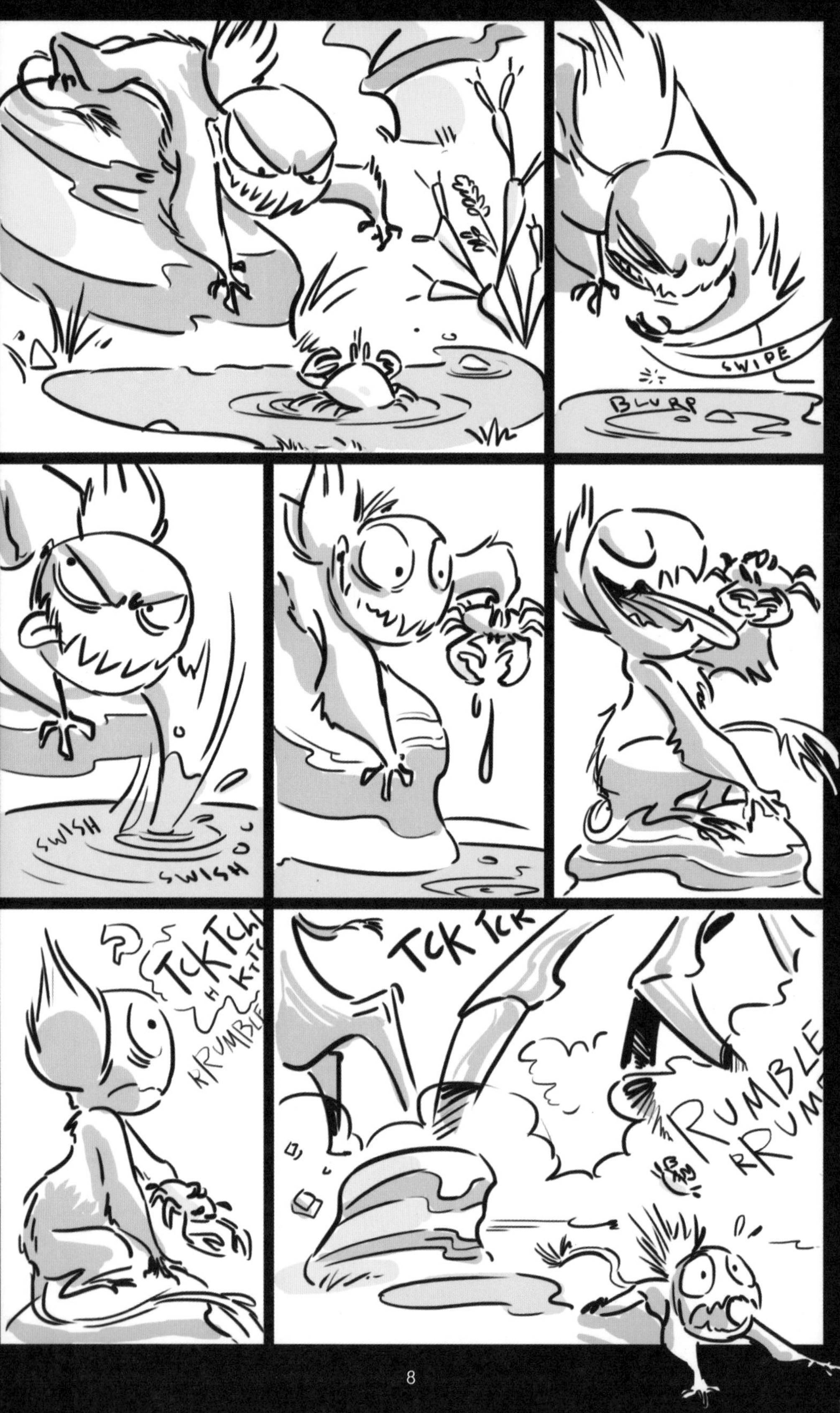
SWIPE
BLURP
SWISH
SWISH
TCK TCK
KTK
RRUMBLE
TCK TCK
RUMBLE
RRUMB

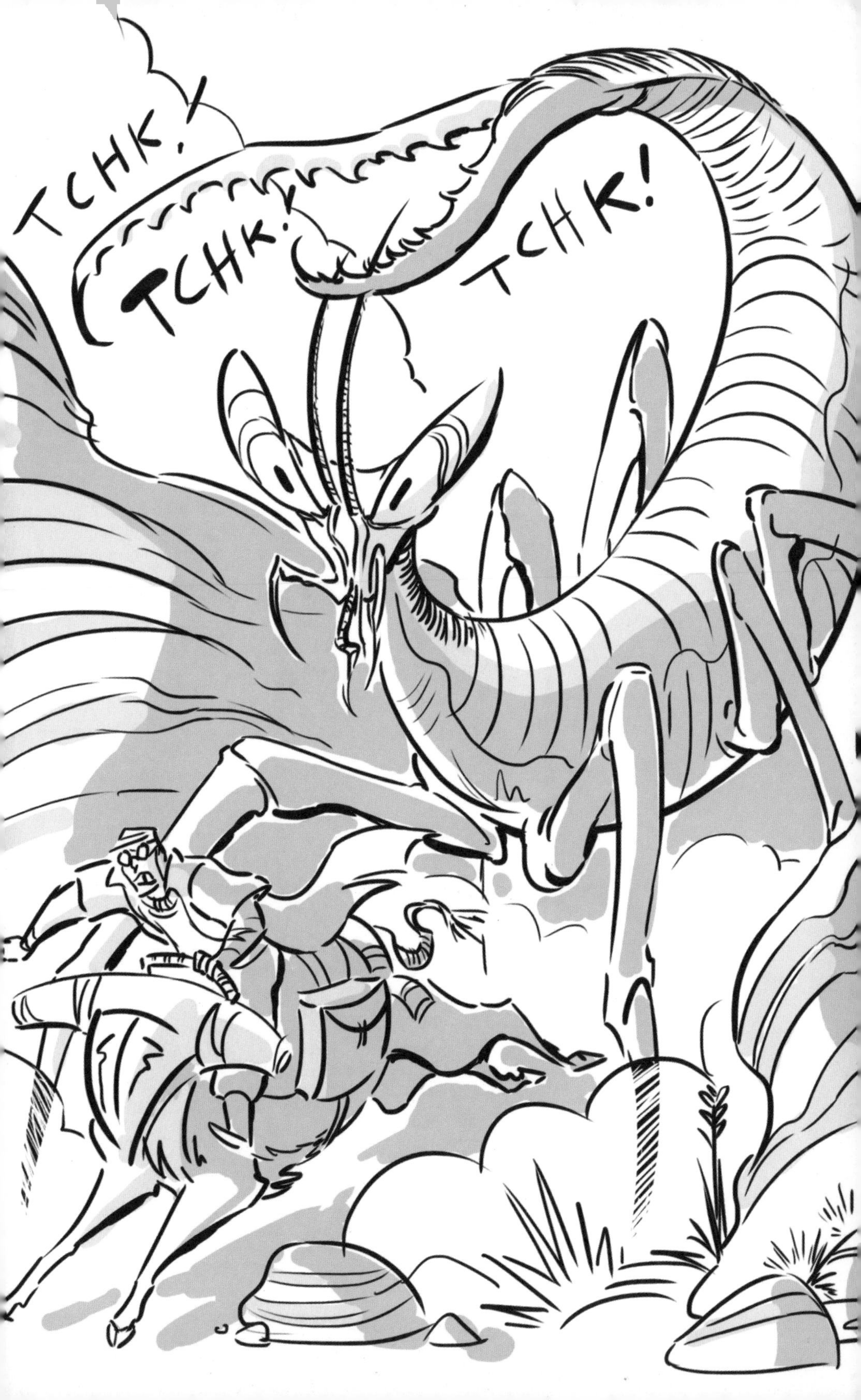
TCHK!
TCHK!
TCHK!

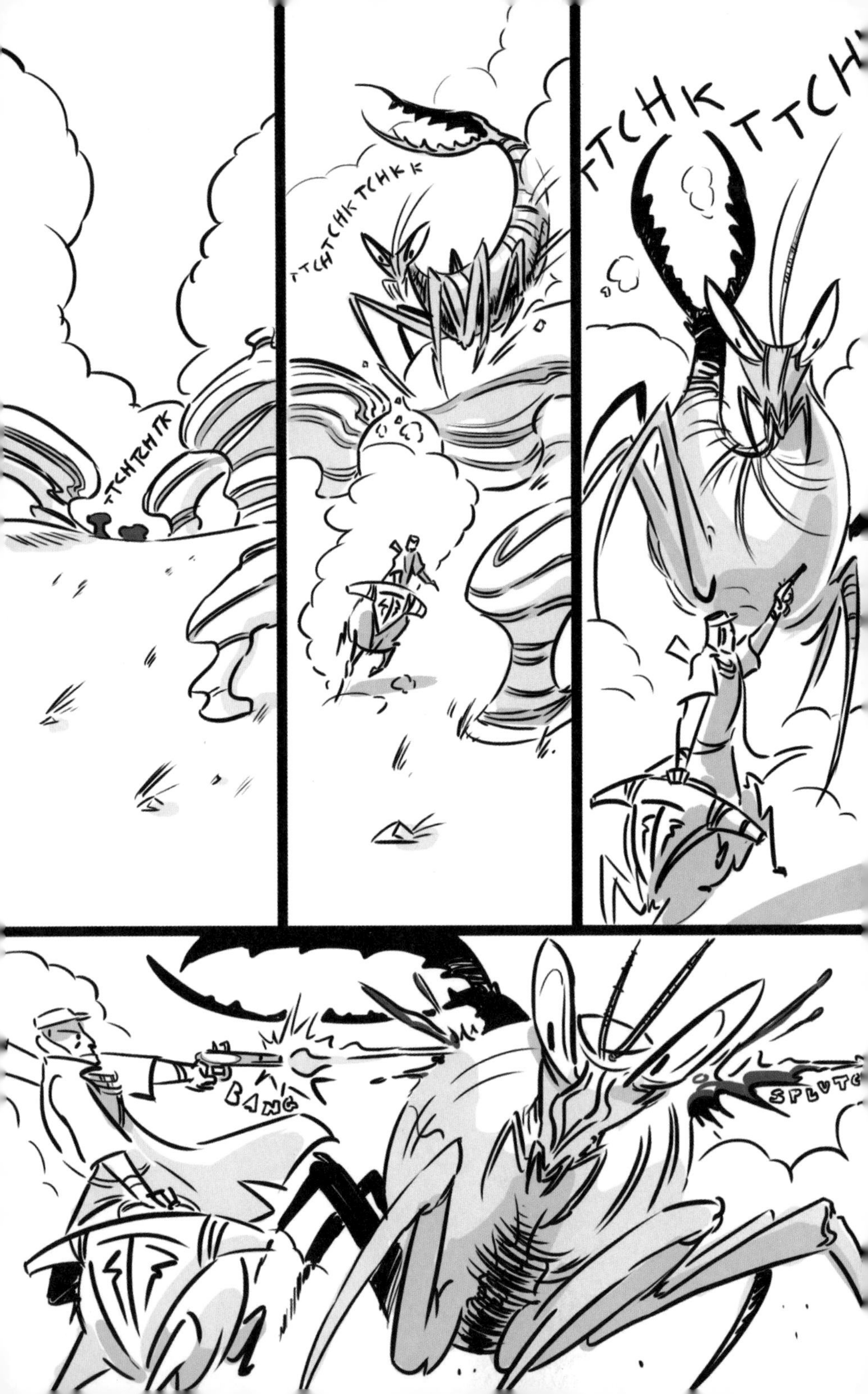
TTCHRCHTK
TTCHTCHKTCHKK
TTCHK
TTCH
BANG
SPLUTC

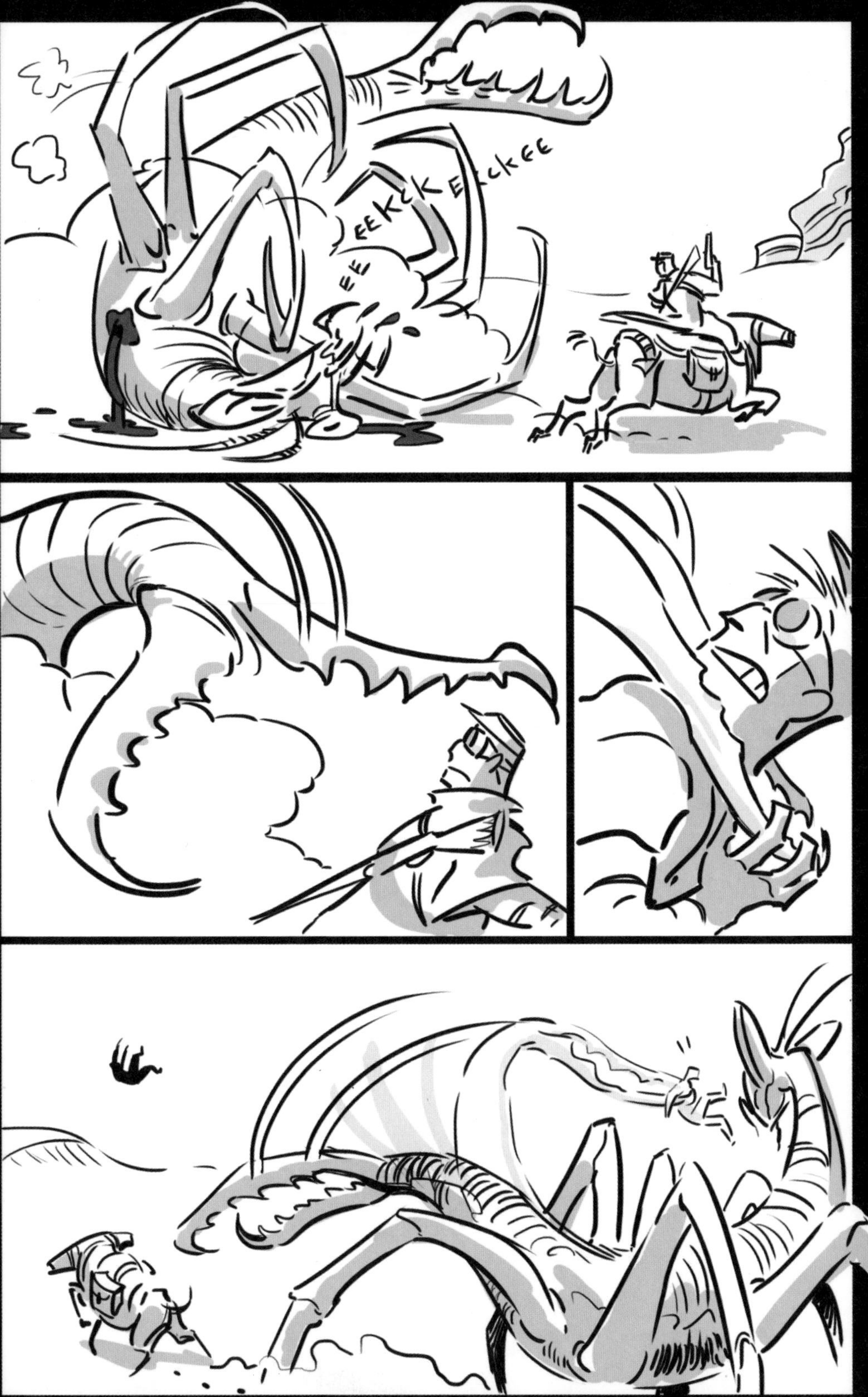
EEEEKKKECKEE

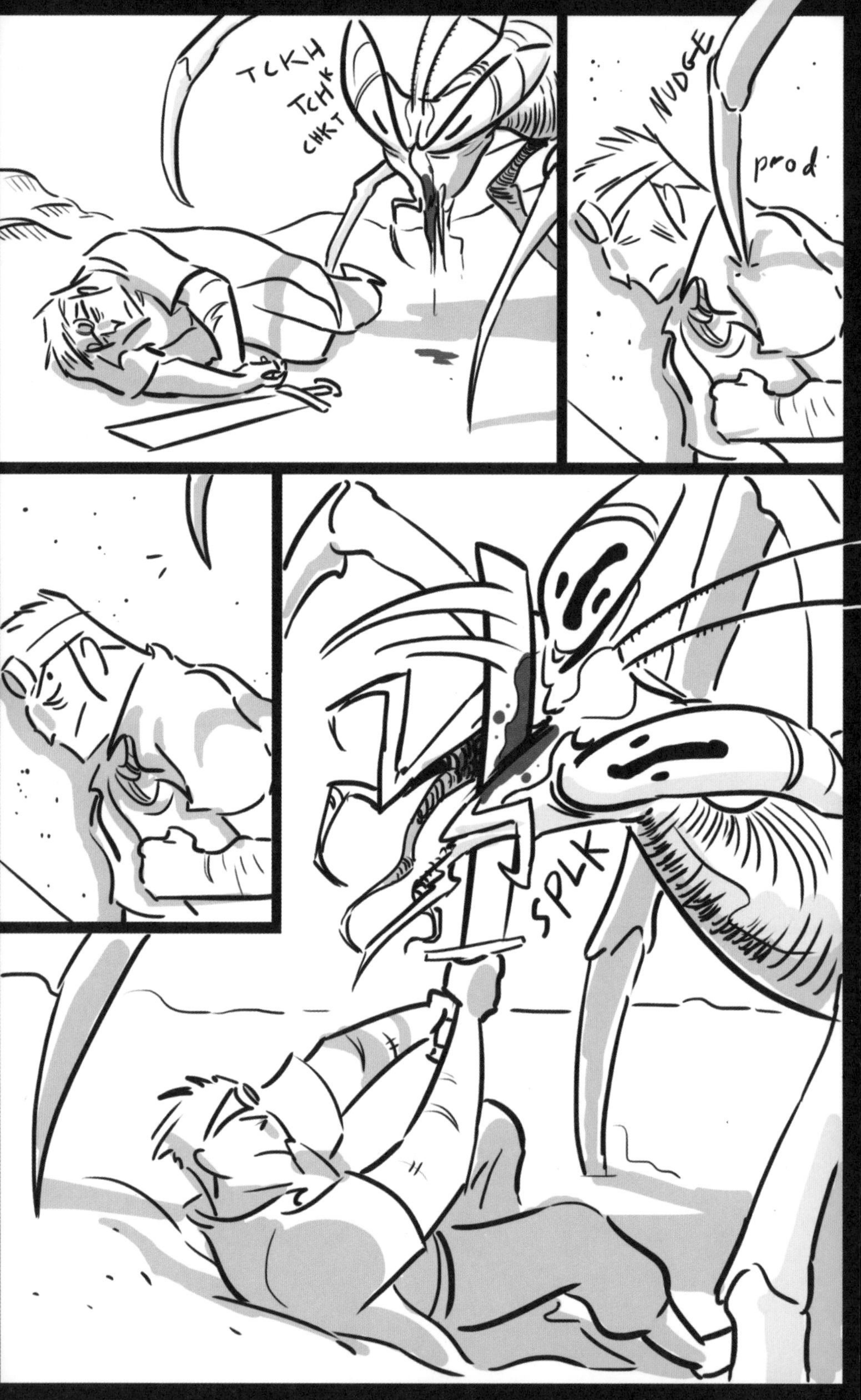
TCKH
TCHK
CHKT
NUDGE
prod
SPLK

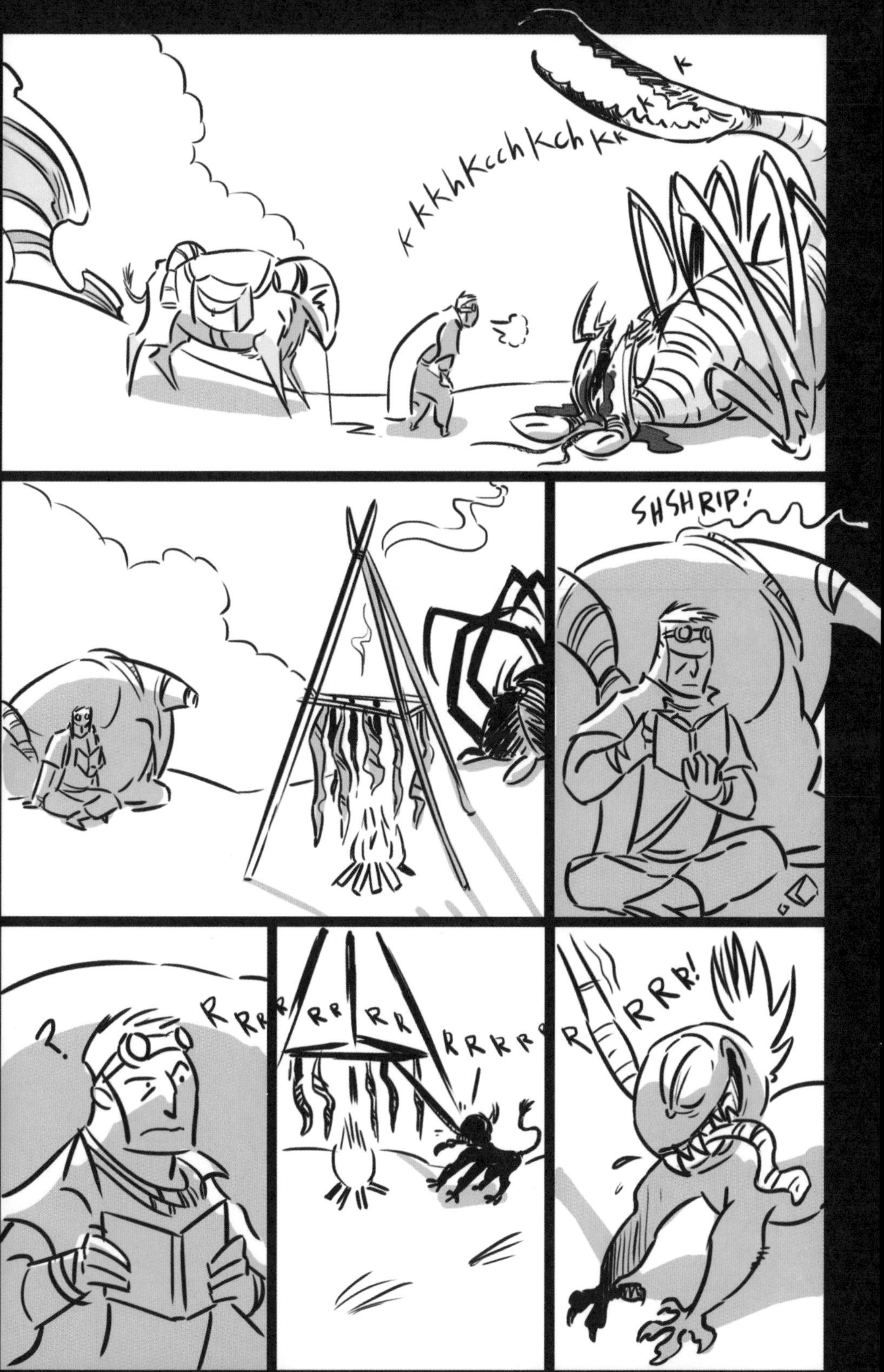
kkkhkcchkchkkkk
SHSHRIP!
?
RRRRRRRRRRRRR
RRR!

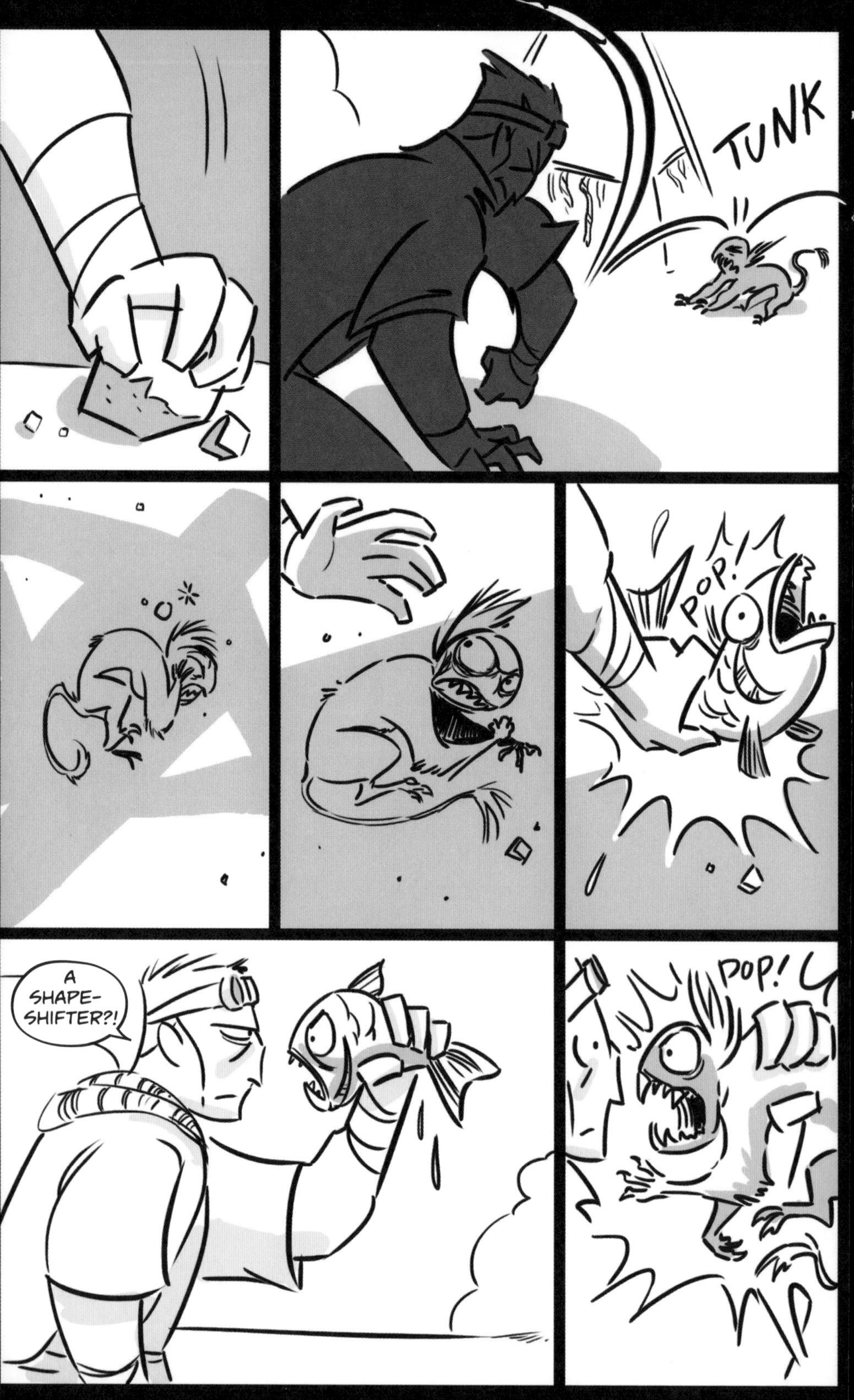
TUNK
POP!
A SHAPE-SHIFTER?!
POP!

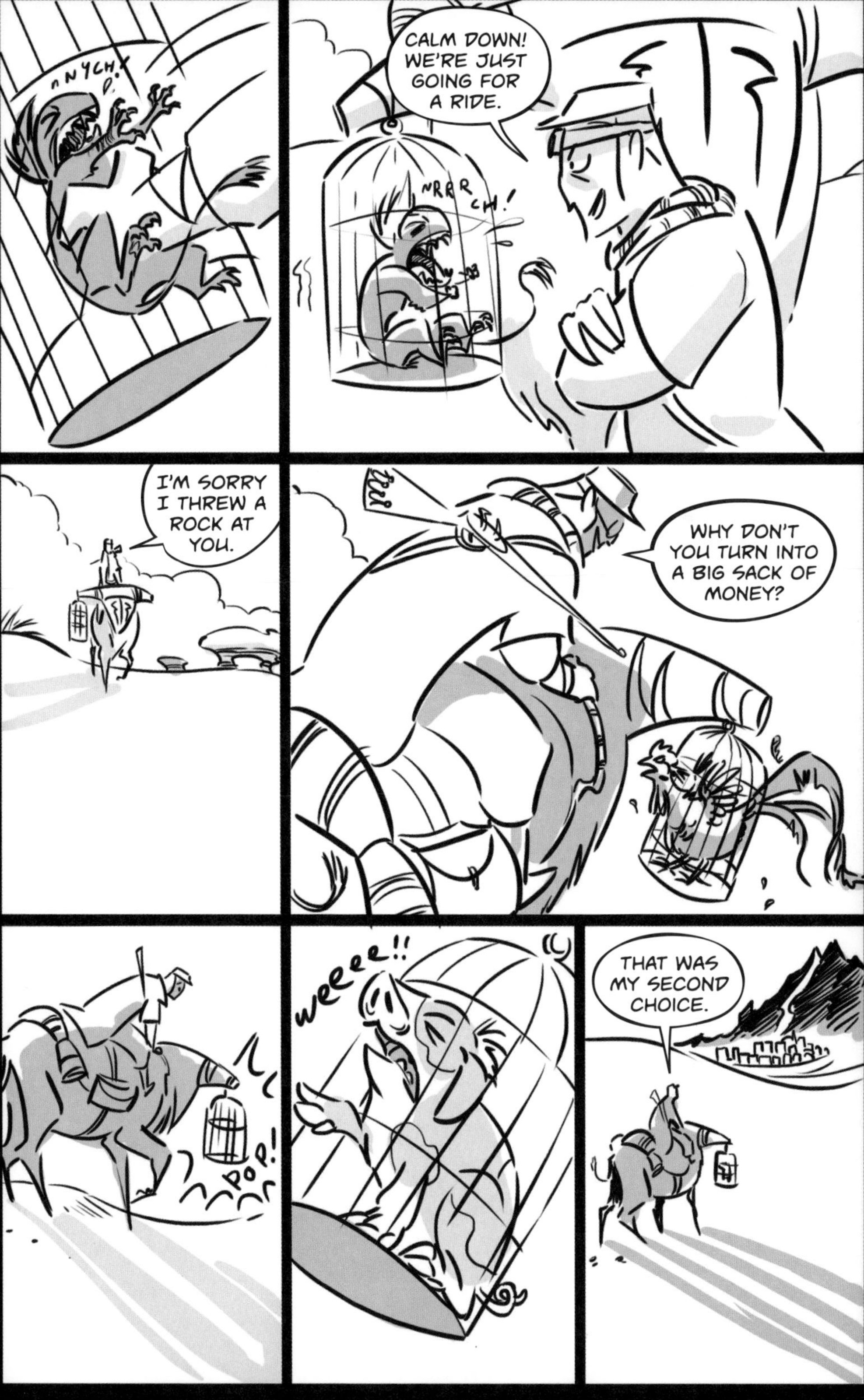

CALM DOWN! WE'RE JUST GOING FOR A RIDE.
I'M SORRY I THREW A ROCK AT YOU.
WHY DON'T YOU TURN INTO A BIG SACK OF MONEY?
POP!
weeee!!
THAT WAS MY SECOND CHOICE.

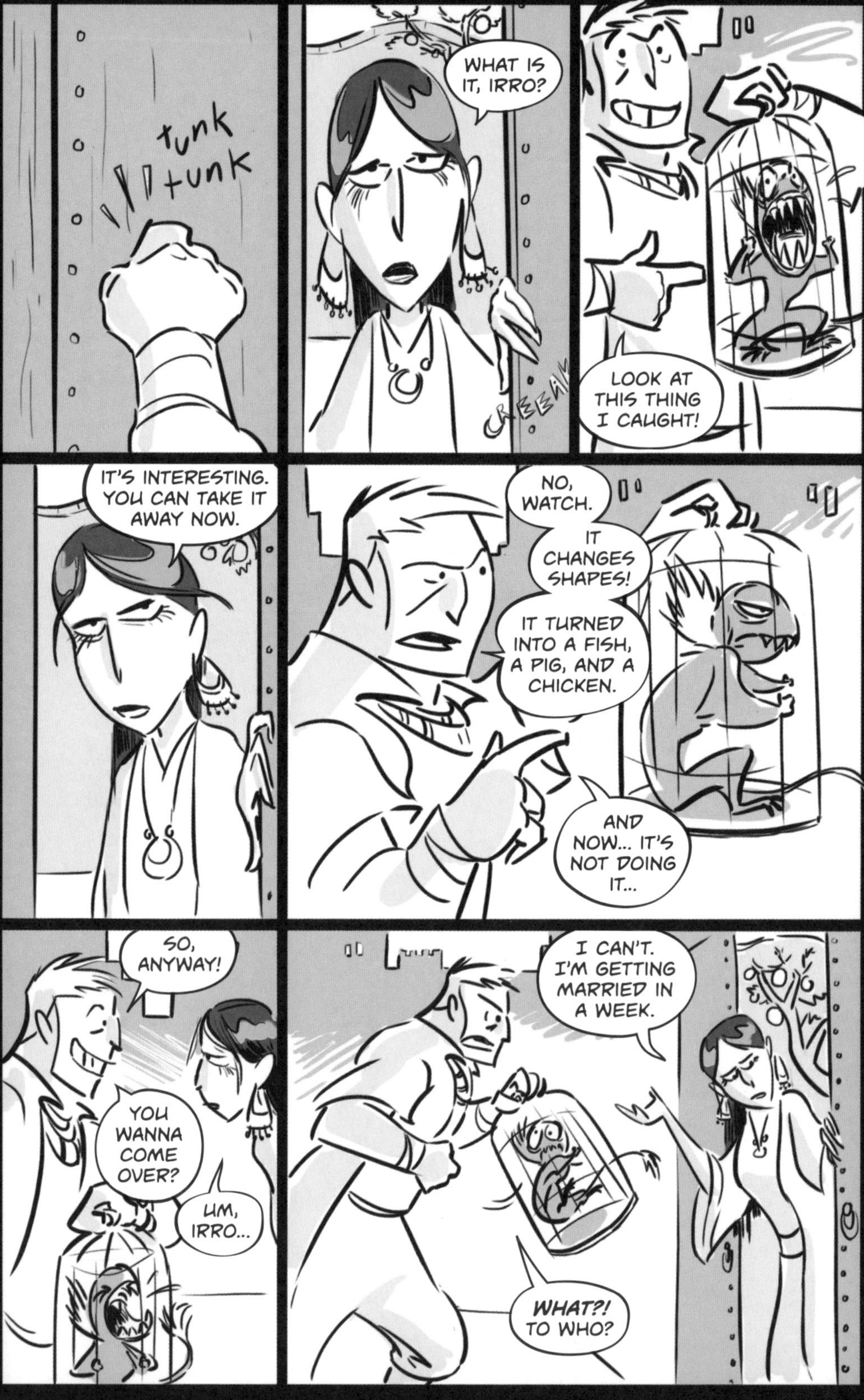
tunk
tunk
WHAT IS IT, IRRO?
CREEAK
LOOK AT THIS THING I CAUGHT!
IT'S INTERESTING. YOU CAN TAKE IT AWAY NOW.
NO, WATCH.
IT CHANGES SHAPES!
IT TURNED INTO A FISH, A PIG, AND A CHICKEN.
AND NOW... IT'S NOT DOING IT...
SO, ANYWAY!
YOU WANNA COME OVER?
UM, IRRO...
I CAN'T. I'M GETTING MARRIED IN A WEEK.
WHAT?! TO WHO?

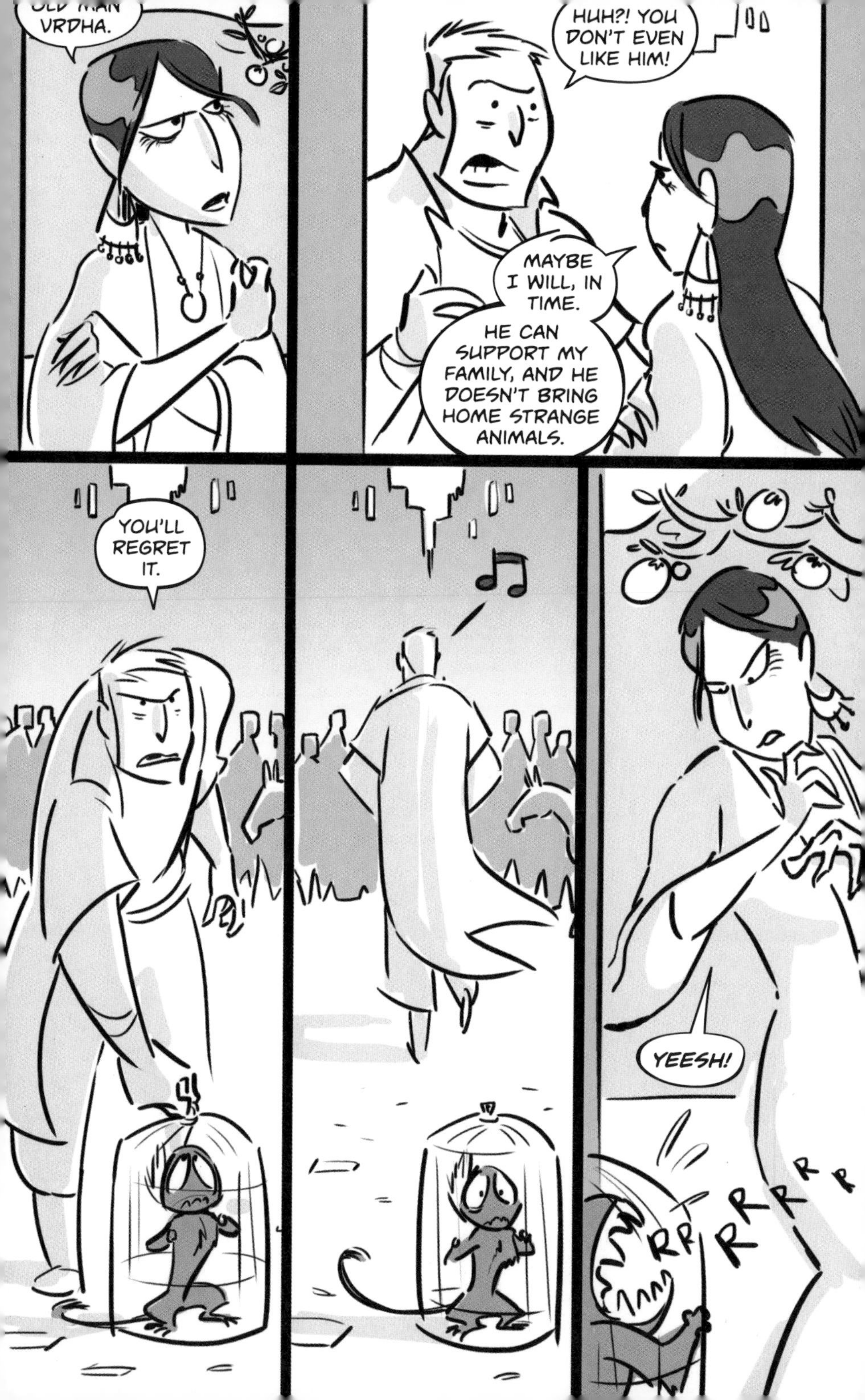
OLD MAN VRDHA.
HUH?! YOU DON'T EVEN LIKE HIM!
MAYBE I WILL, IN TIME.
HE CAN SUPPORT MY FAMILY, AND HE DOESN'T BRING HOME STRANGE ANIMALS.
YOU'LL REGRET IT.
YEESH!
RRRRRRR

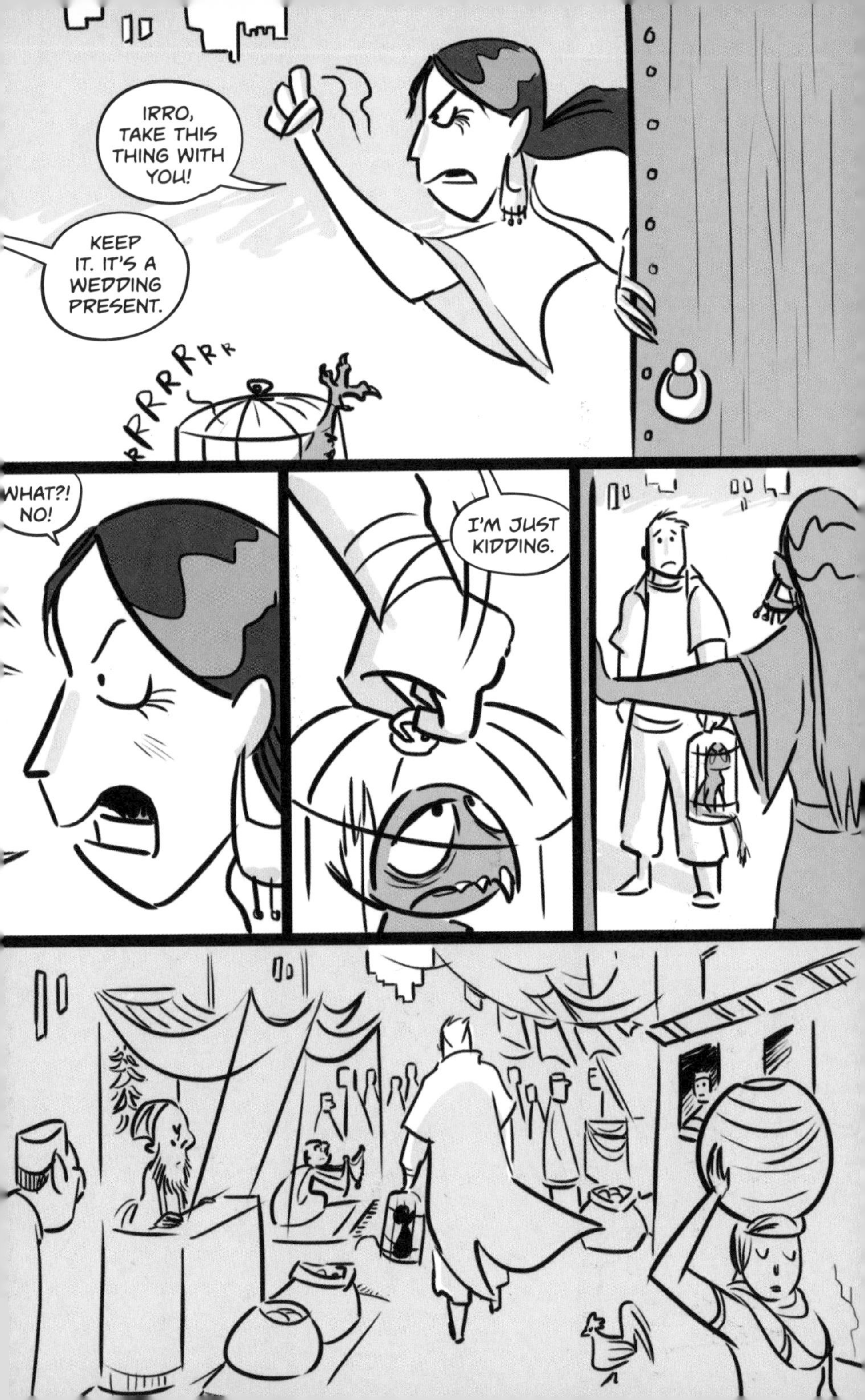
IRRO, TAKE THIS THING WITH YOU!
KEEP IT. IT'S A WEDDING PRESENT.
RRRRRRRR
WHAT?! NO!
I'M JUST KIDDING.

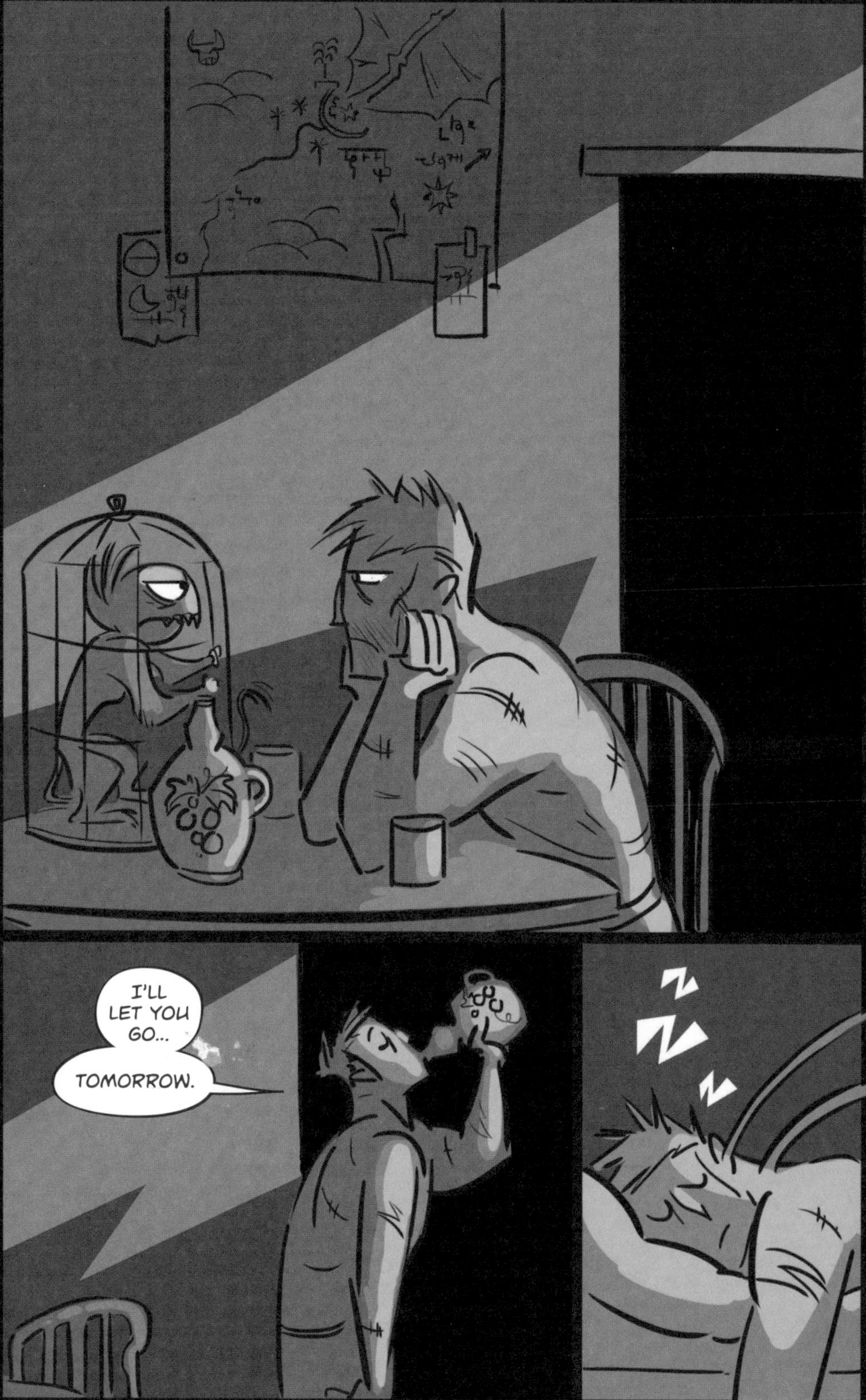
I'LL LET YOU GO...
TOMORROW.
Z
Z
Z

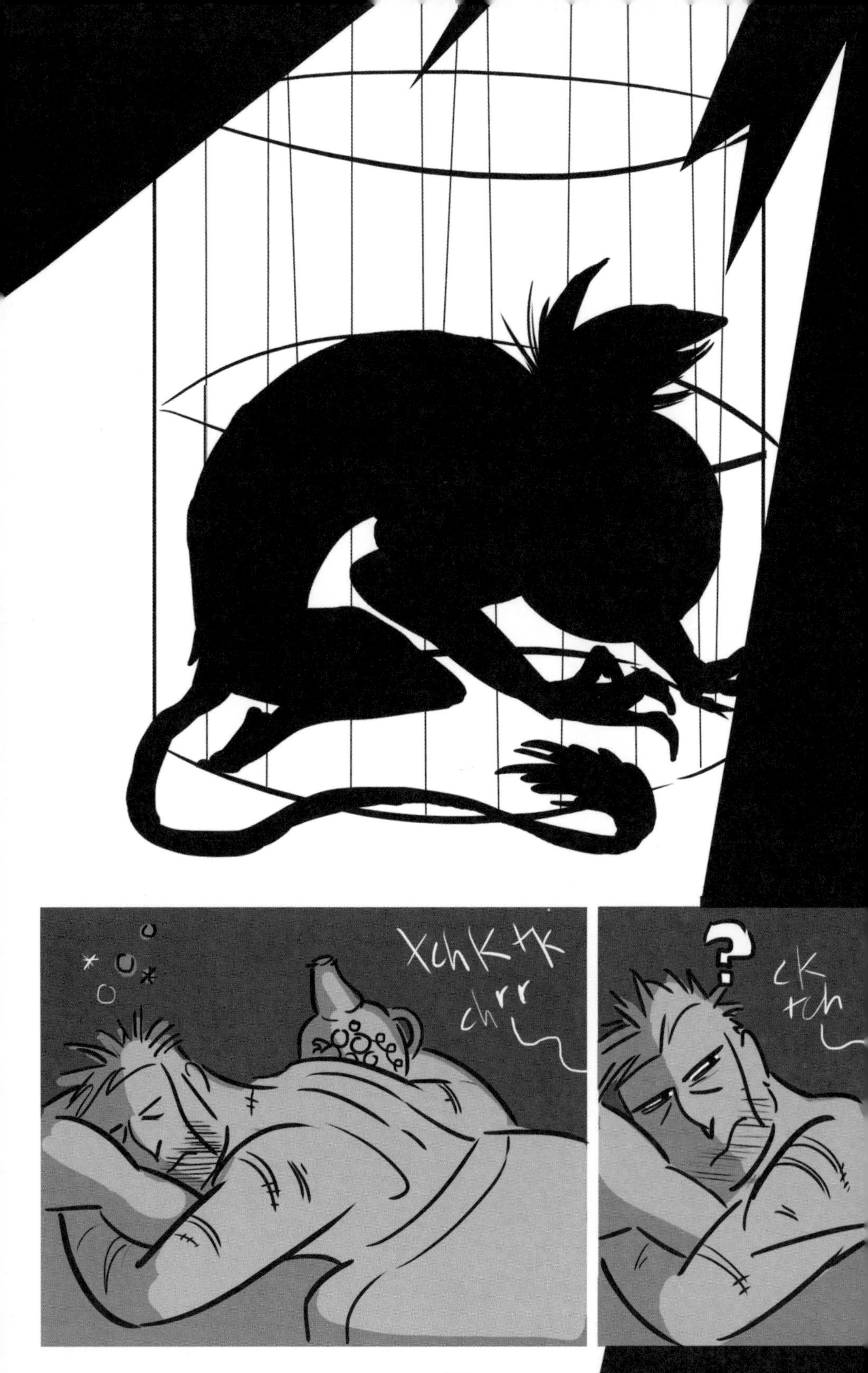

XchKtk
chrr
ck
tch

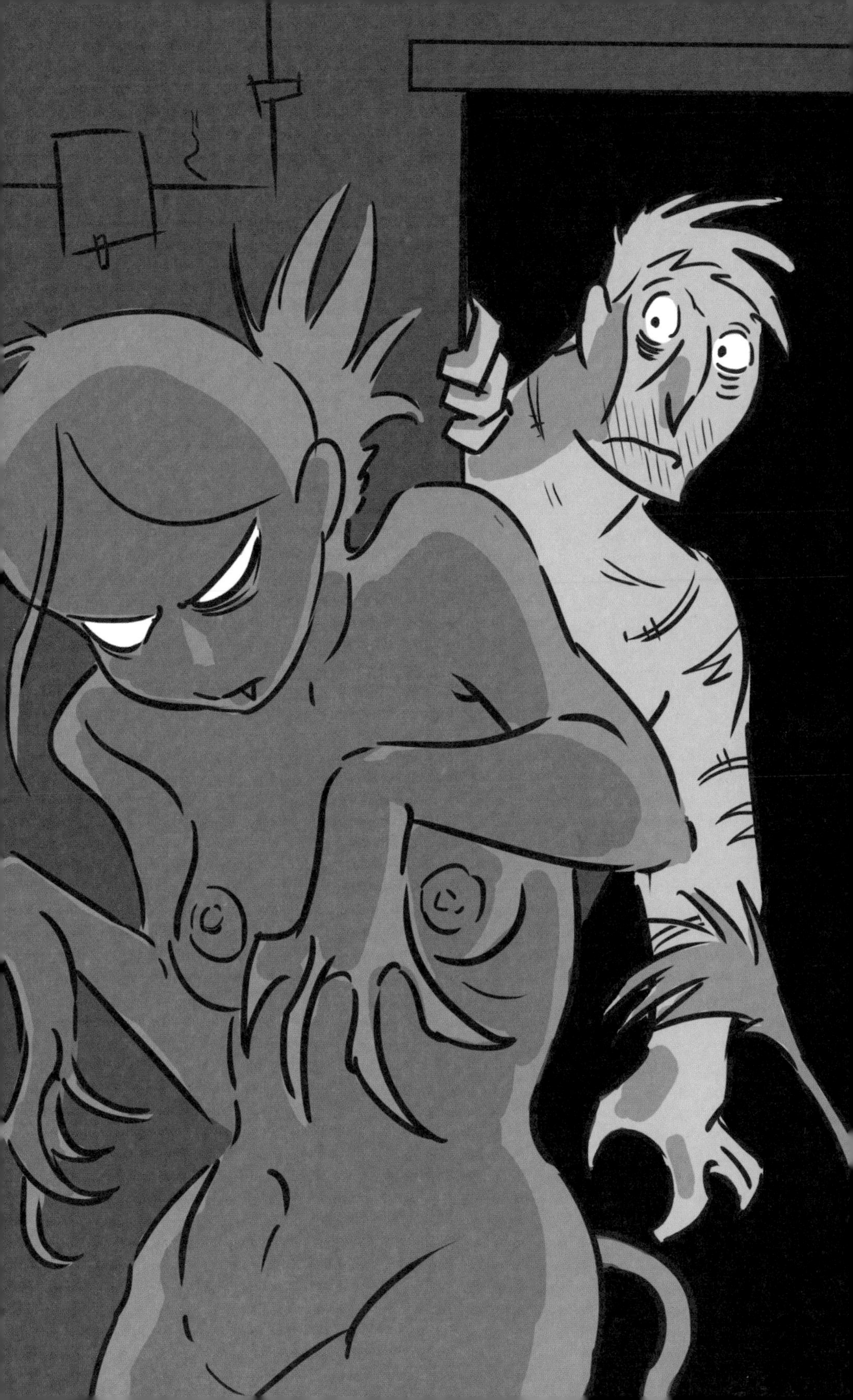

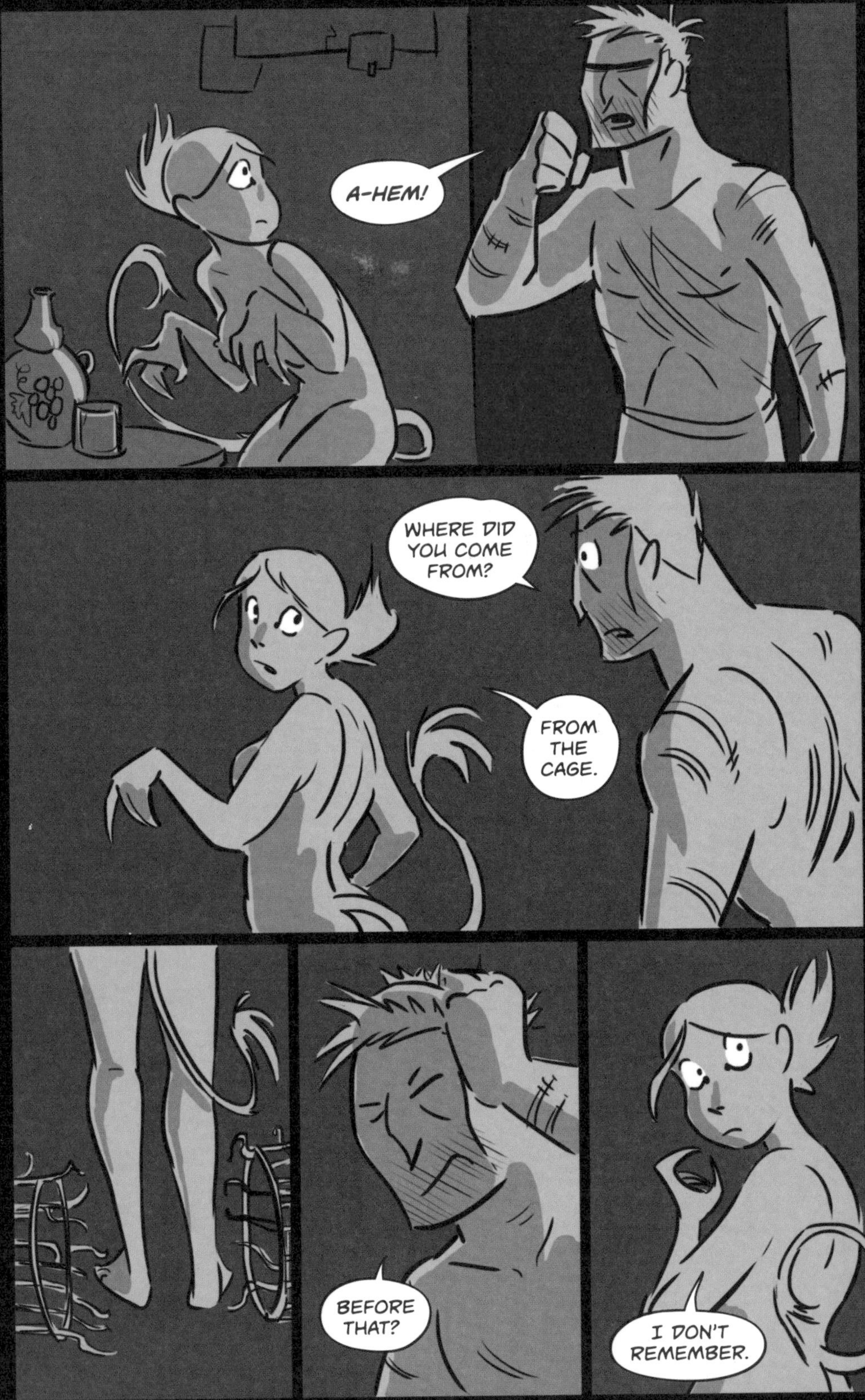
A-HEM!
WHERE DID YOU COME FROM?
FROM THE CAGE.
BEFORE THAT?
I DON'T REMEMBER.

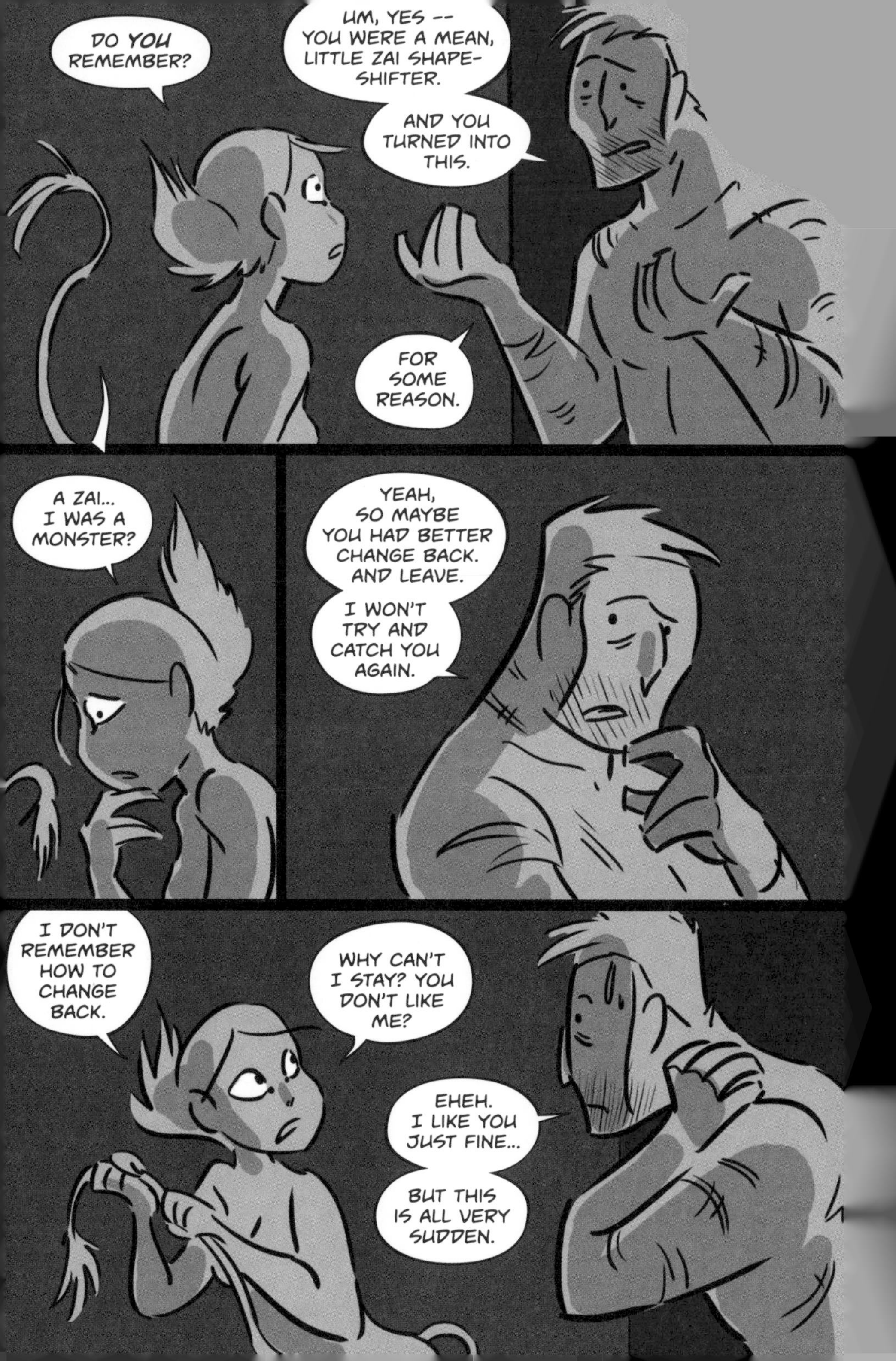
DO YOU REMEMBER?
UM, YES -- YOU WERE A MEAN, LITTLE ZAI SHAPE-SHIFTER.
AND YOU TURNED INTO THIS.
FOR SOME REASON.
A ZAI... I WAS A MONSTER?
YEAH, SO MAYBE YOU HAD BETTER CHANGE BACK. AND LEAVE.
I WON'T TRY AND CATCH YOU AGAIN.
I DON'T REMEMBER HOW TO CHANGE BACK.
WHY CAN'T I STAY? YOU DON'T LIKE ME?
EHEH. I LIKE YOU JUST FINE...
BUT THIS IS ALL VERY SUDDEN.

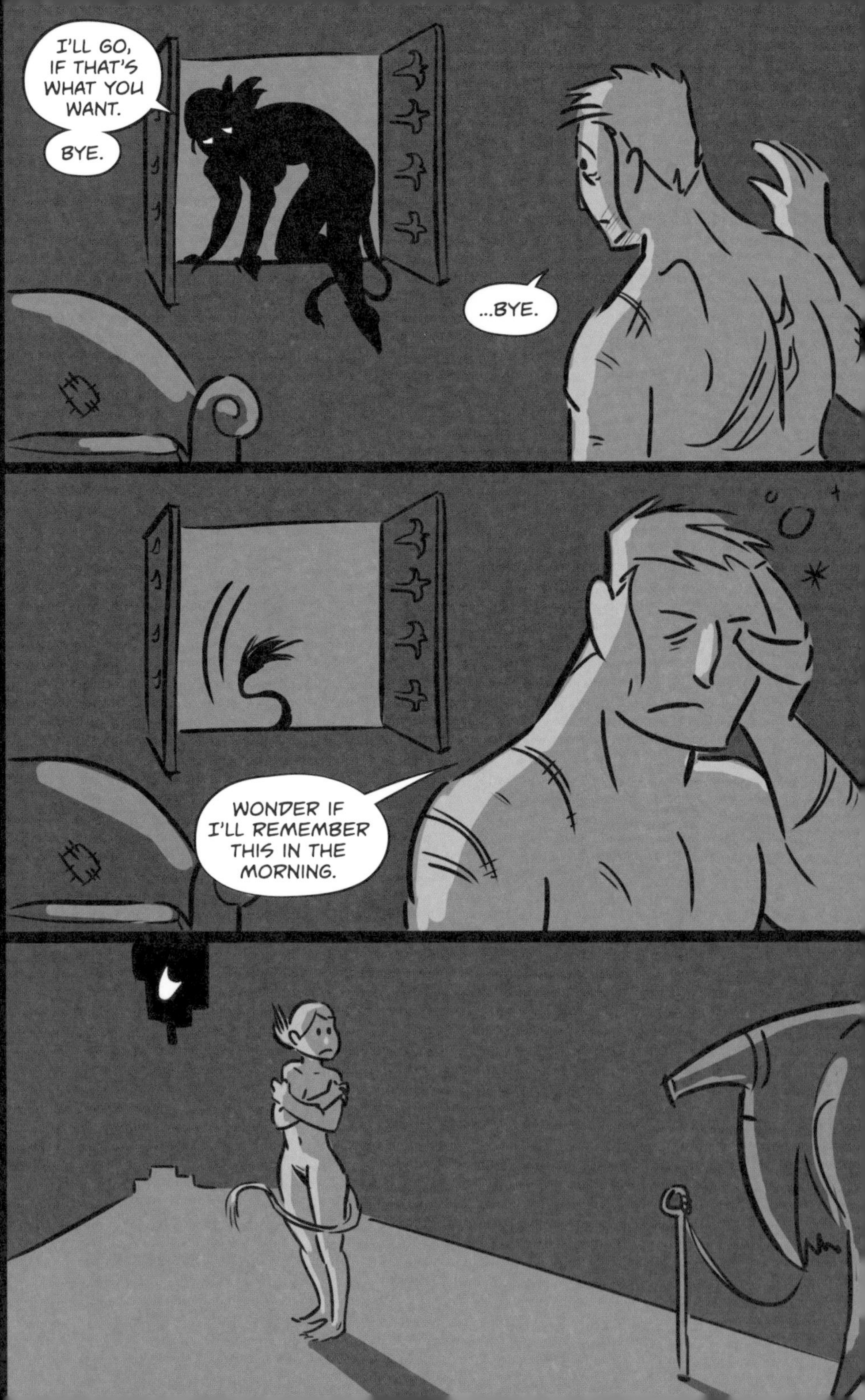

I'LL GO, IF THAT'S WHAT YOU WANT.
BYE.
...BYE.
WONDER IF I'LL REMEMBER THIS IN THE MORNING.

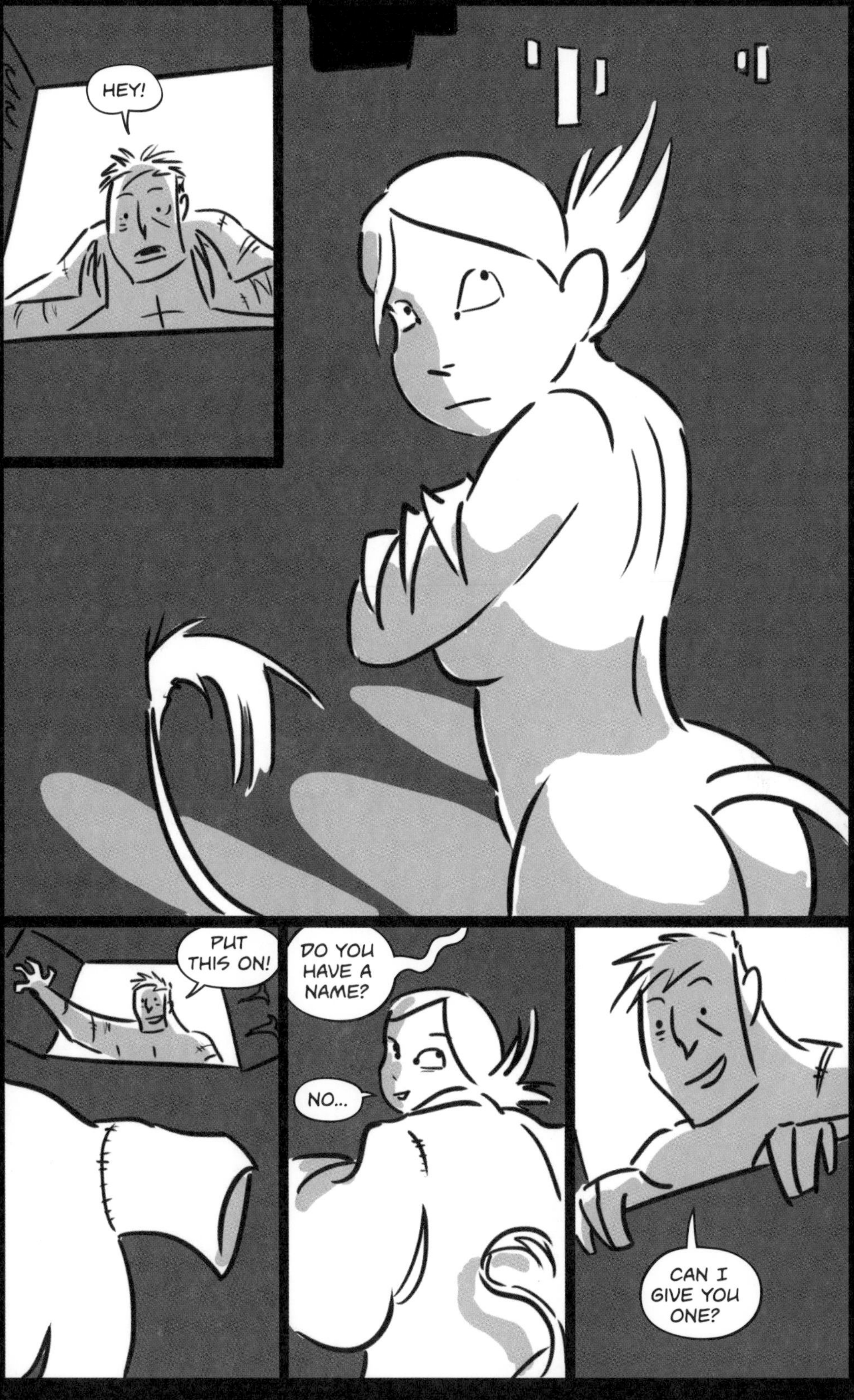
HEY!
PUT THIS ON!
DO YOU HAVE A NAME?
NO...
CAN I GIVE YOU ONE?

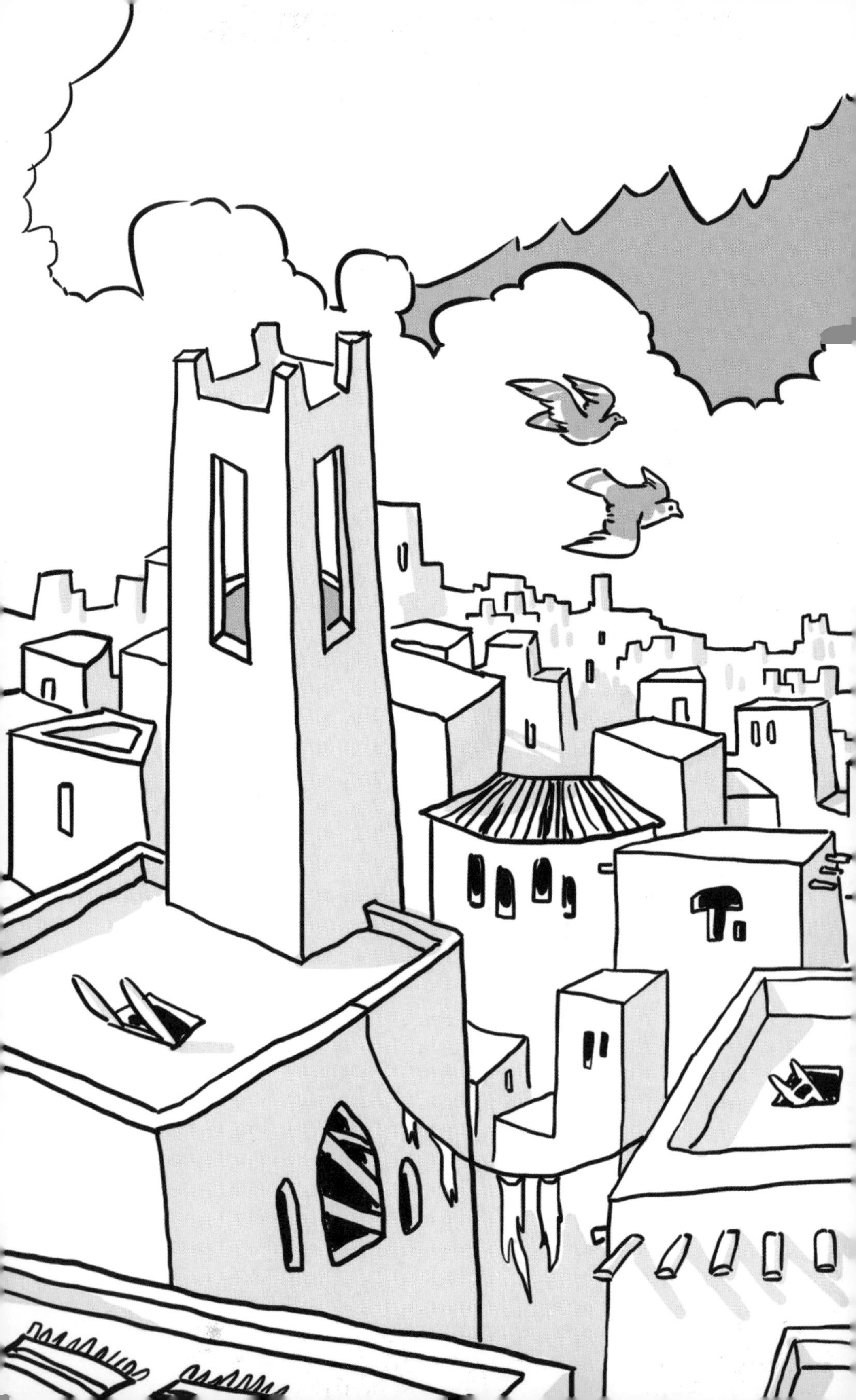

MORO ROGERS'

# CITY IN THE DESERT

## THE SERPENT CROWN

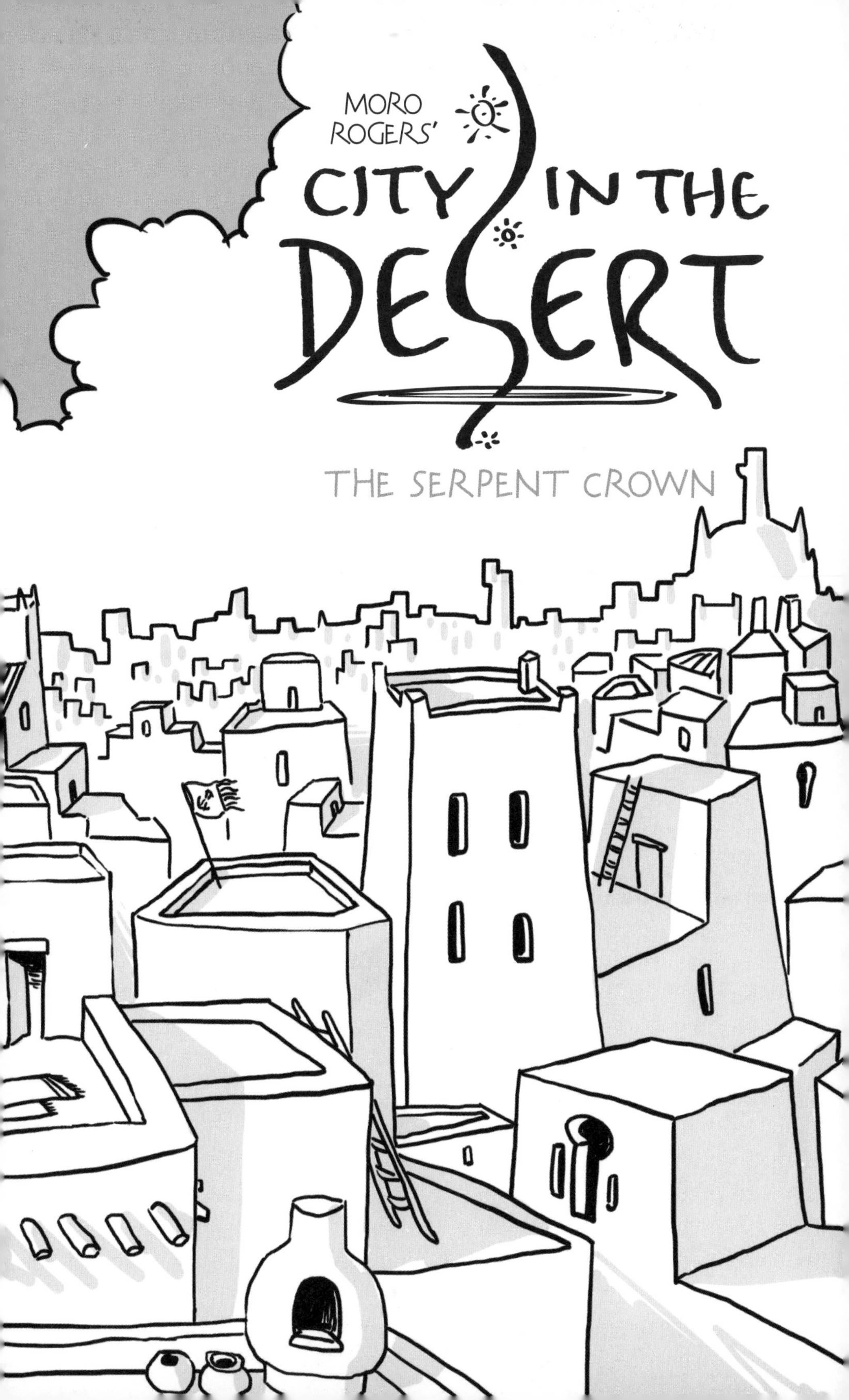

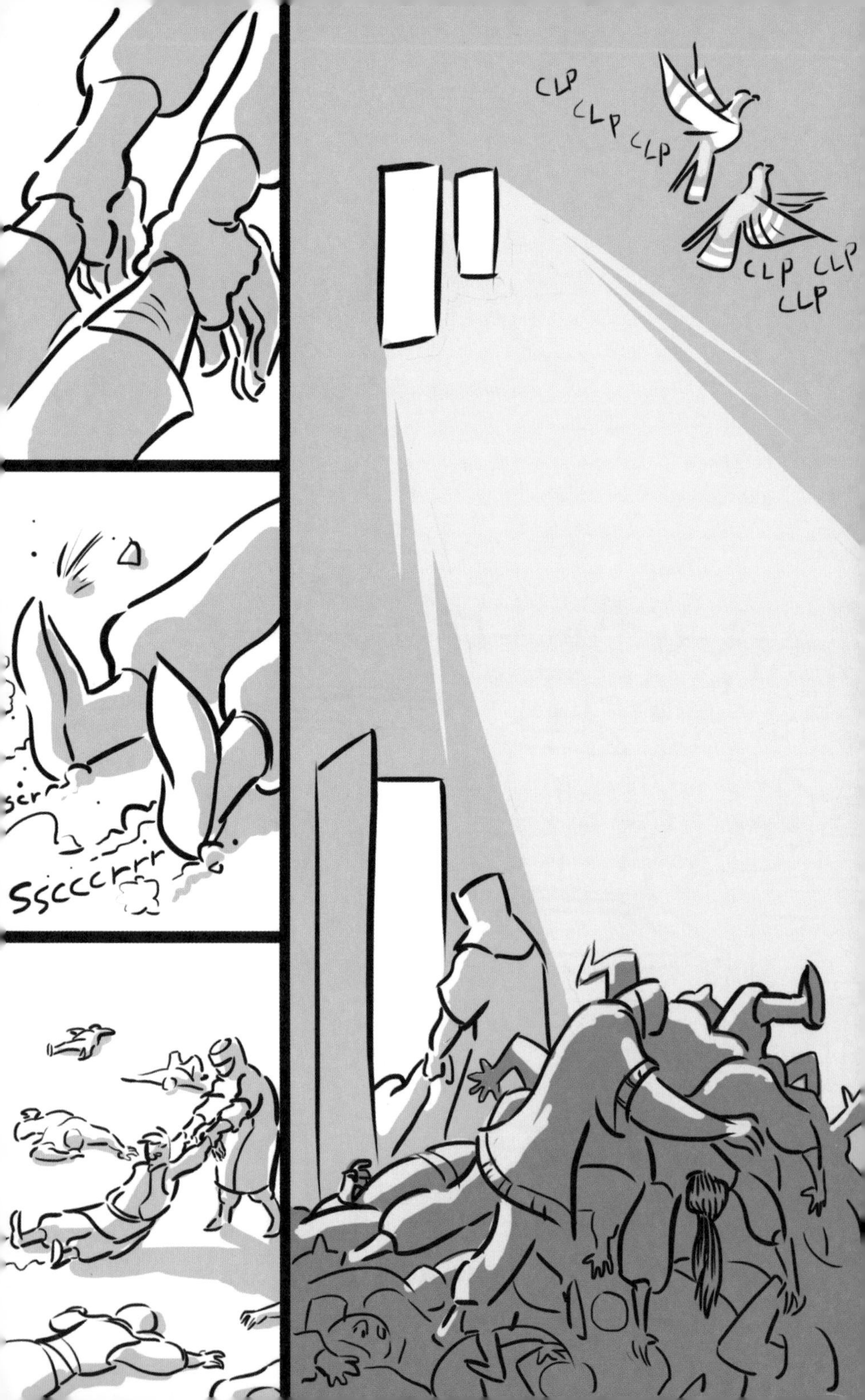
scr
SSCCCrrr
CLP CLP CLP
CLP CLP CLP

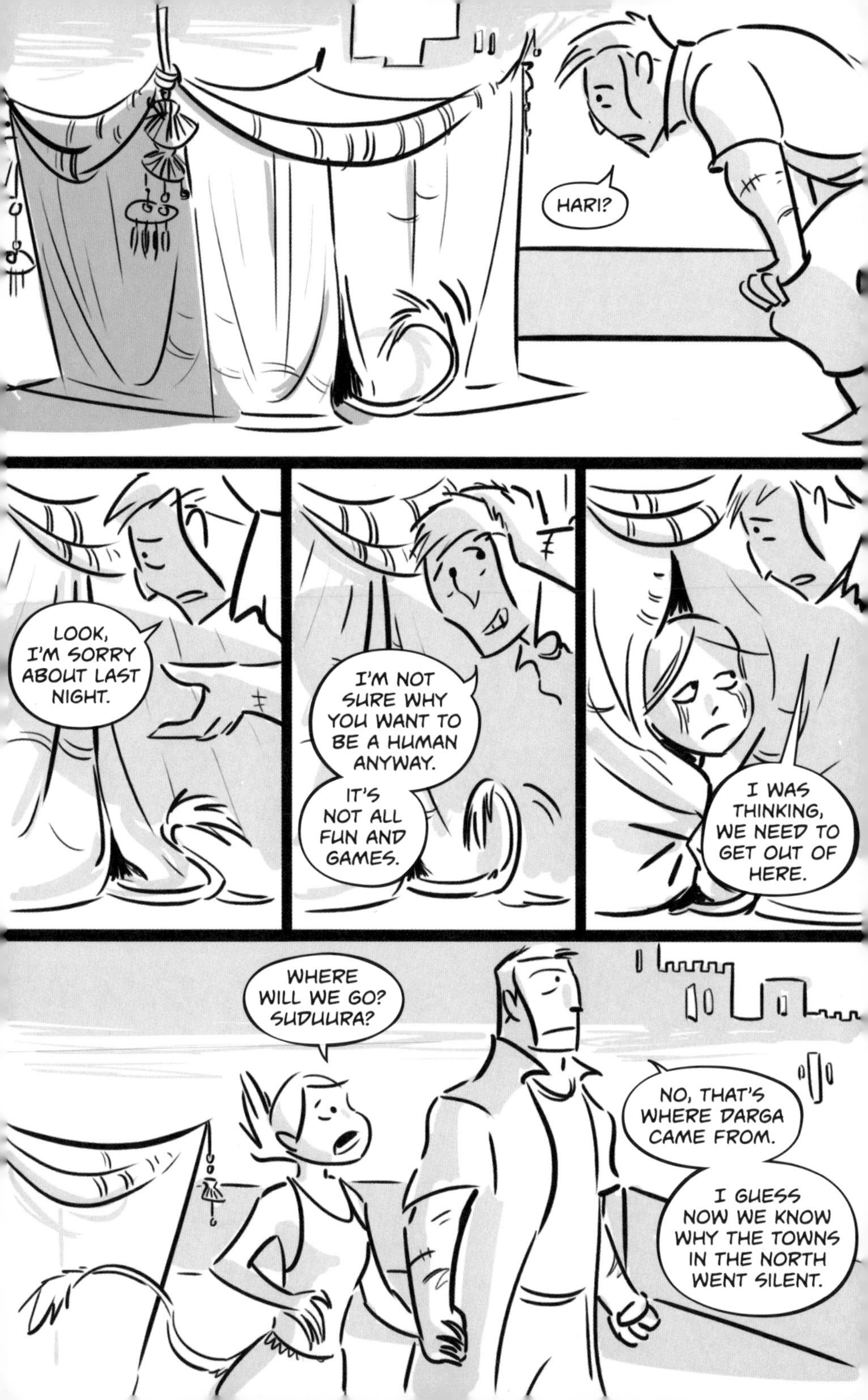
HARI?
LOOK, I'M SORRY ABOUT LAST NIGHT.
I'M NOT SURE WHY YOU WANT TO BE A HUMAN ANYWAY.
IT'S NOT ALL FUN AND GAMES.
I WAS THINKING, WE NEED TO GET OUT OF HERE.
WHERE WILL WE GO? SUDUURA?
NO, THAT'S WHERE DARGA CAME FROM.
I GUESS NOW WE KNOW WHY THE TOWNS IN THE NORTH WENT SILENT.

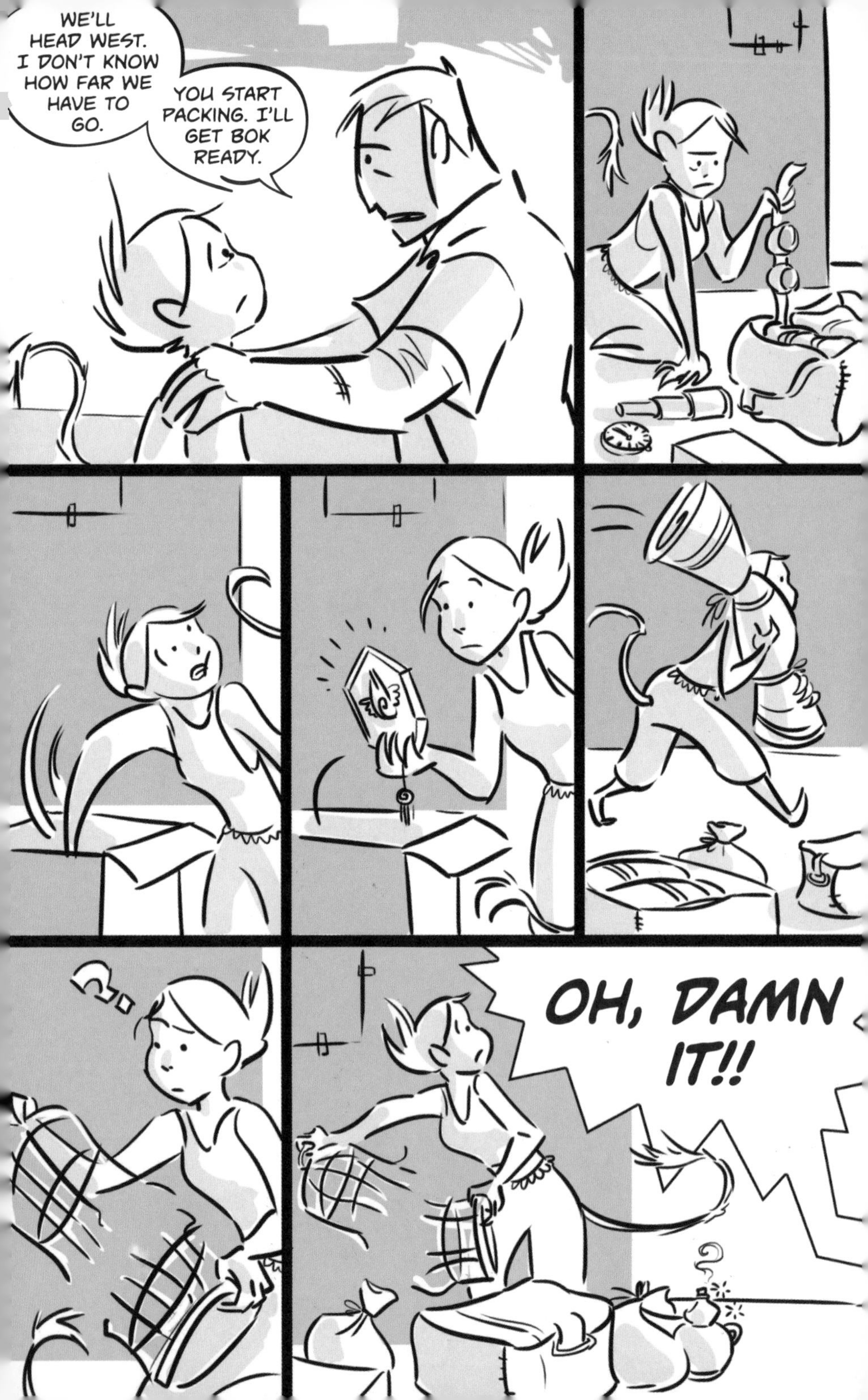
WE'LL HEAD WEST. I DON'T KNOW HOW FAR WE HAVE TO GO.
YOU START PACKING. I'LL GET BOK READY.
?!
OH, DAMN IT!!

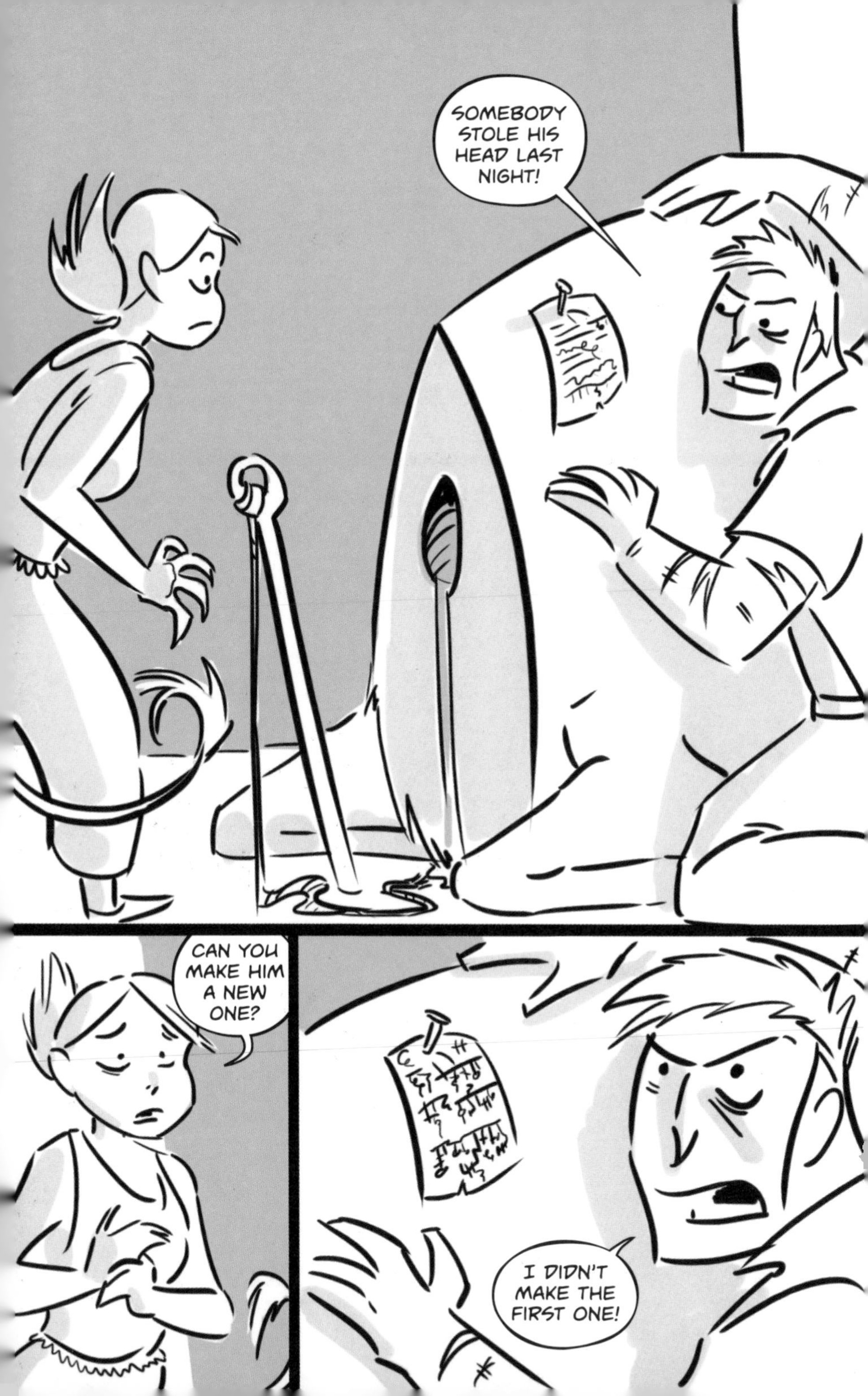
SOMEBODY STOLE HIS HEAD LAST NIGHT!
CAN YOU MAKE HIM A NEW ONE?
I DIDN'T MAKE THE FIRST ONE!

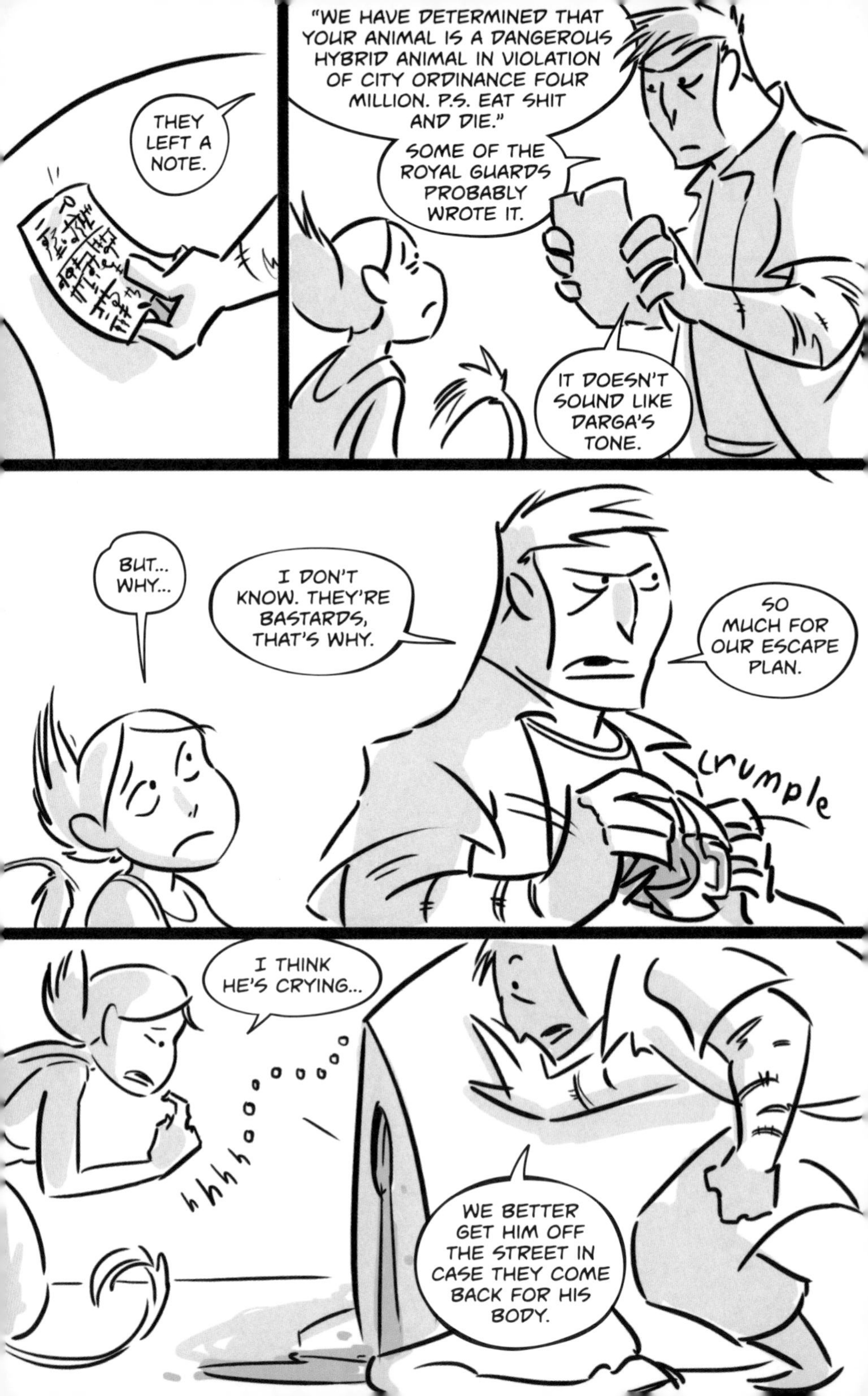
THEY LEFT A NOTE.
"WE HAVE DETERMINED THAT YOUR ANIMAL IS A DANGEROUS HYBRID ANIMAL IN VIOLATION OF CITY ORDINANCE FOUR MILLION. P.S. EAT SHIT AND DIE."
SOME OF THE ROYAL GUARDS PROBABLY WROTE IT.
IT DOESN'T SOUND LIKE DARGA'S TONE.
BUT... WHY...
I DON'T KNOW. THEY'RE BASTARDS, THAT'S WHY.
SO MUCH FOR OUR ESCAPE PLAN.
crumple
I THINK HE'S CRYING...
hhhhooooooo
WE BETTER GET HIM OFF THE STREET IN CASE THEY COME BACK FOR HIS BODY.

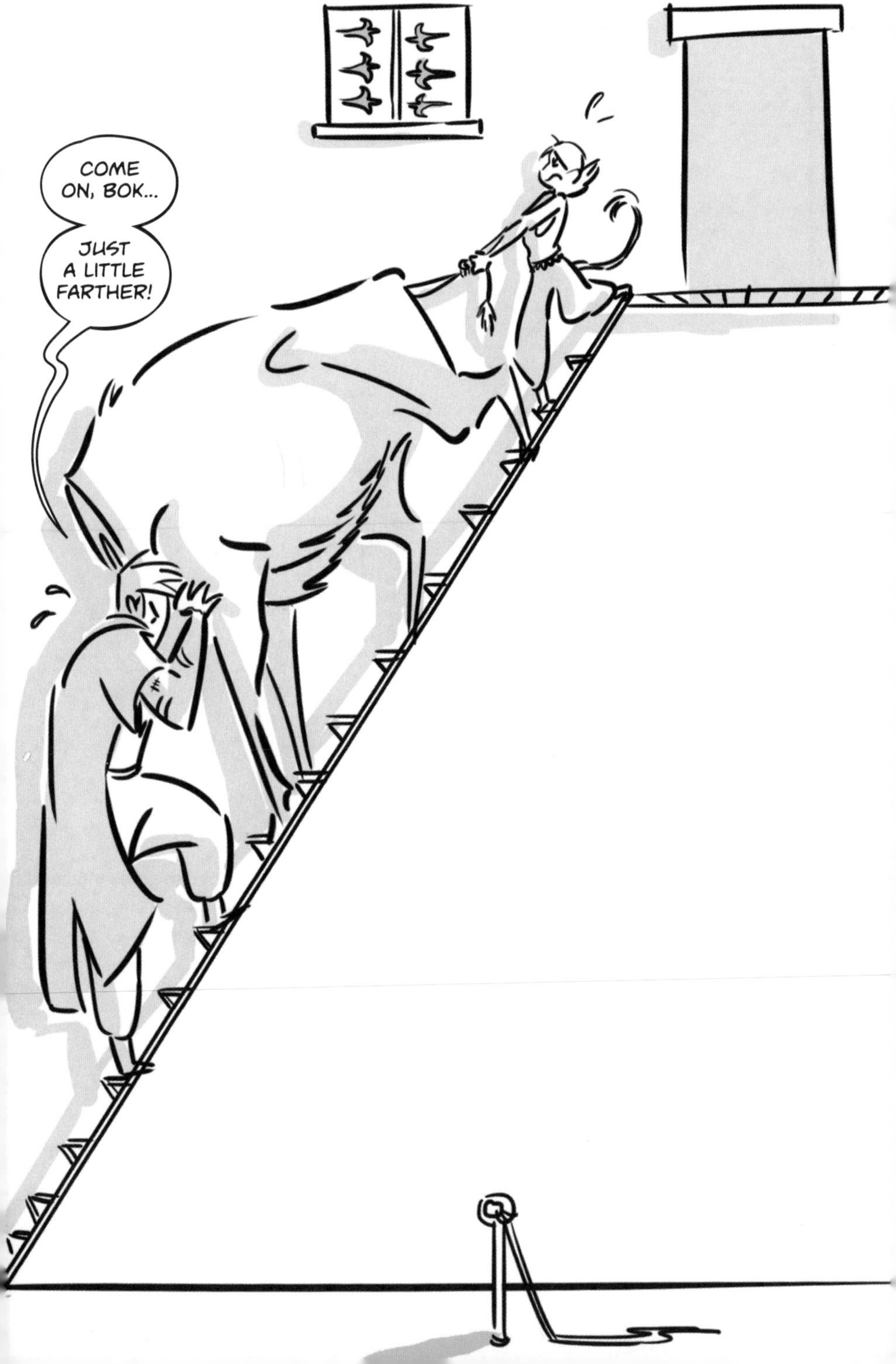
COME ON, BOK...
JUST A LITTLE FARTHER!

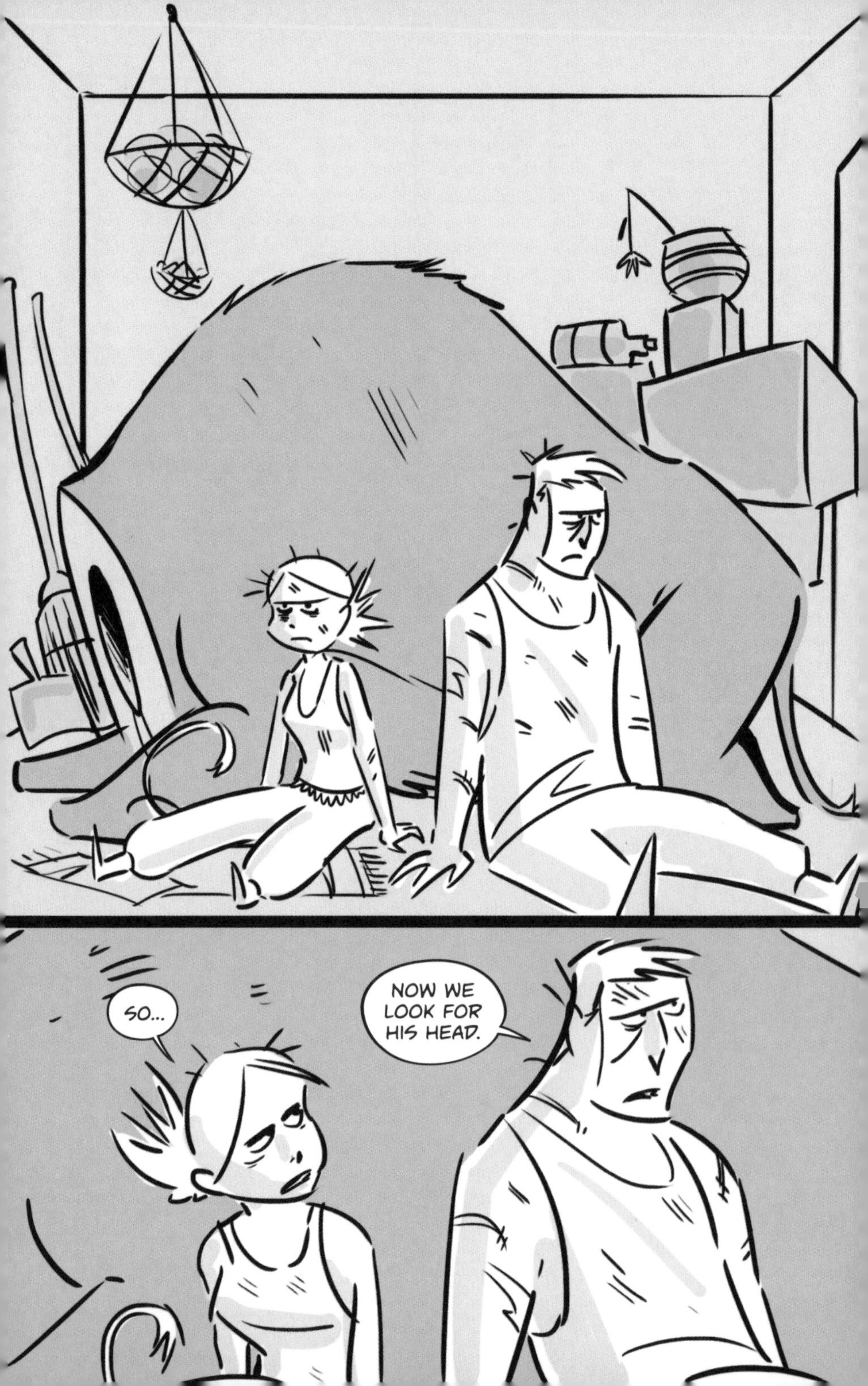
SO...
NOW WE LOOK FOR HIS HEAD.

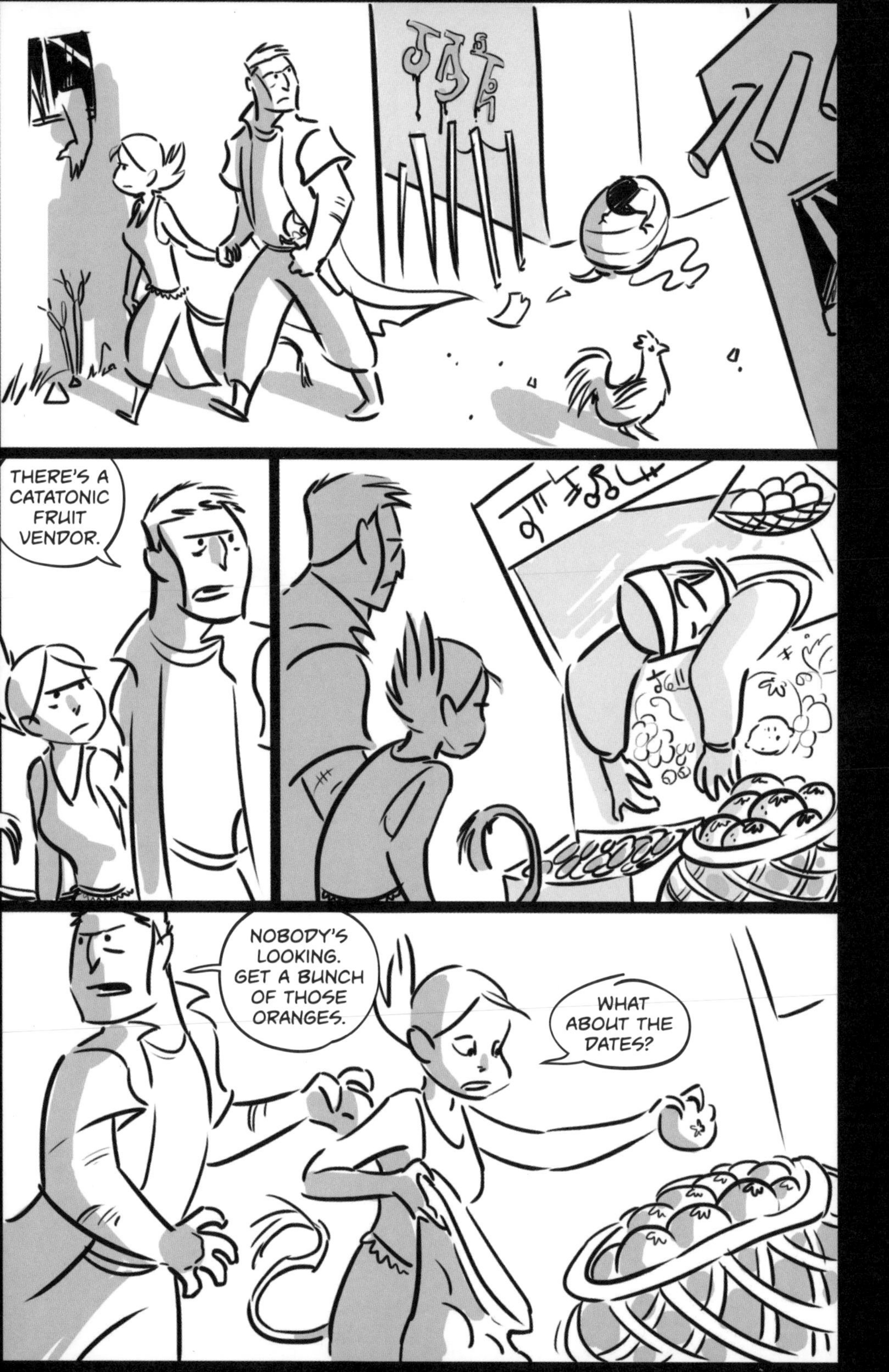
THERE'S A CATATONIC FRUIT VENDOR.
NOBODY'S LOOKING. GET A BUNCH OF THOSE ORANGES.
WHAT ABOUT THE DATES?

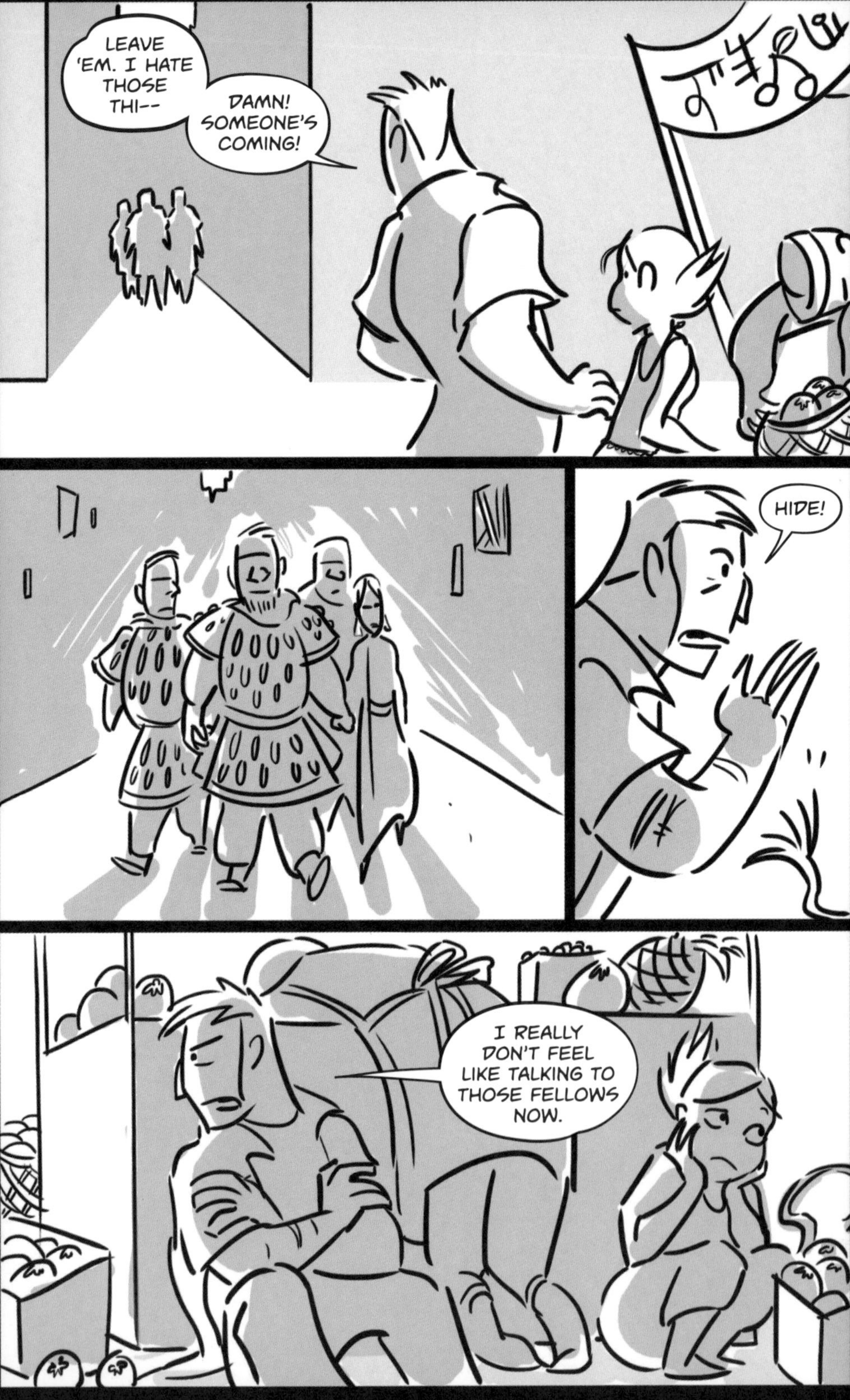
LEAVE 'EM. I HATE THOSE THI--
DAMN! SOMEONE'S COMING!
HIDE!
I REALLY DON'T FEEL LIKE TALKING TO THOSE FELLOWS NOW.

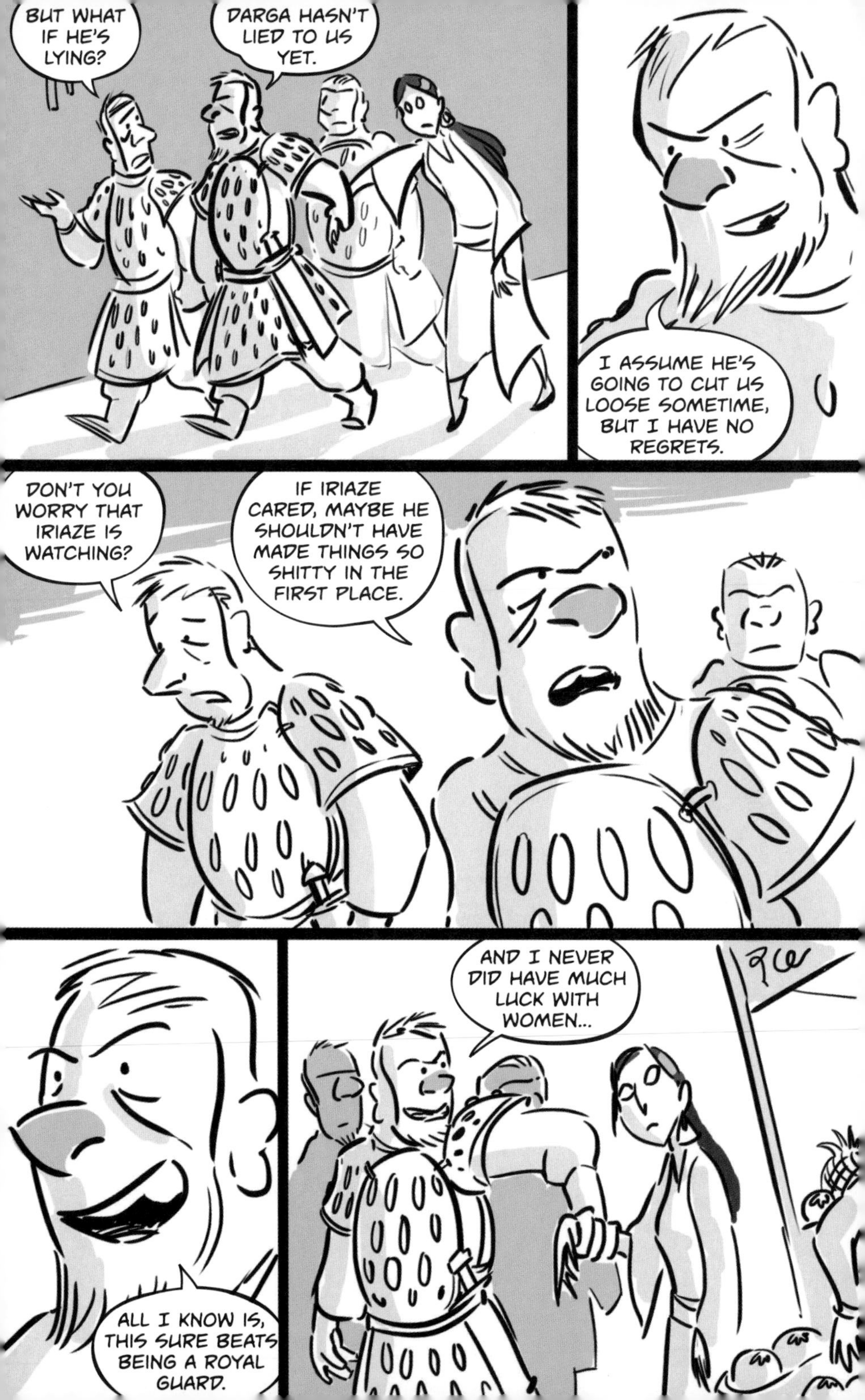
BUT WHAT IF HE'S LYING?
DARGA HASN'T LIED TO US YET.
I ASSUME HE'S GOING TO CUT US LOOSE SOMETIME, BUT I HAVE NO REGRETS.
DON'T YOU WORRY THAT IRIAZE IS WATCHING?
IF IRIAZE CARED, MAYBE HE SHOULDN'T HAVE MADE THINGS SO SHITTY IN THE FIRST PLACE.
ALL I KNOW IS, THIS SURE BEATS BEING A ROYAL GUARD.
AND I NEVER DID HAVE MUCH LUCK WITH WOMEN...

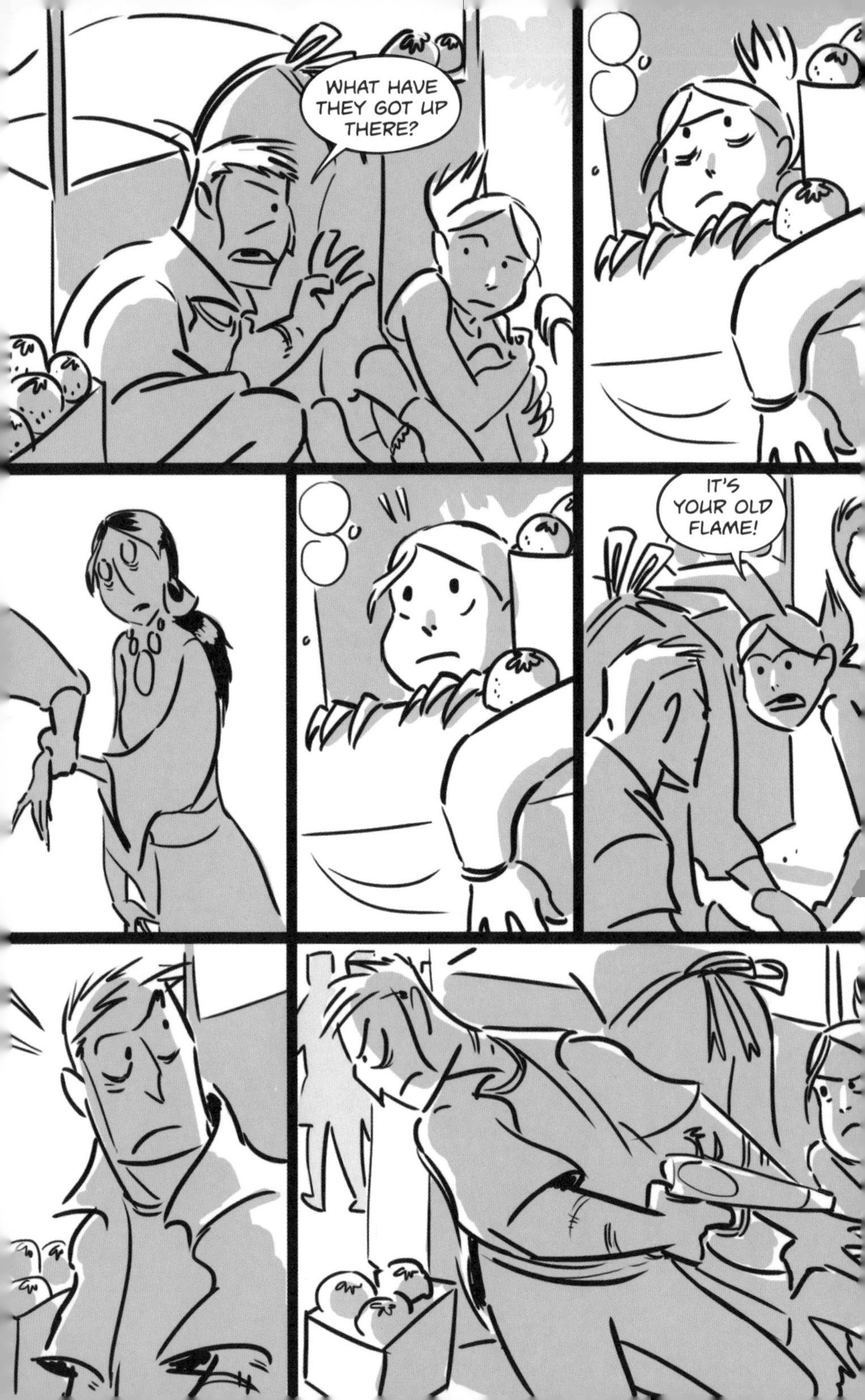
WHAT HAVE THEY GOT UP THERE?
IT'S YOUR OLD FLAME!

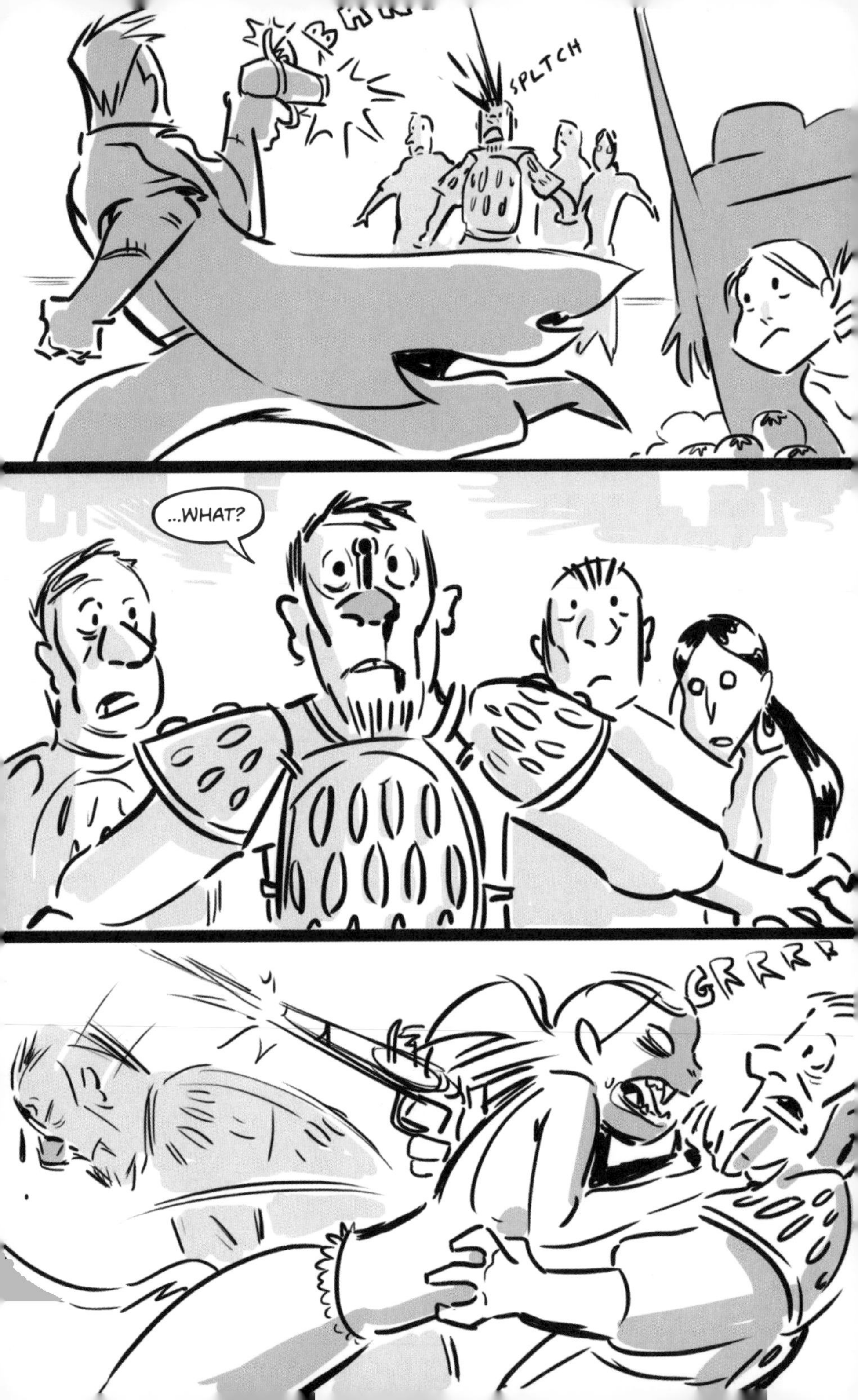
SPLTCH
...WHAT?
GRRRR

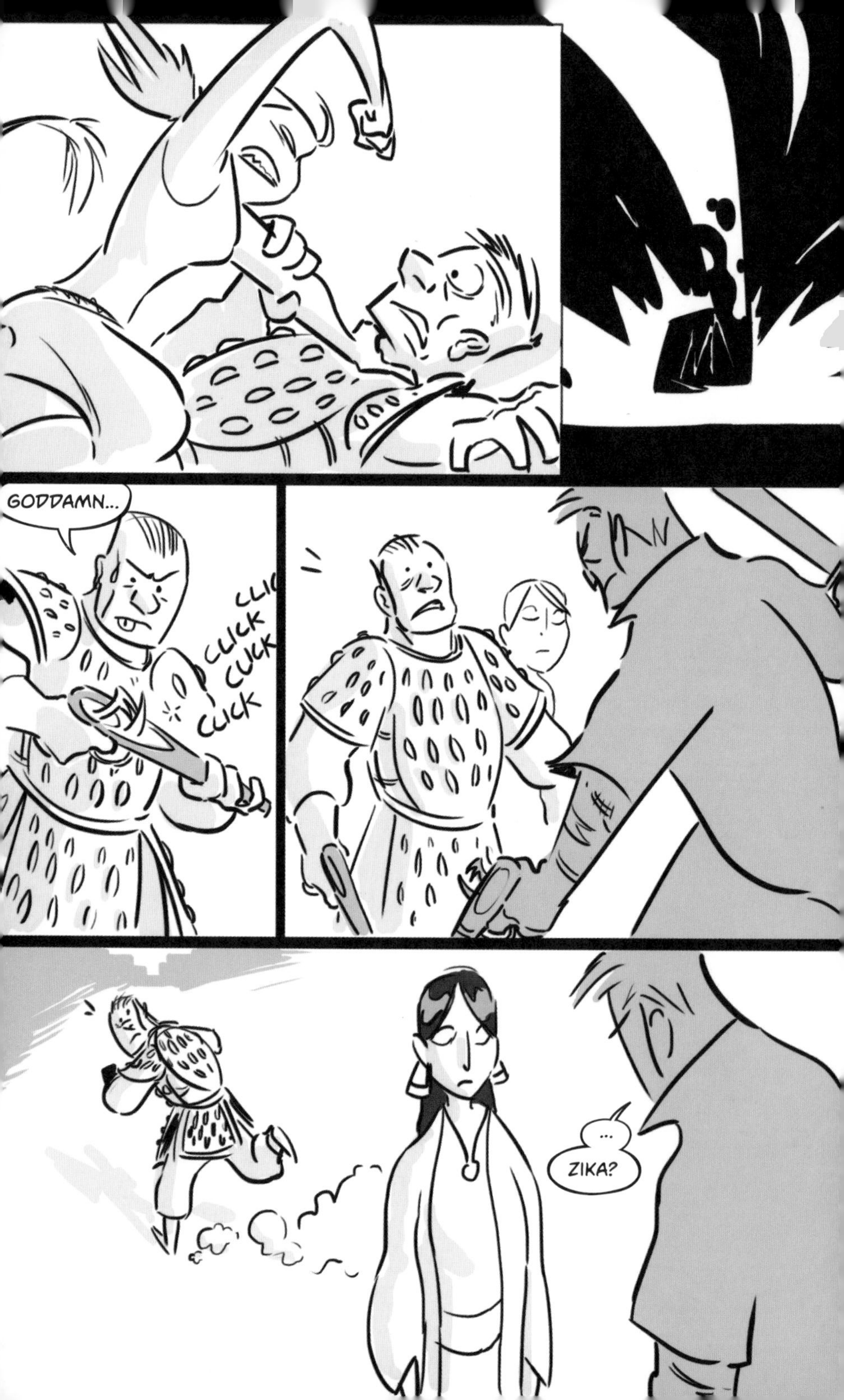
GODDAMN...
CLIC
CLICK
CLICK
CLICK
...
ZIKA?

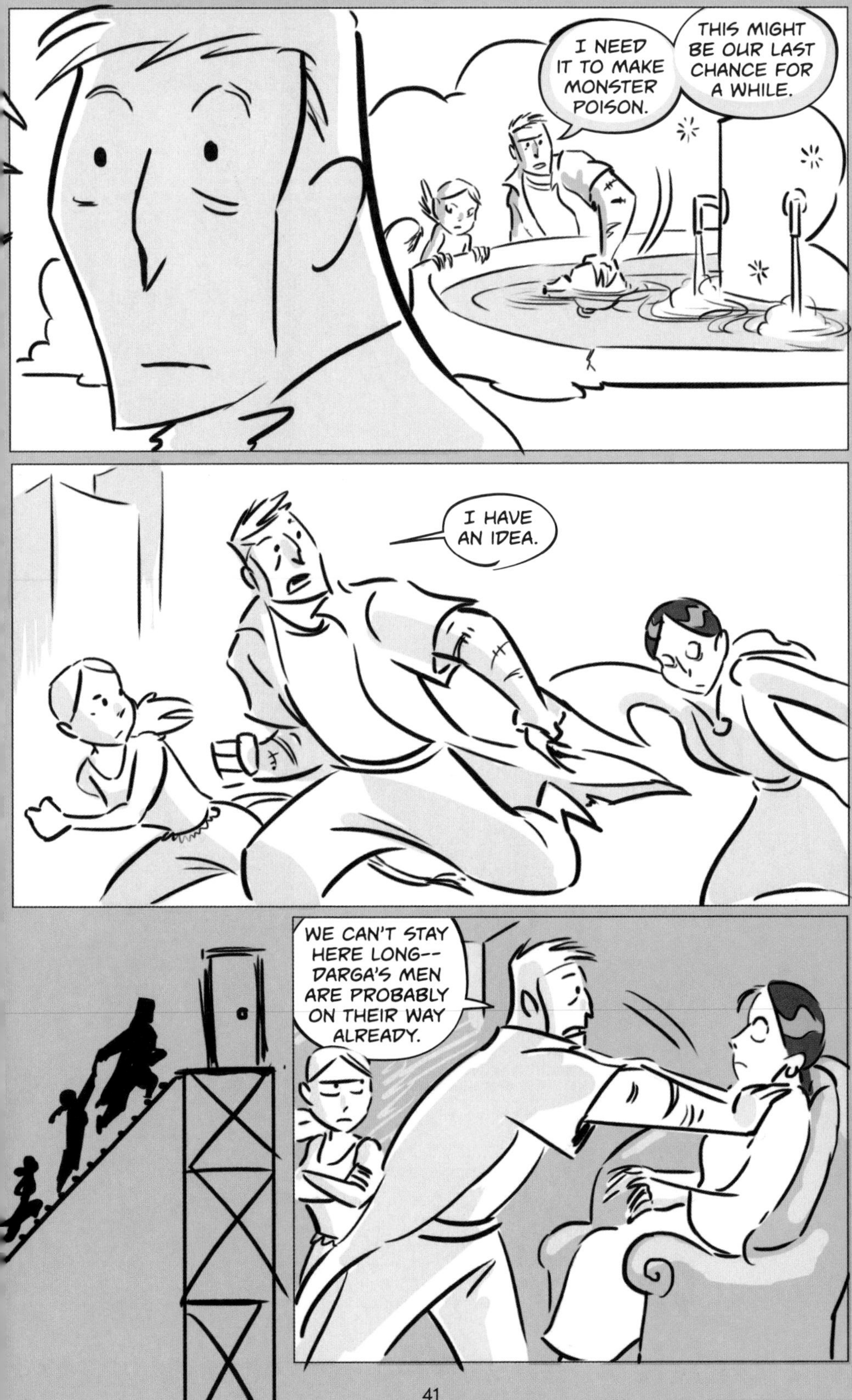
I NEED IT TO MAKE MONSTER POISON.
THIS MIGHT BE OUR LAST CHANCE FOR A WHILE.
I HAVE AN IDEA.
WE CAN'T STAY HERE LONG-- DARGA'S MEN ARE PROBABLY ON THEIR WAY ALREADY.

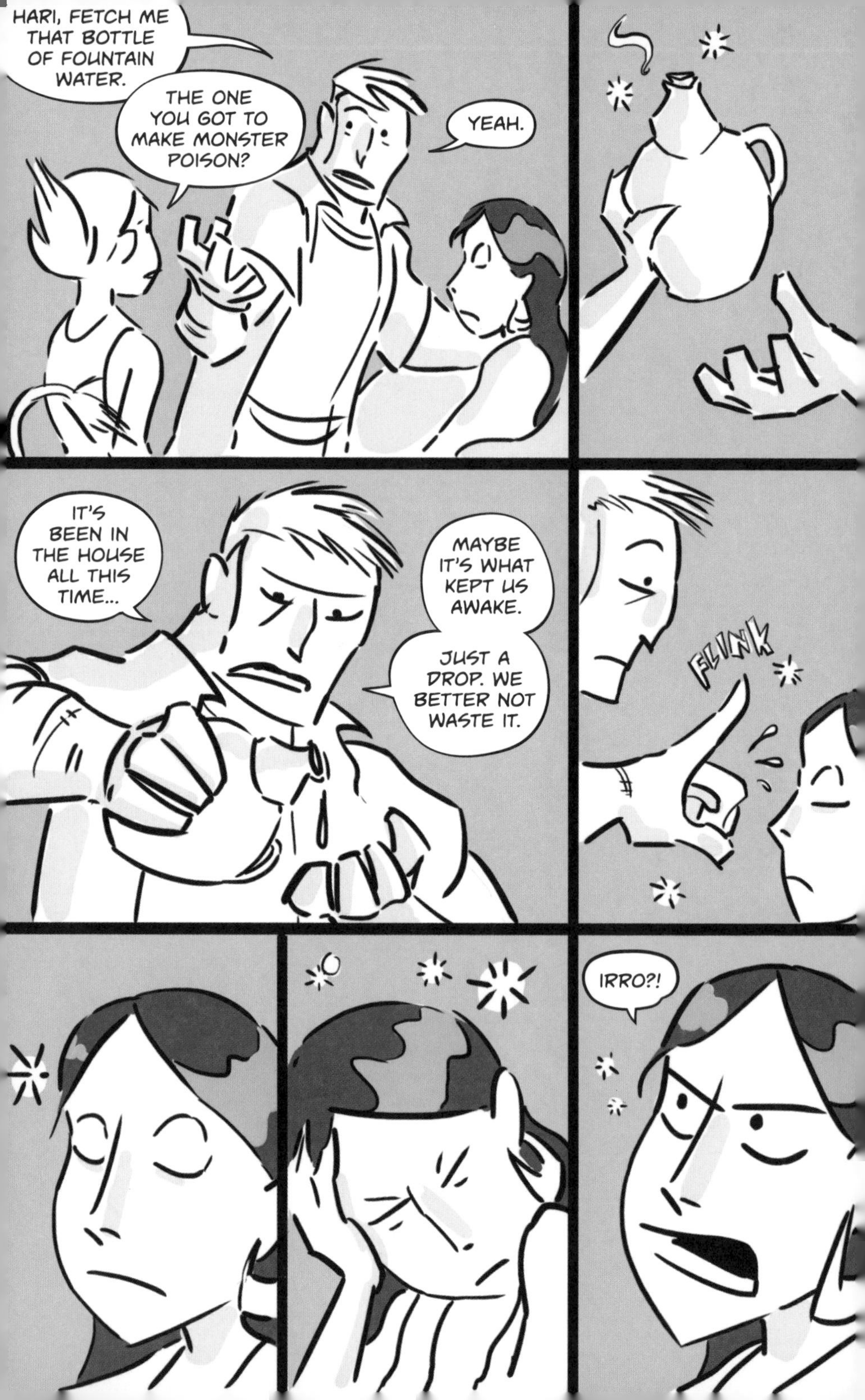
HARI, FETCH ME THAT BOTTLE OF FOUNTAIN WATER.
THE ONE YOU GOT TO MAKE MONSTER POISON?
YEAH.
IT'S BEEN IN THE HOUSE ALL THIS TIME...
MAYBE IT'S WHAT KEPT US AWAKE.
JUST A DROP. WE BETTER NOT WASTE IT.
FLINK
IRRO?!

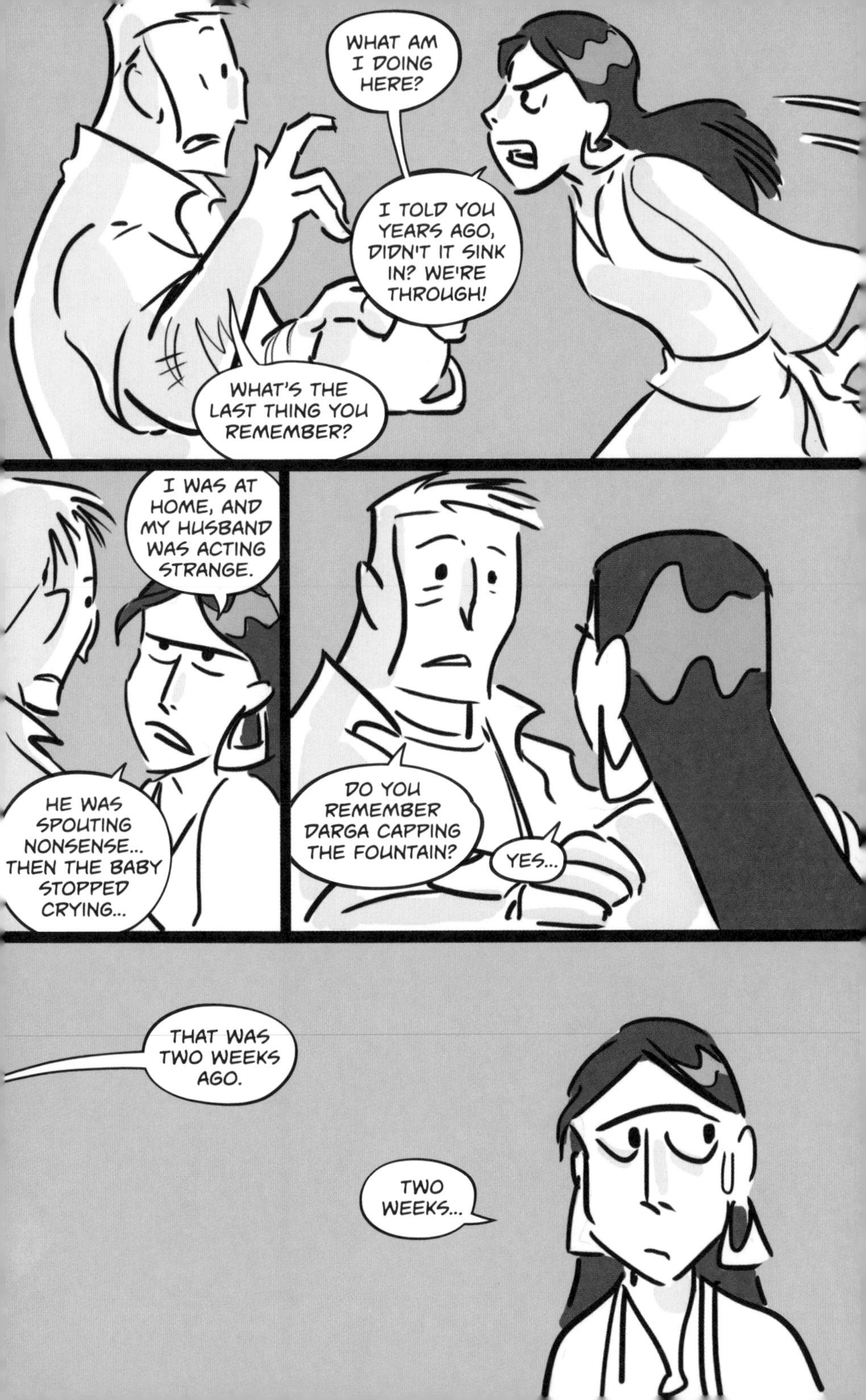
WHAT AM I DOING HERE?
I TOLD YOU YEARS AGO, DIDN'T IT SINK IN? WE'RE THROUGH!
WHAT'S THE LAST THING YOU REMEMBER?
I WAS AT HOME, AND MY HUSBAND WAS ACTING STRANGE.
HE WAS SPOUTING NONSENSE... THEN THE BABY STOPPED CRYING...
DO YOU REMEMBER DARGA CAPPING THE FOUNTAIN?
YES...
THAT WAS TWO WEEKS AGO.
TWO WEEKS...

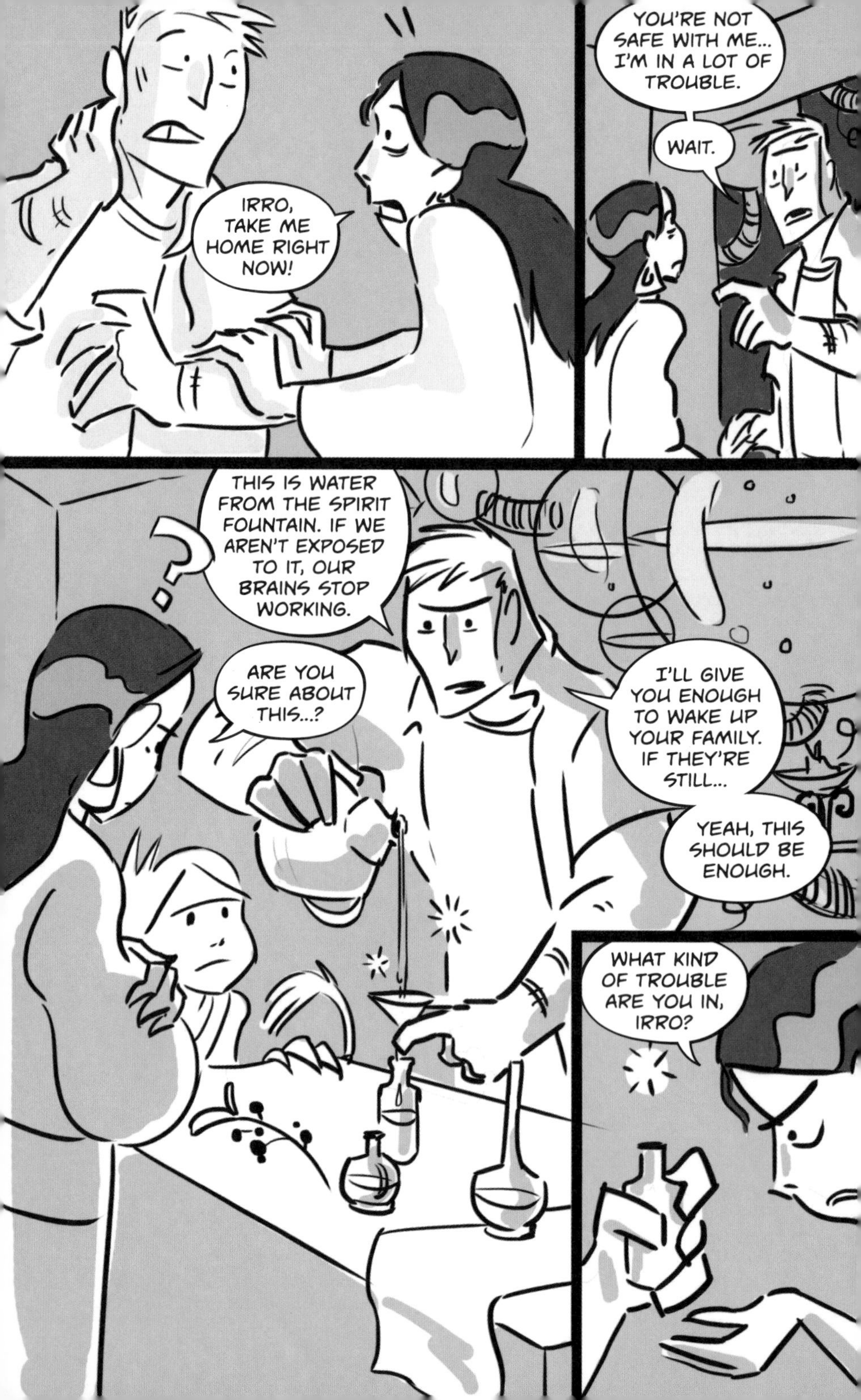
IRRO, TAKE ME HOME RIGHT NOW!
YOU'RE NOT SAFE WITH ME... I'M IN A LOT OF TROUBLE.
WAIT.
THIS IS WATER FROM THE SPIRIT FOUNTAIN. IF WE AREN'T EXPOSED TO IT, OUR BRAINS STOP WORKING.
ARE YOU SURE ABOUT THIS...?
I'LL GIVE YOU ENOUGH TO WAKE UP YOUR FAMILY. IF THEY'RE STILL...
YEAH, THIS SHOULD BE ENOUGH.
WHAT KIND OF TROUBLE ARE YOU IN, IRRO?

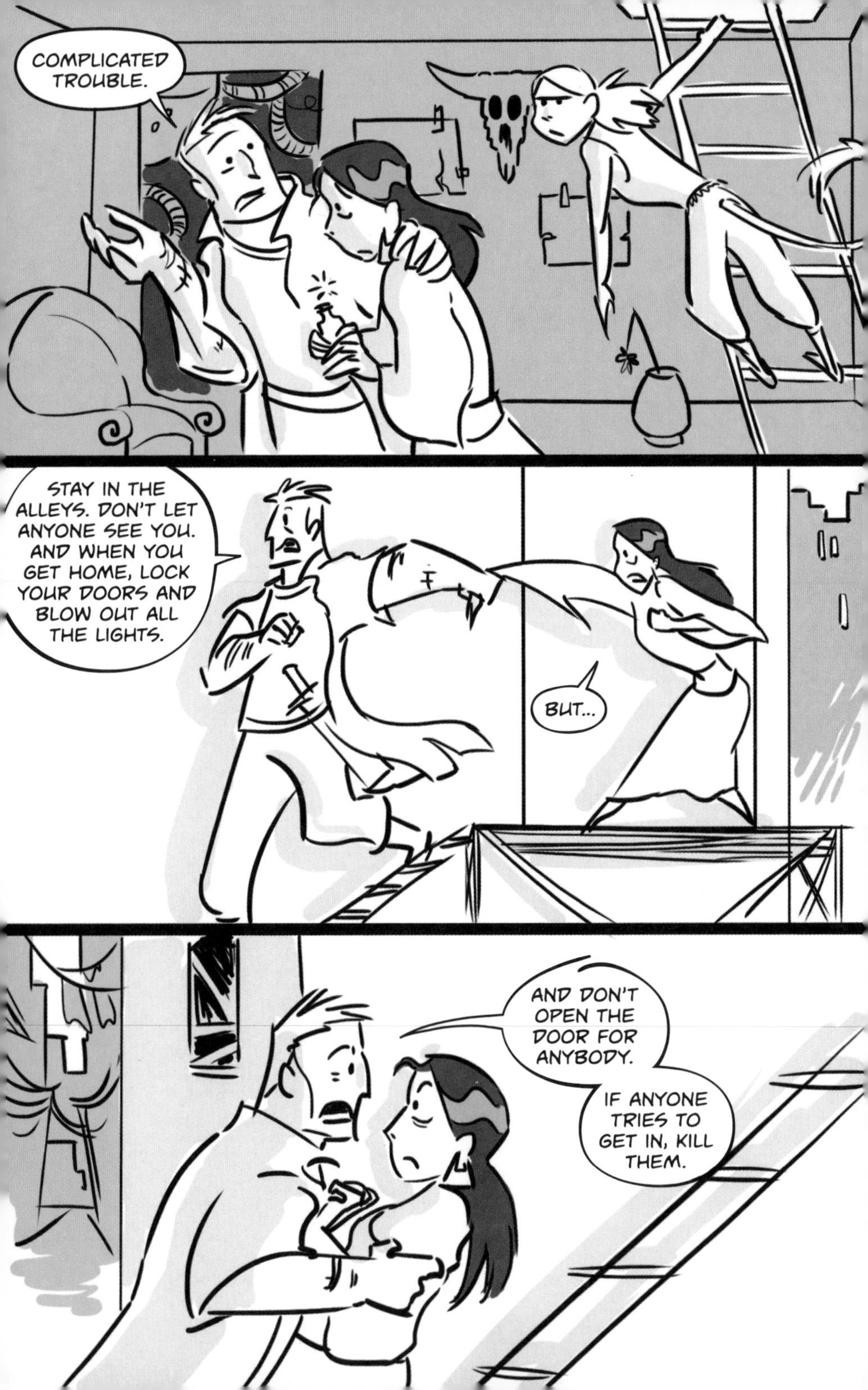
COMPLICATED TROUBLE.
STAY IN THE ALLEYS. DON'T LET ANYONE SEE YOU. AND WHEN YOU GET HOME, LOCK YOUR DOORS AND BLOW OUT ALL THE LIGHTS.
BUT...
AND DON'T OPEN THE DOOR FOR ANYBODY.
IF ANYONE TRIES TO GET IN, KILL THEM.

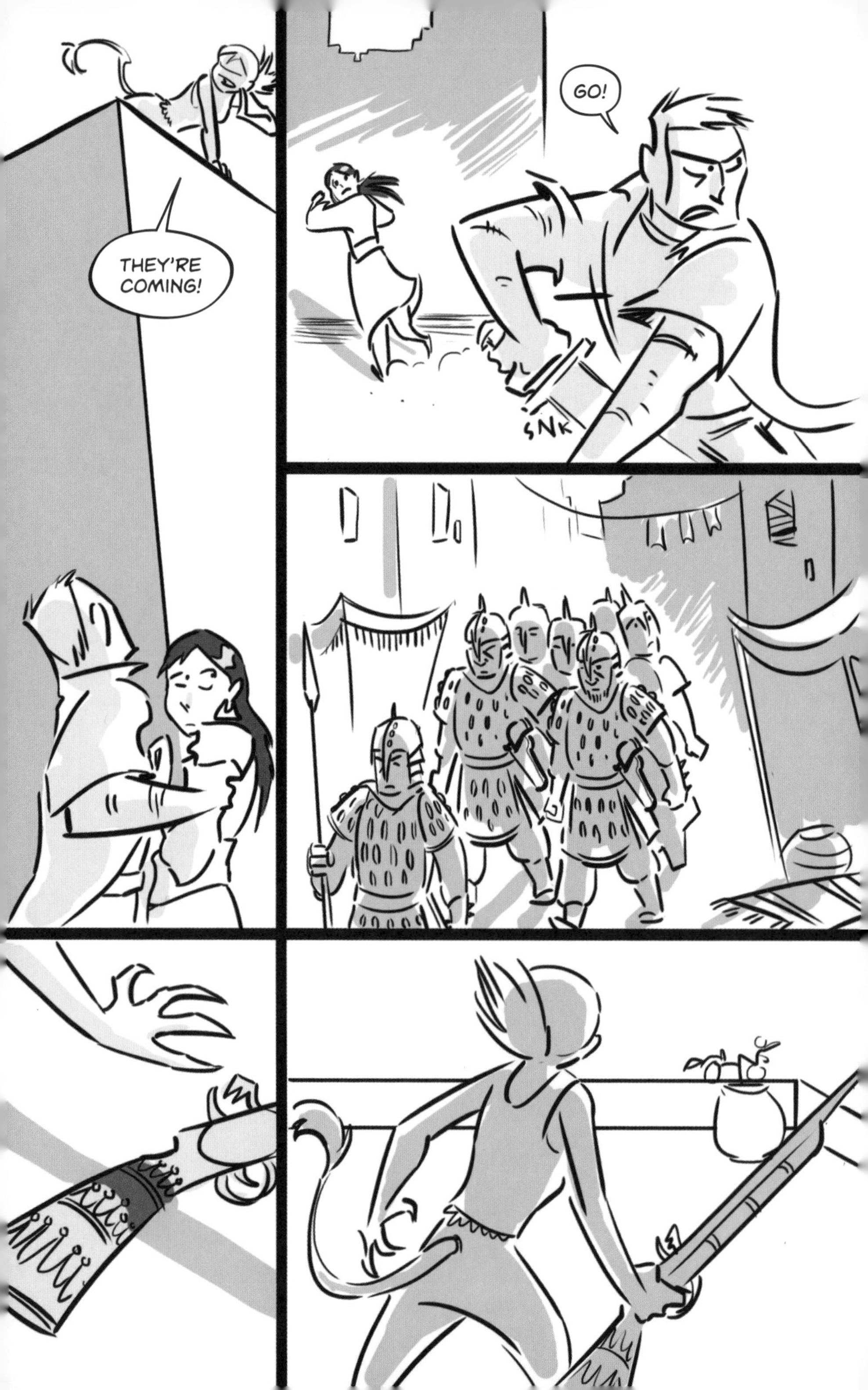
THEY'RE COMING!
GO!
SNK

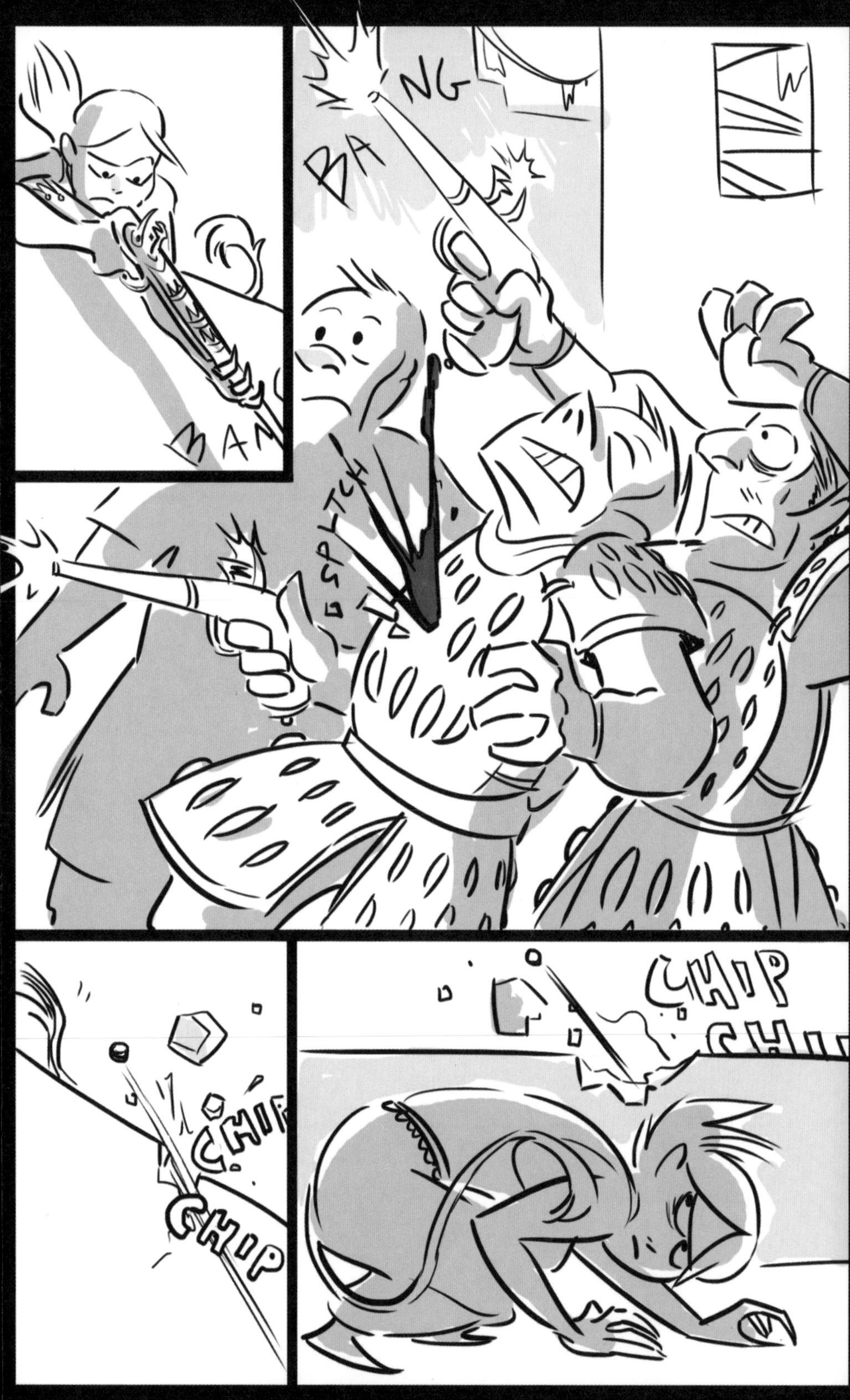
BAM
BANG
BANG
SPLTCH
CHIP
CHIP
CHIP
CHIP

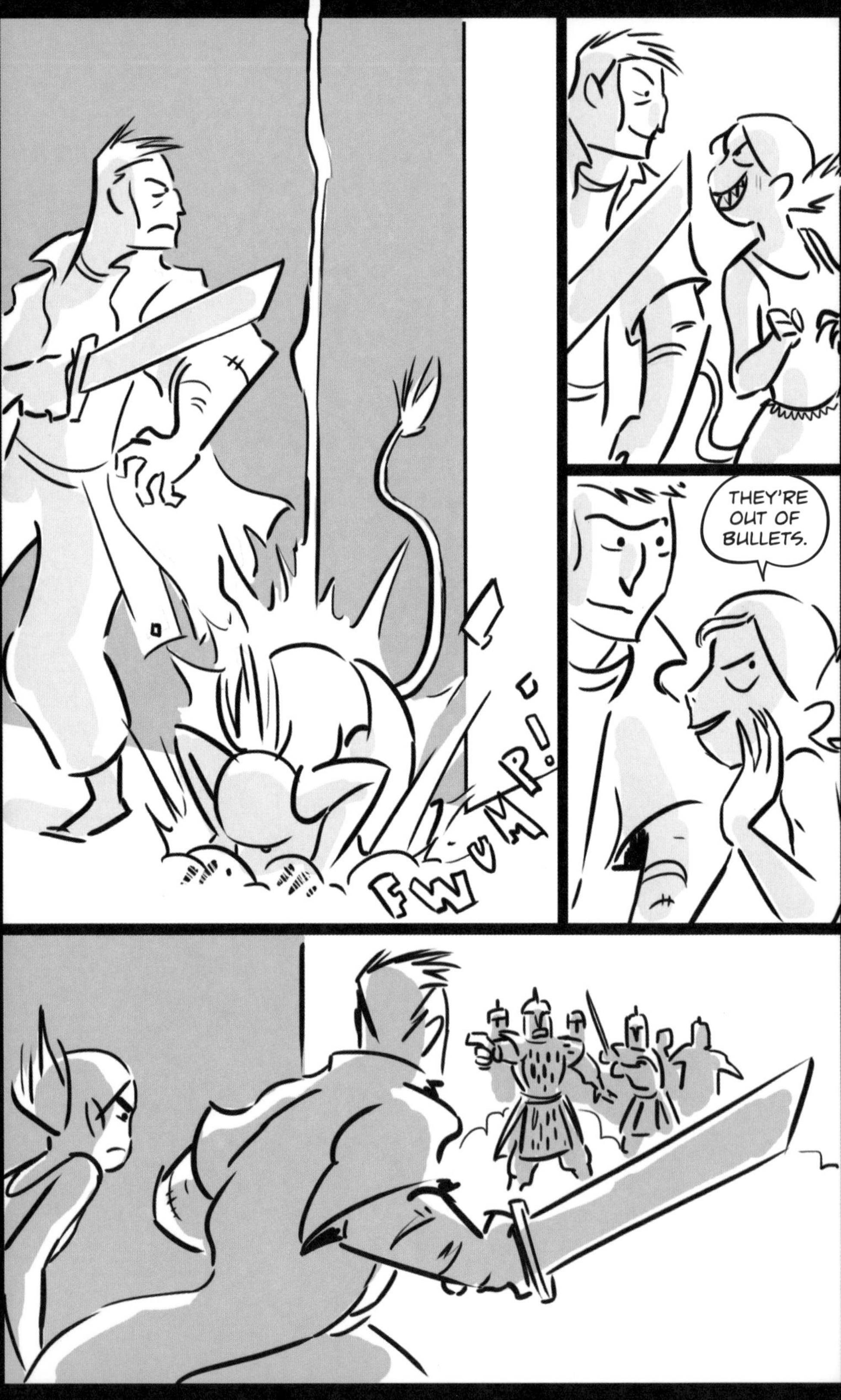
FWUMP!
THEY'RE OUT OF BULLETS.

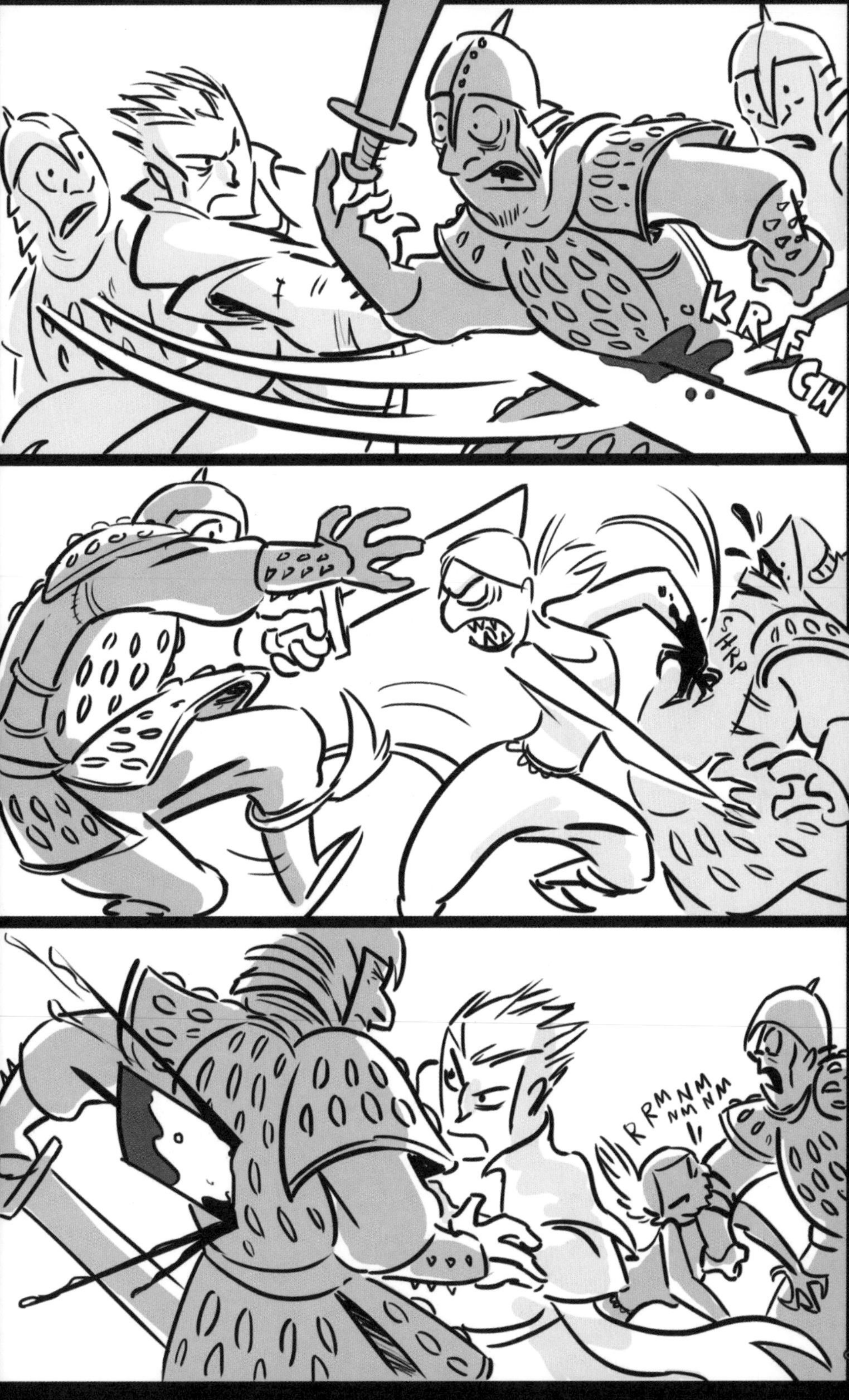
KRFCH
SHRP
RRMNMNMNM

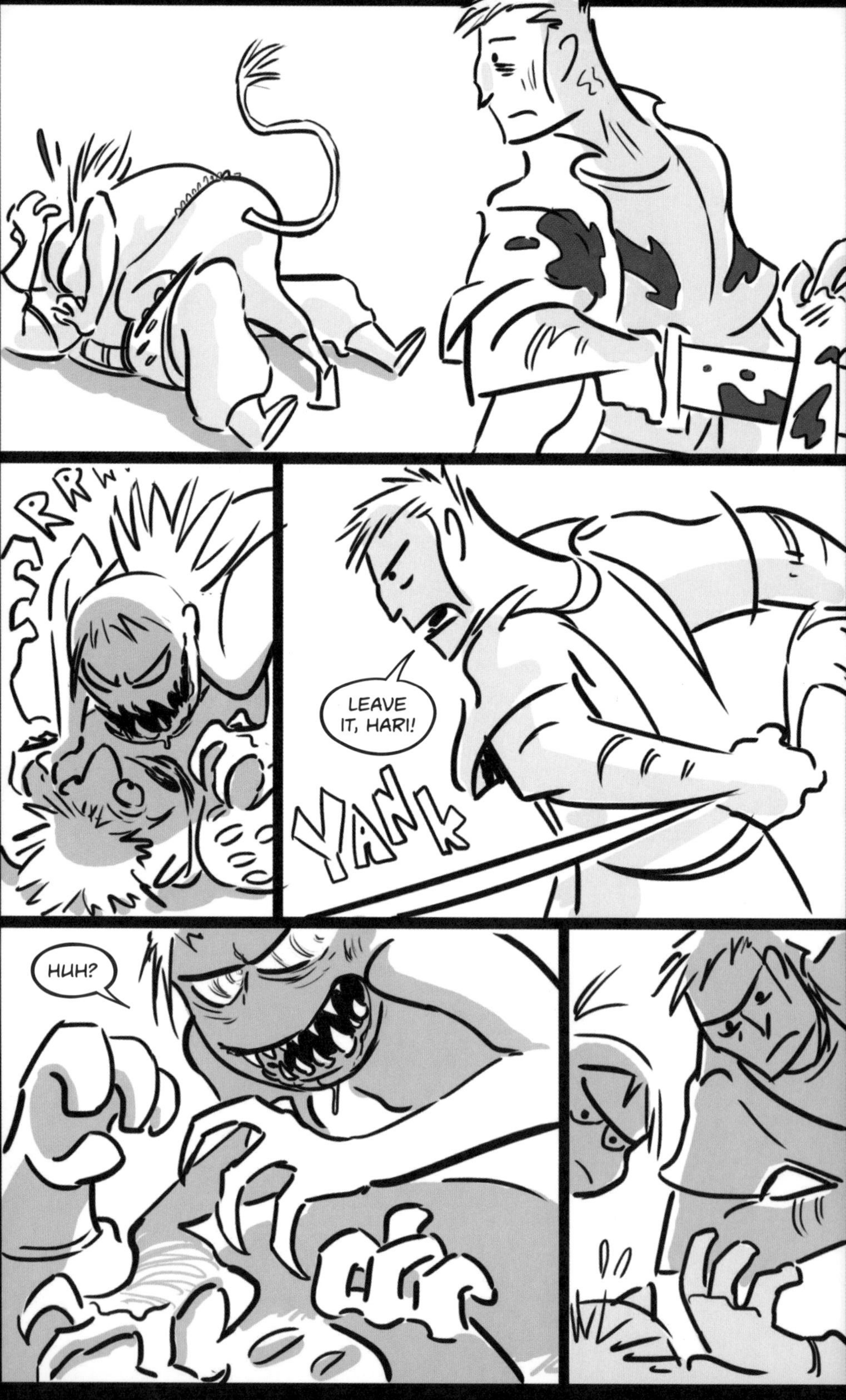
RRRW
LEAVE IT, HARI!
YANK
HUH?

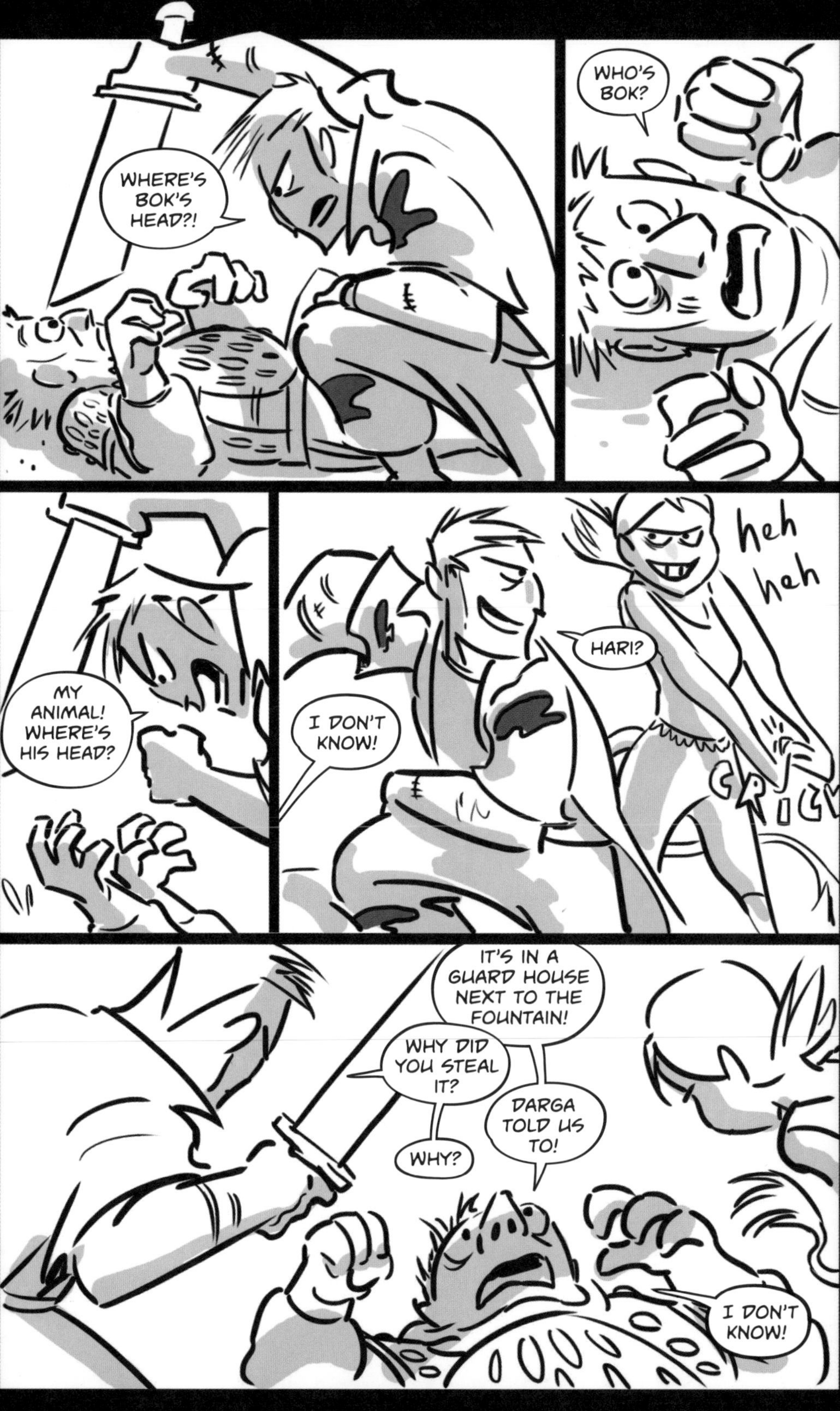
WHERE'S BOK'S HEAD?!
WHO'S BOK?
MY ANIMAL! WHERE'S HIS HEAD?
I DON'T KNOW!
HARI?
heh heh
IT'S IN A GUARD HOUSE NEXT TO THE FOUNTAIN!
WHY DID YOU STEAL IT?
DARGA TOLD US TO!
WHY?
I DON'T KNOW!

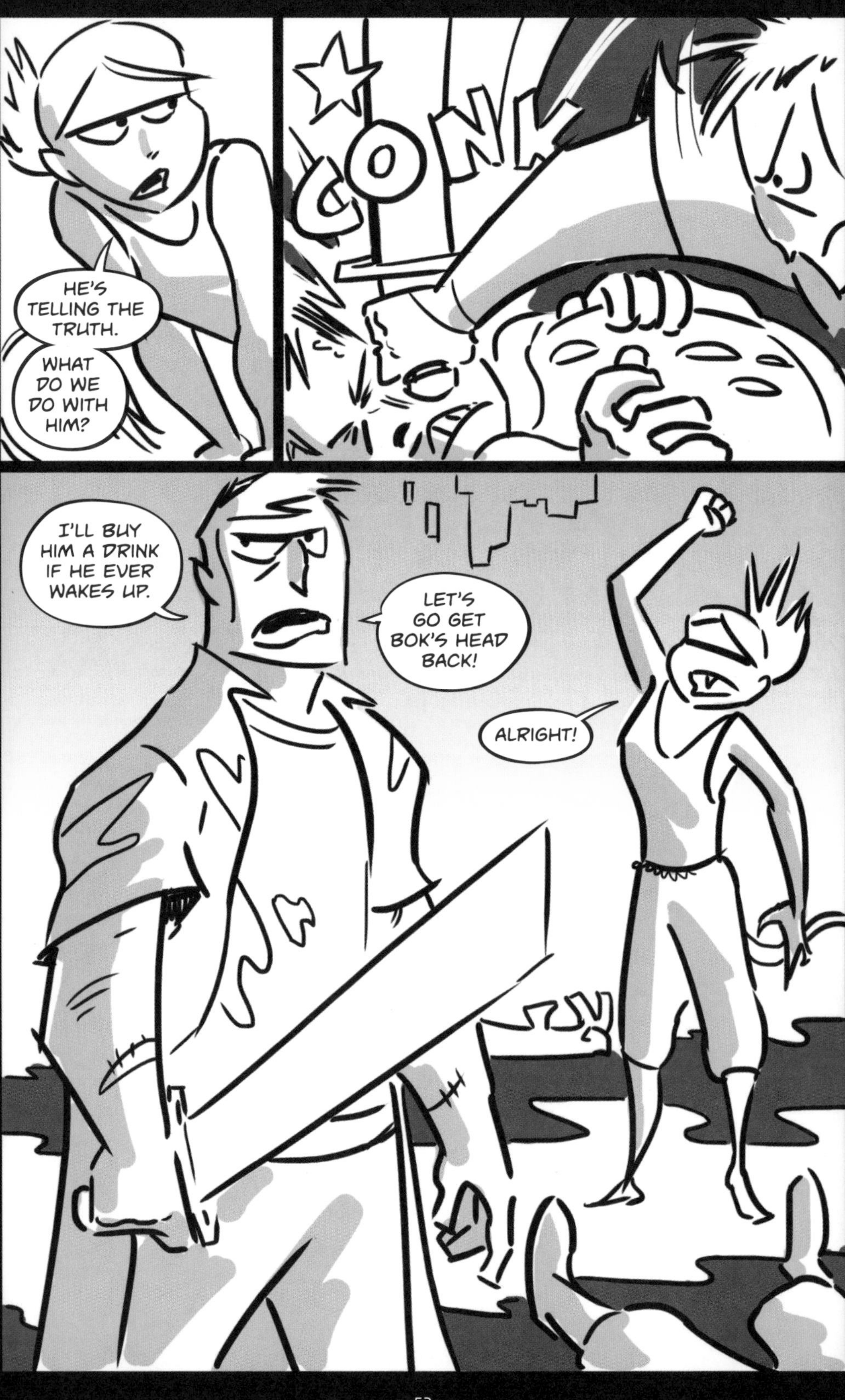
HE'S TELLING THE TRUTH.
WHAT DO WE DO WITH HIM?
CONK
I'LL BUY HIM A DRINK IF HE EVER WAKES UP.
LET'S GO GET BOK'S HEAD BACK!
ALRIGHT!

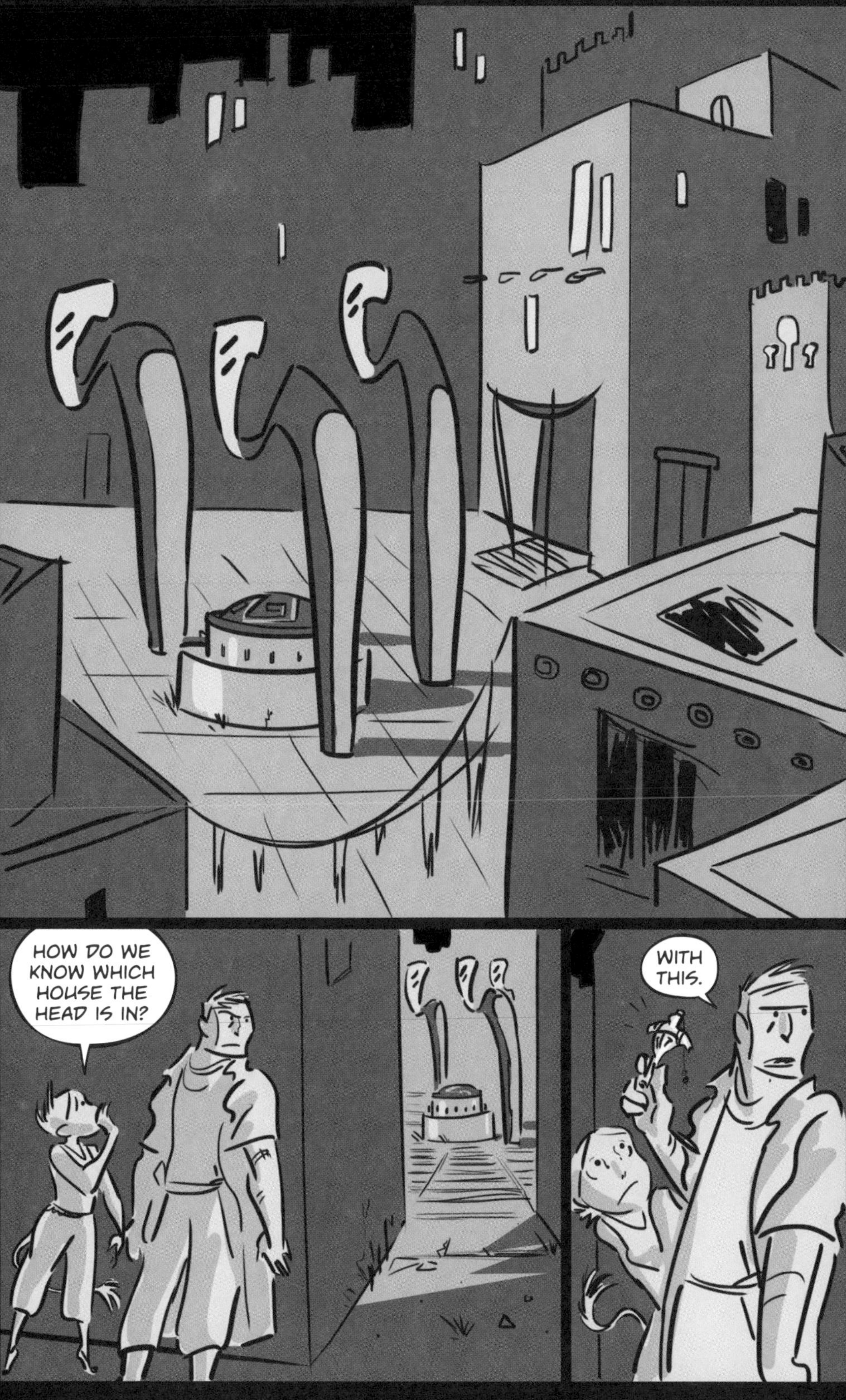
HOW DO WE KNOW WHICH HOUSE THE HEAD IS IN?
WITH THIS.

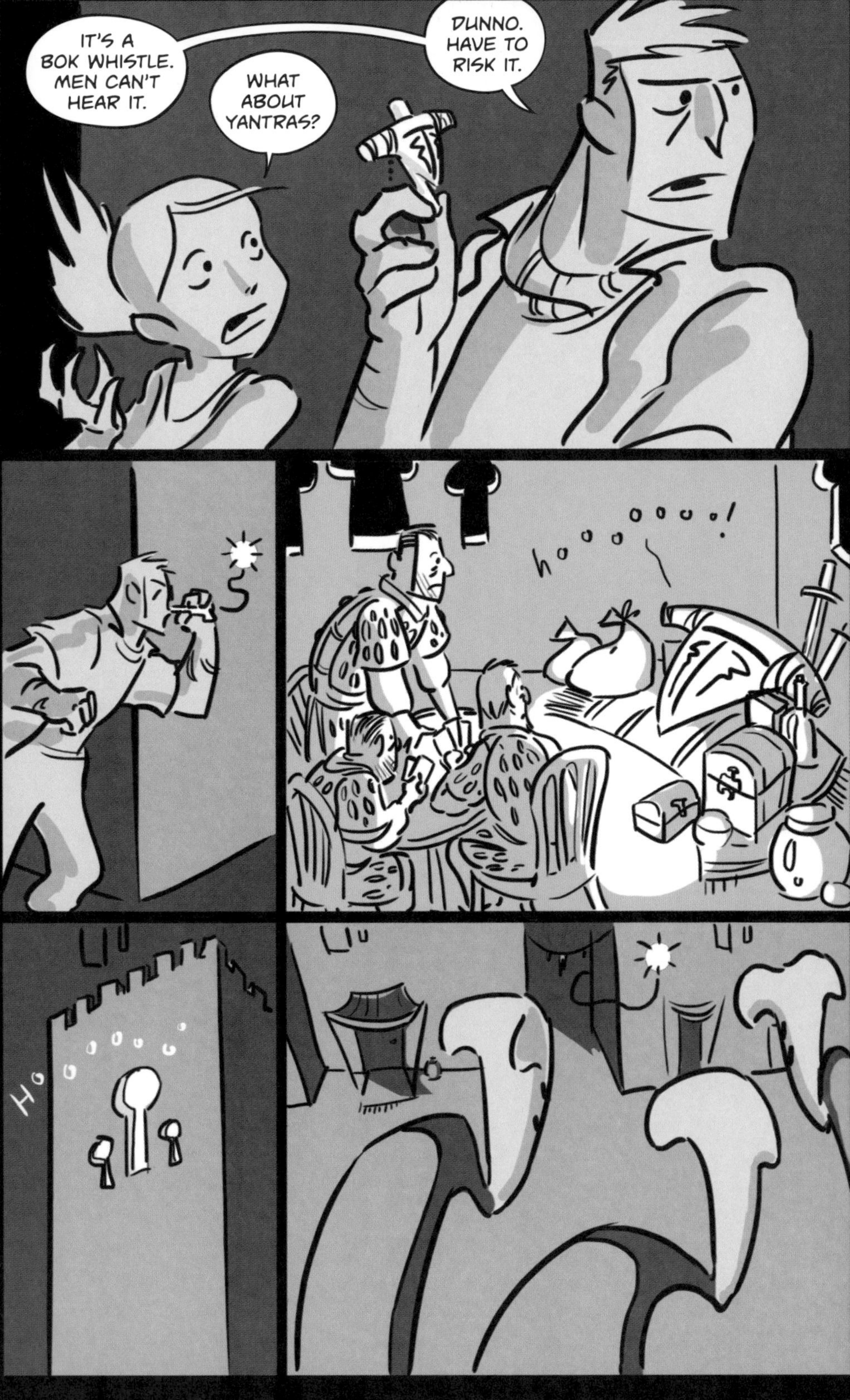
IT'S A BOK WHISTLE. MEN CAN'T HEAR IT.
WHAT ABOUT YANTRAS?
DUNNO. HAVE TO RISK IT.
hooooo!
HOOOOOO

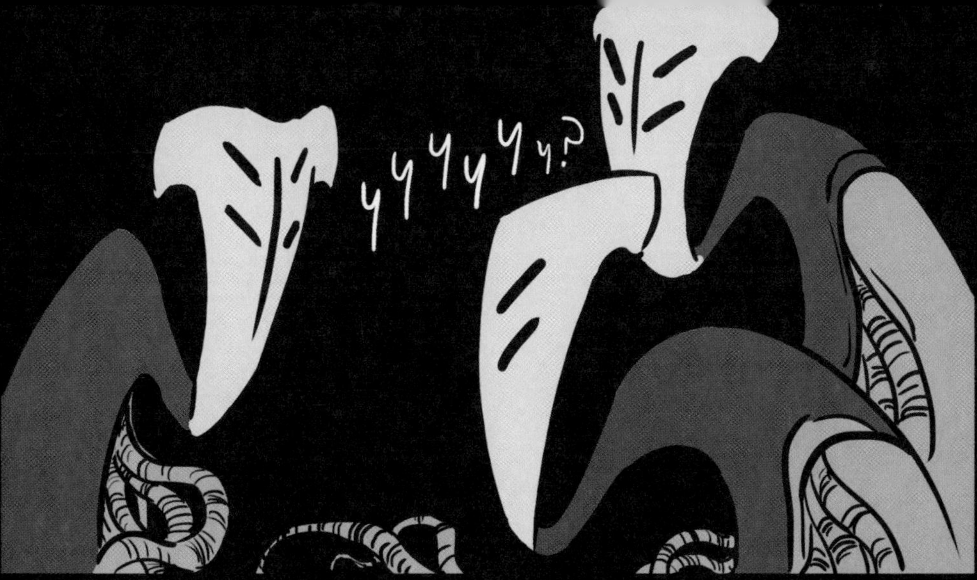
yyyyyy?

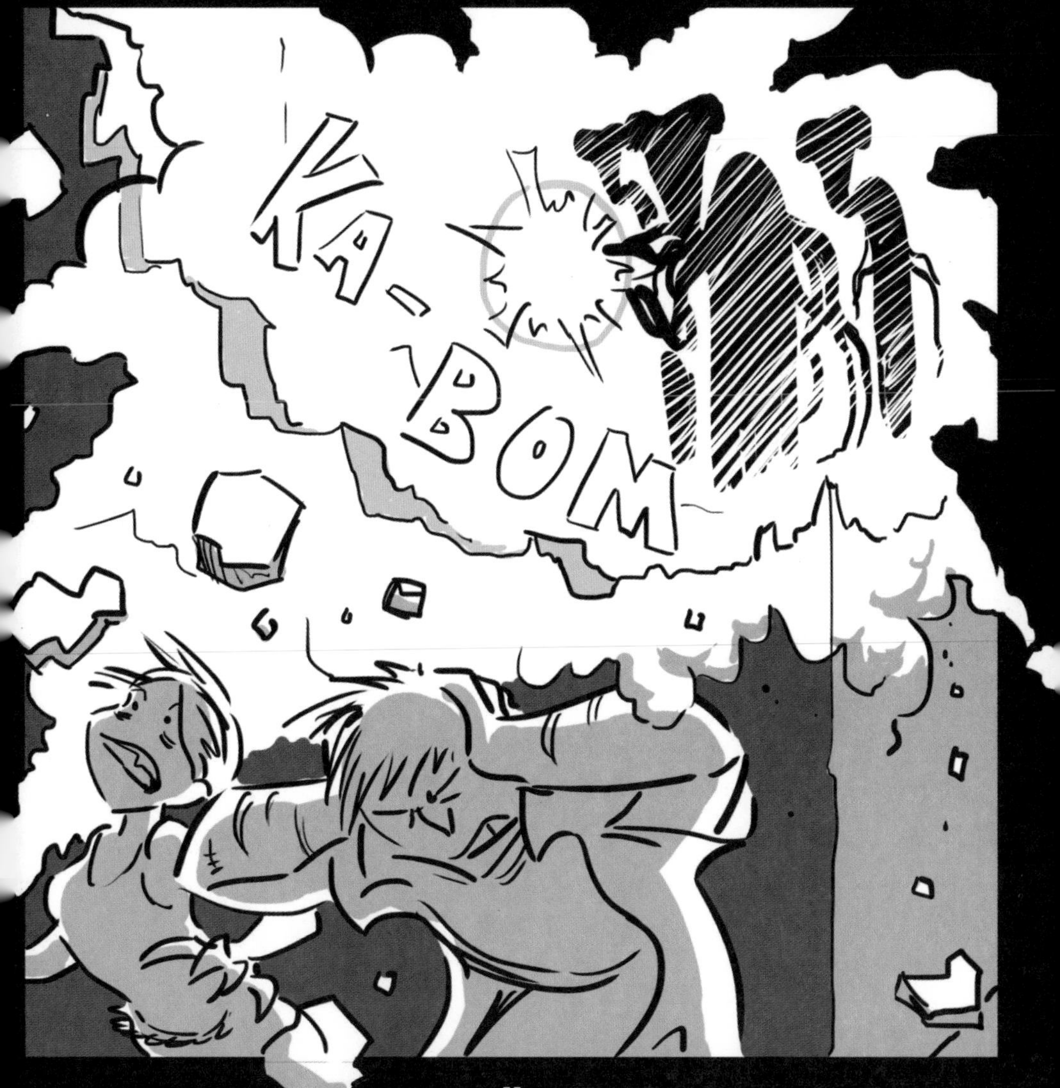
KA-BOM

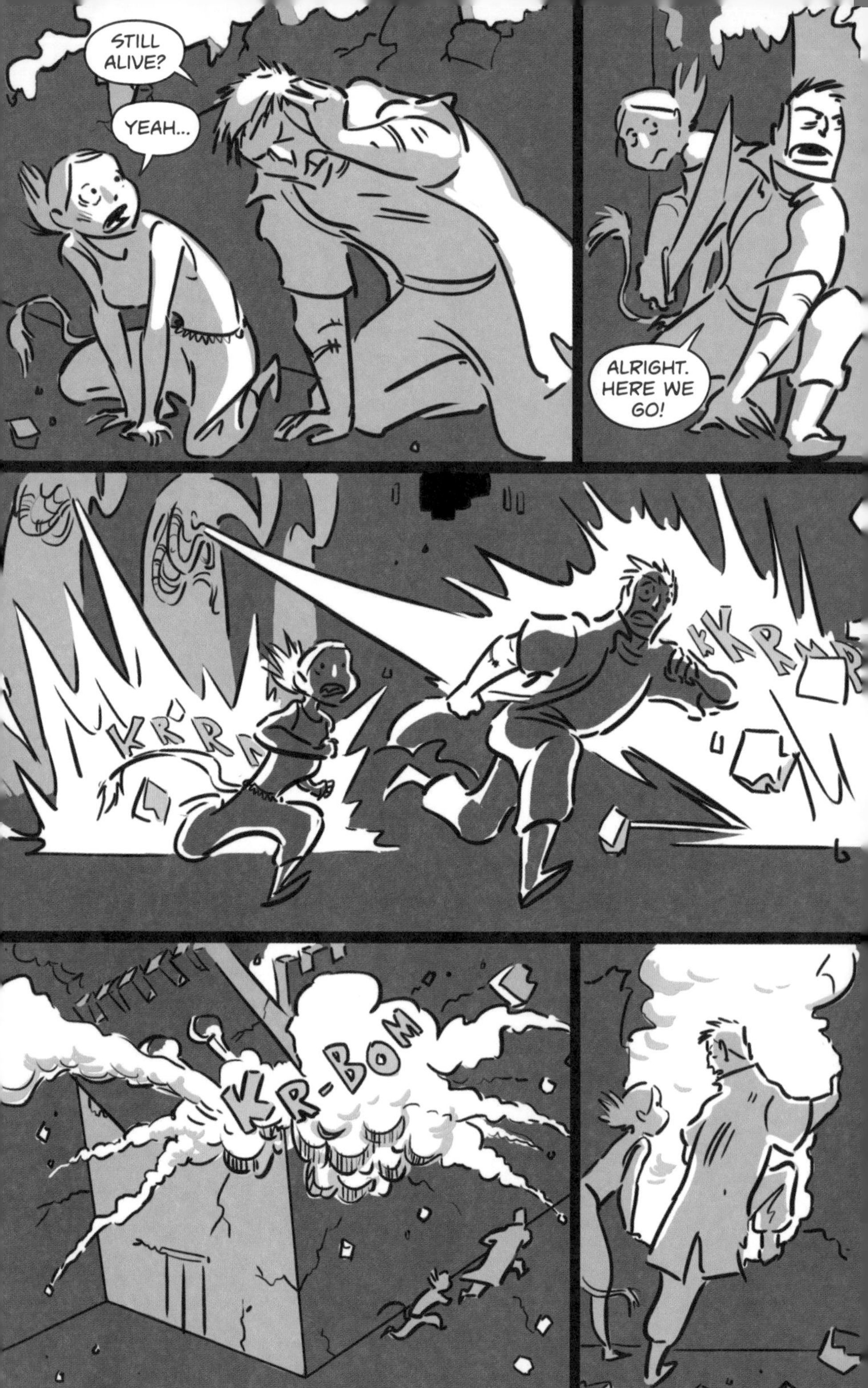
STILL ALIVE?
YEAH...
ALRIGHT. HERE WE GO!
KR-BOM

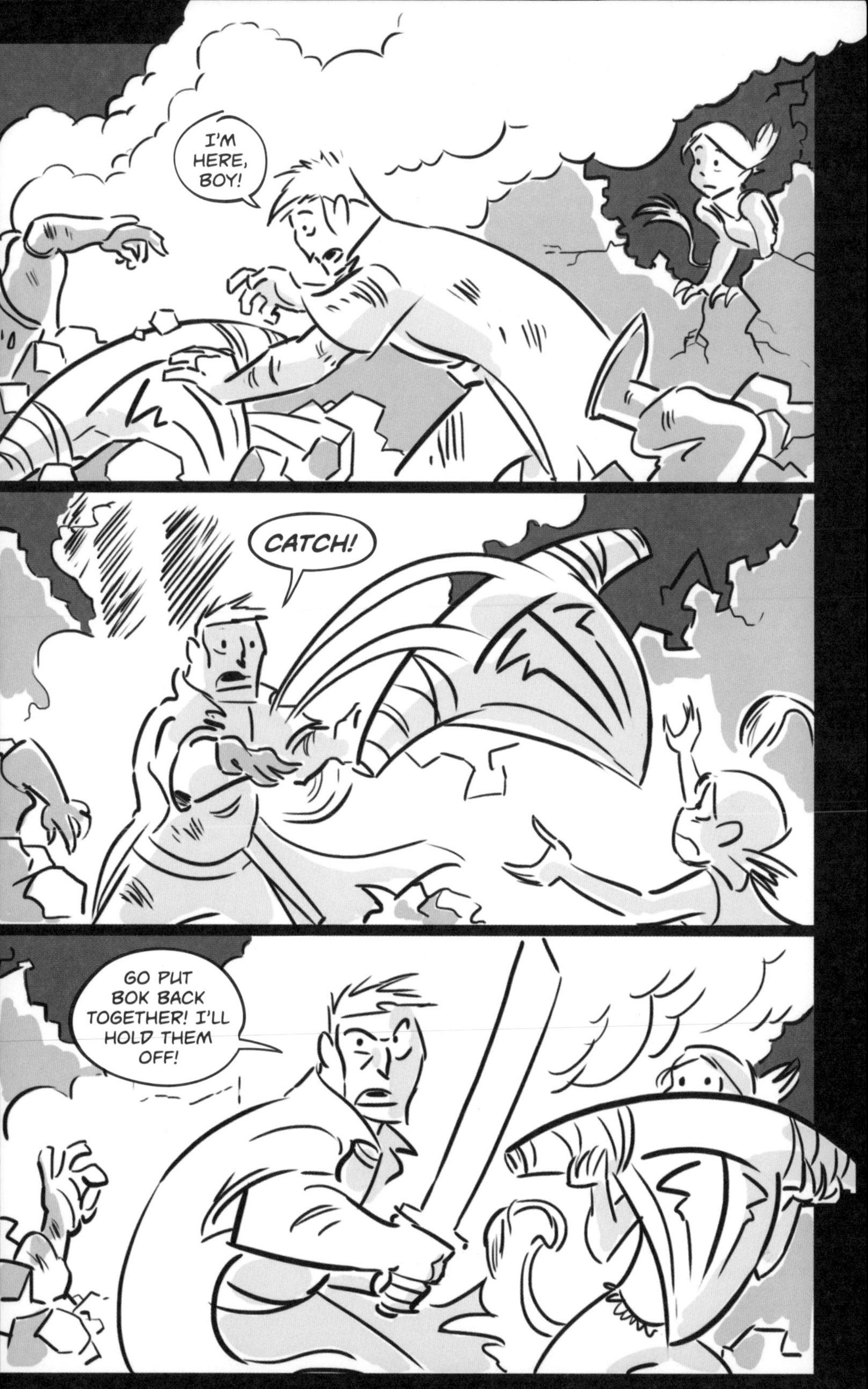
I'M HERE, BOY!
CATCH!
GO PUT BOK BACK TOGETHER! I'LL HOLD THEM OFF!

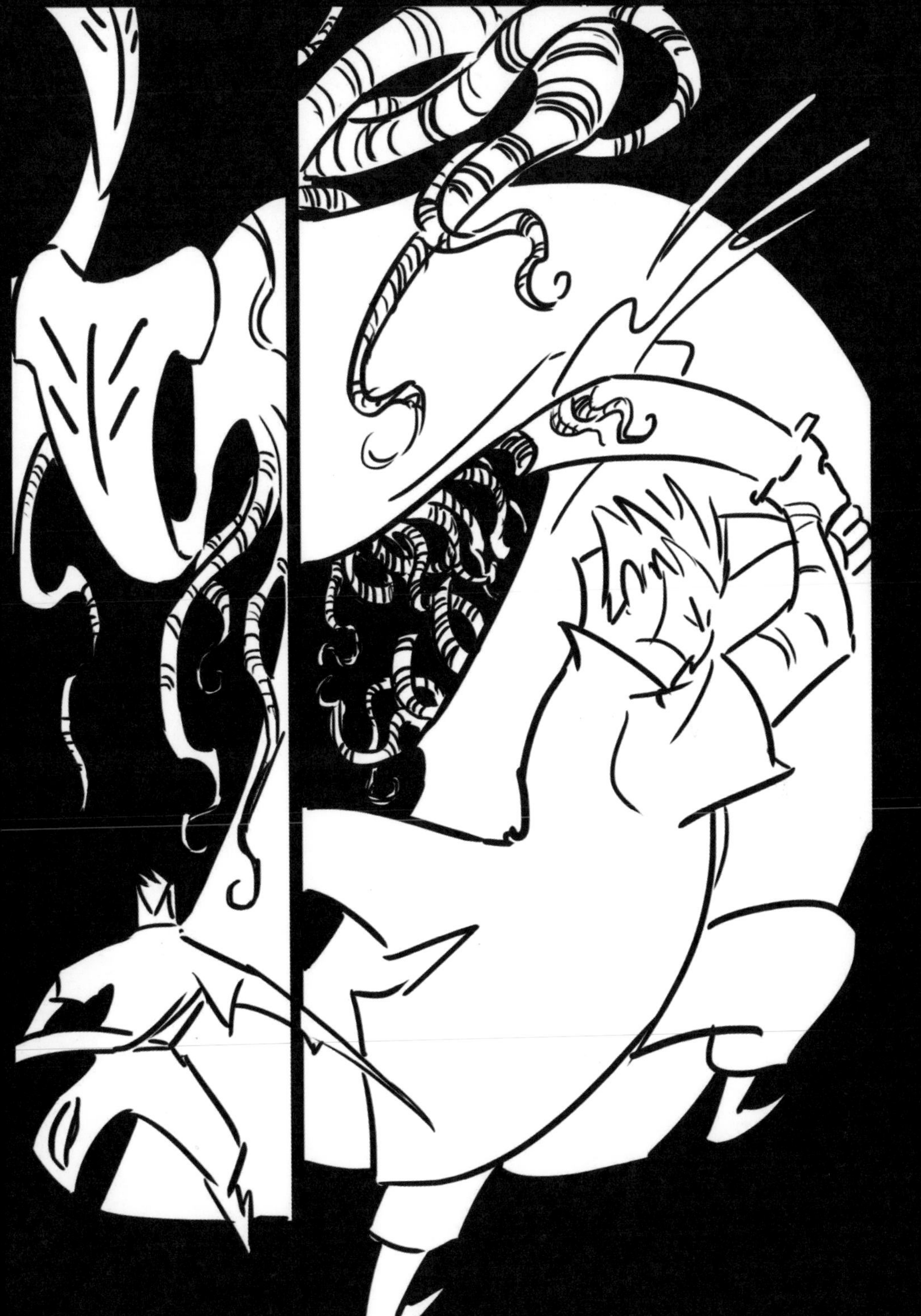

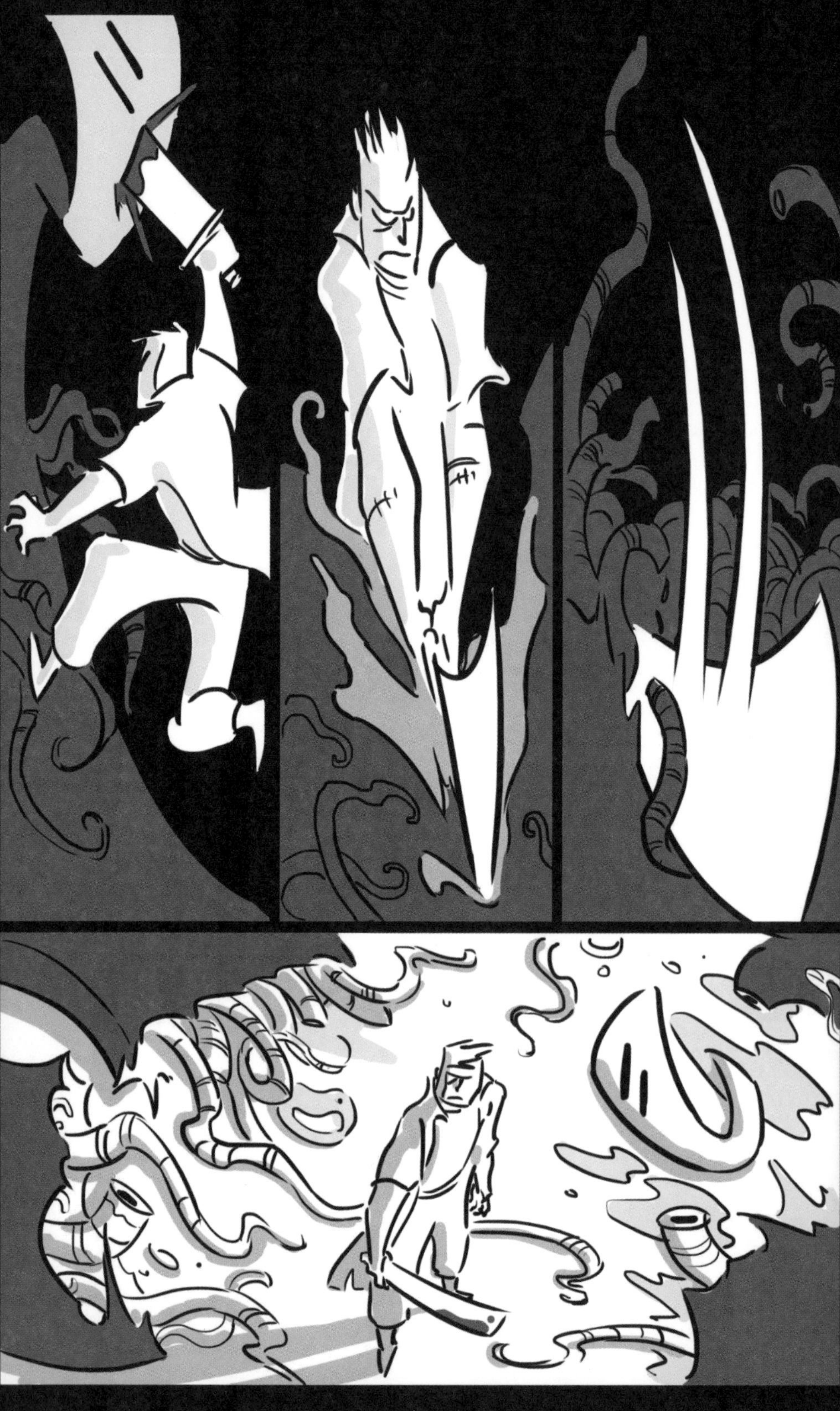

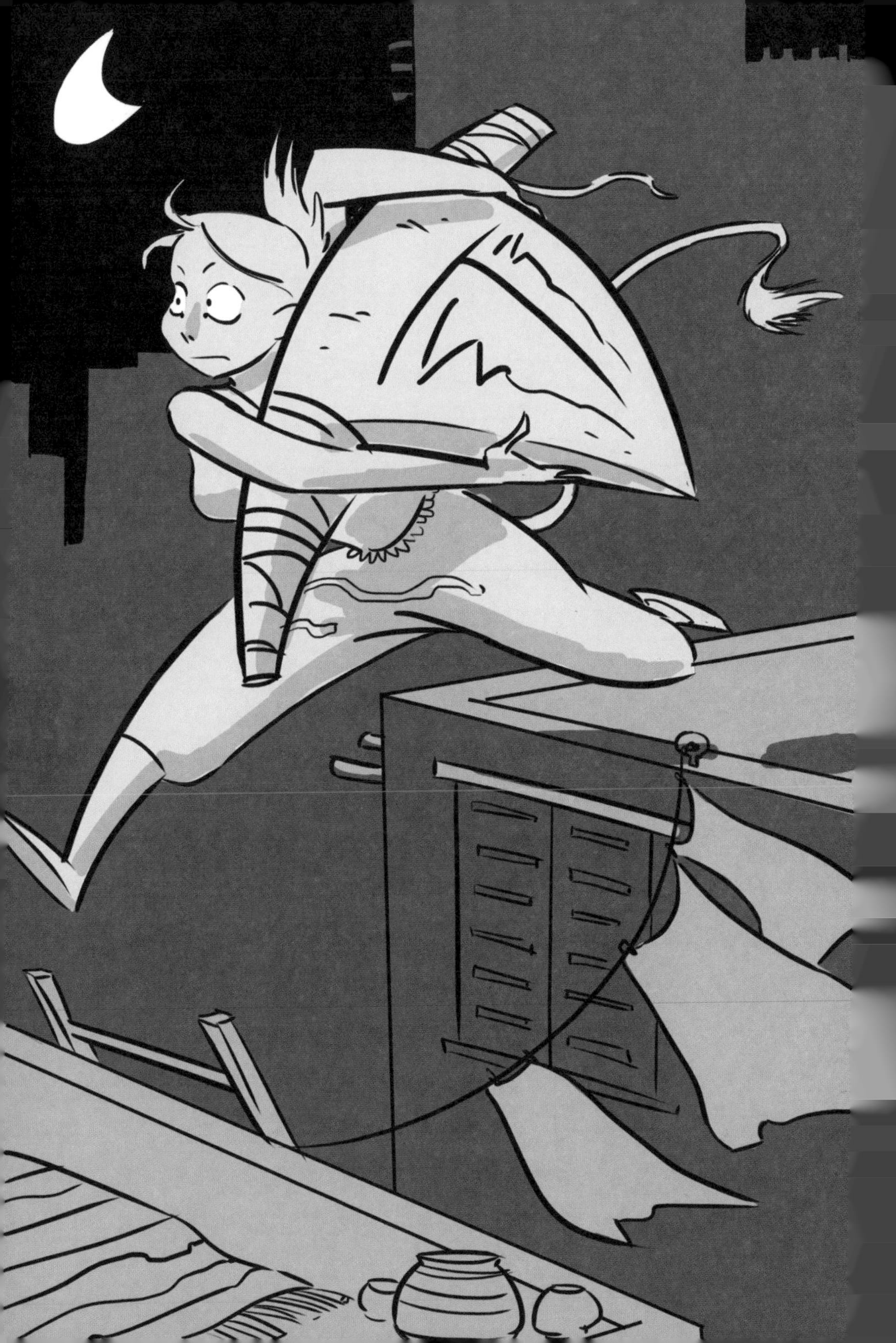

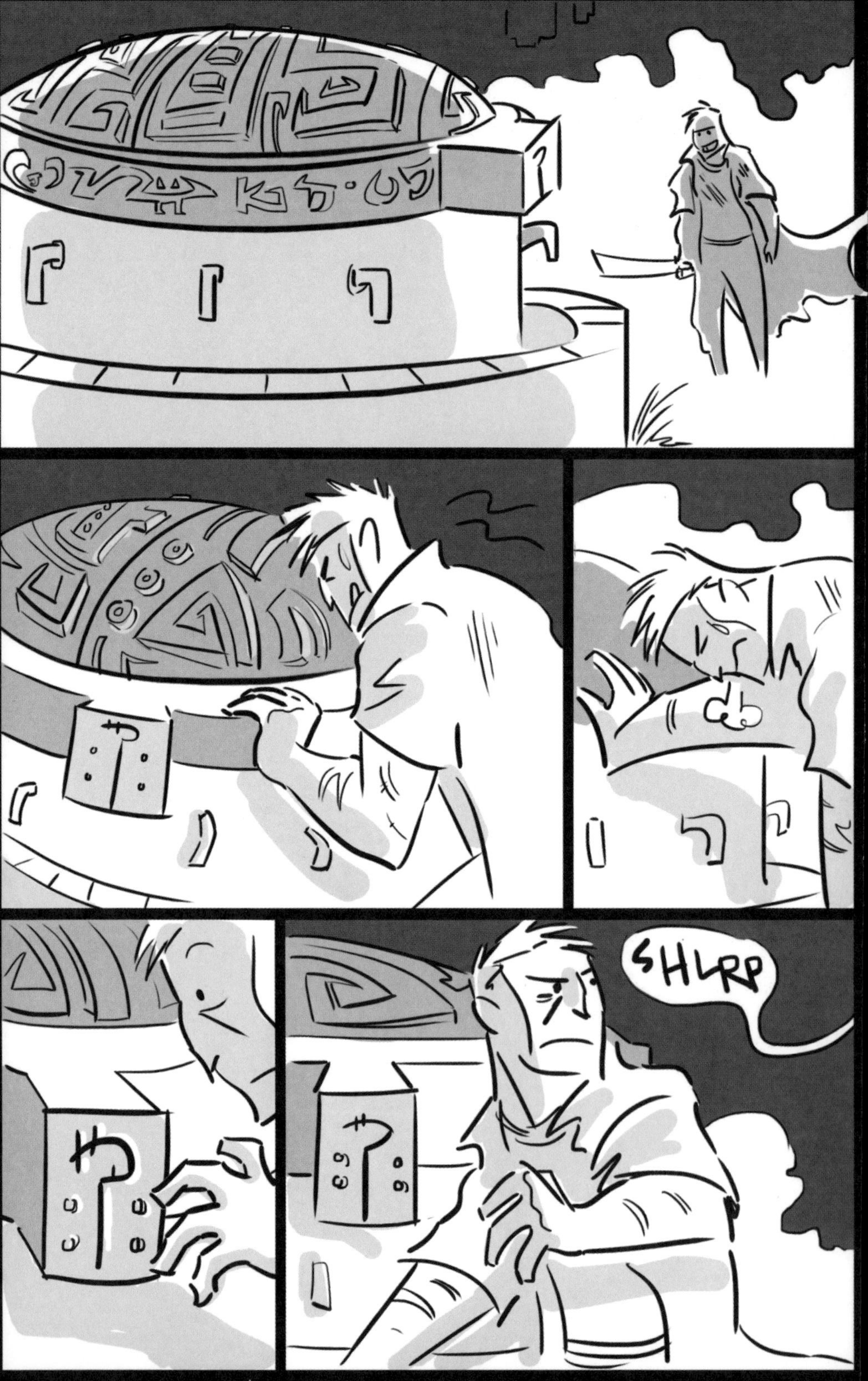
SHLRP

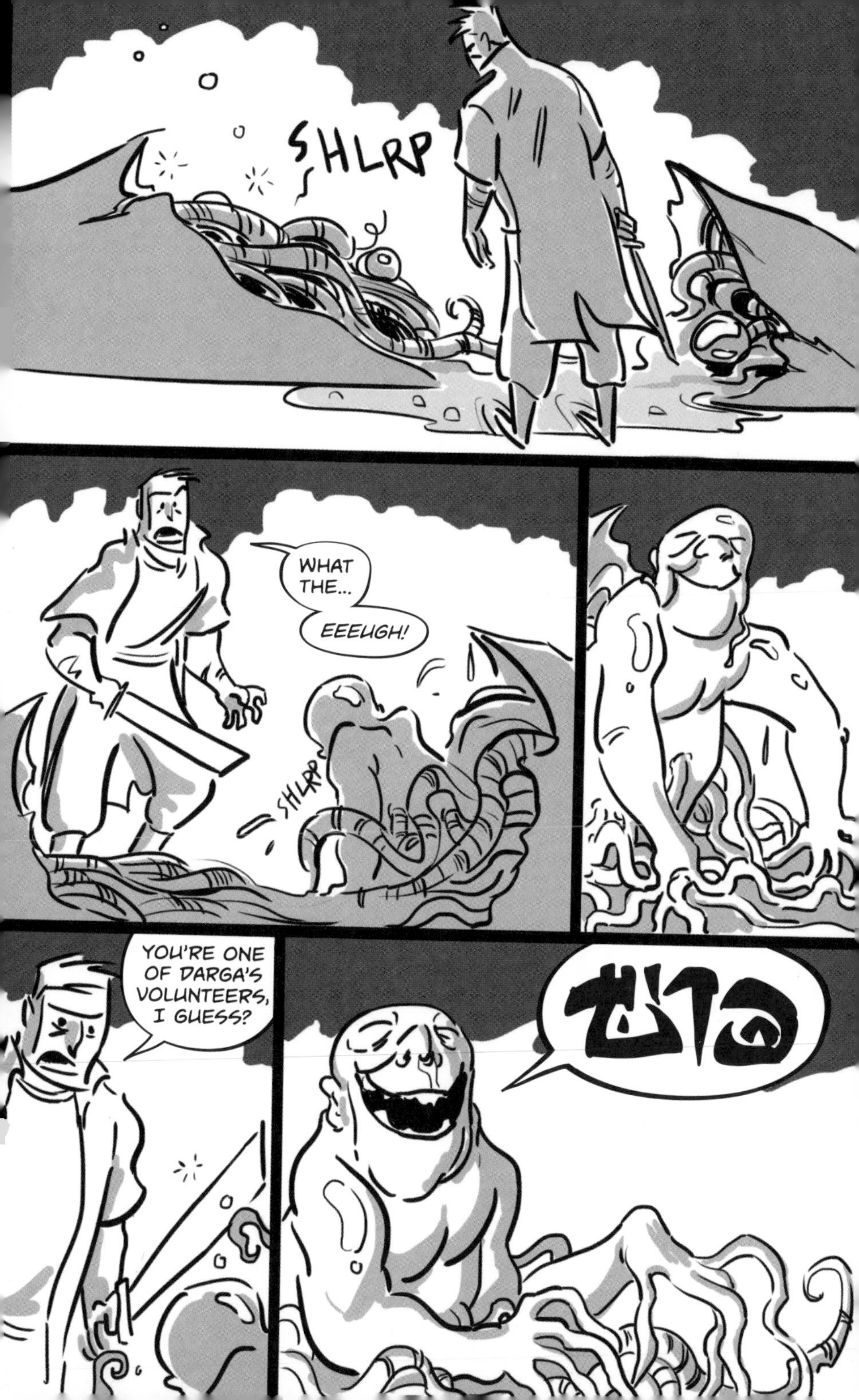
SHLRP
WHAT THE...
EEEUGH!
SHLRP
YOU'RE ONE OF DARGA'S VOLUNTEERS, I GUESS?

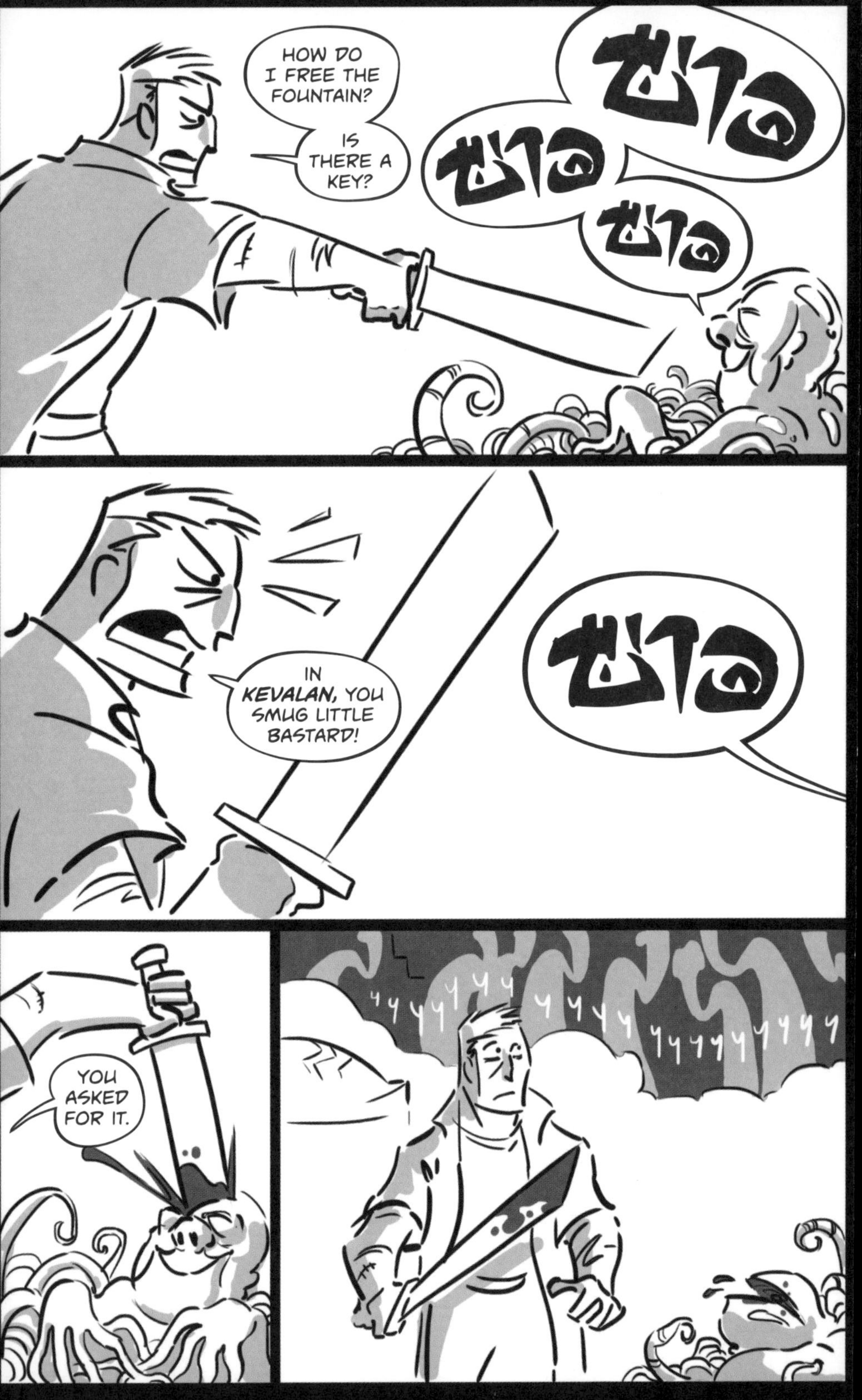
HOW DO I FREE THE FOUNTAIN?
IS THERE A KEY?
IN KEVALAN, YOU SMUG LITTLE BASTARD!
YOU ASKED FOR IT.

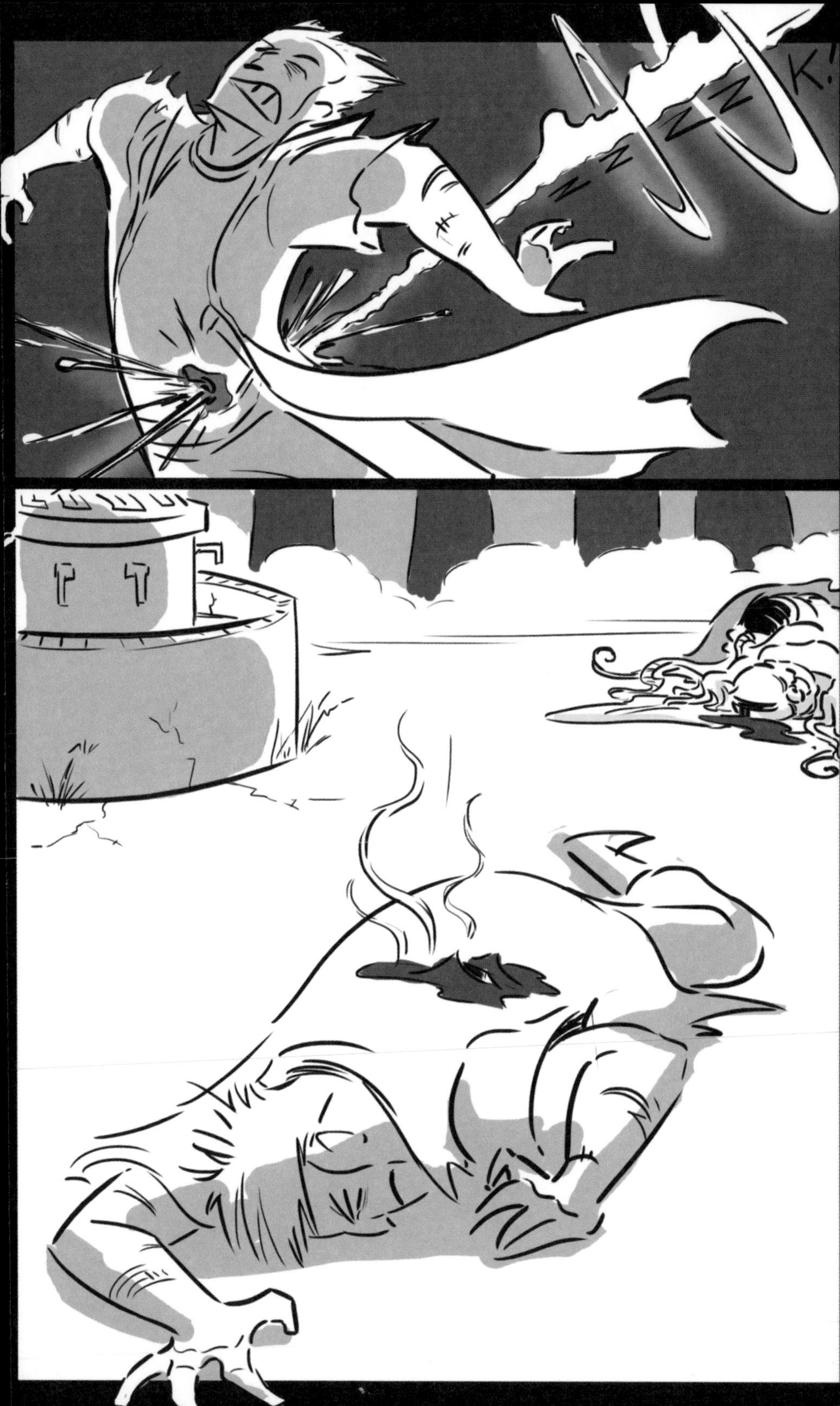
ZZZZK!

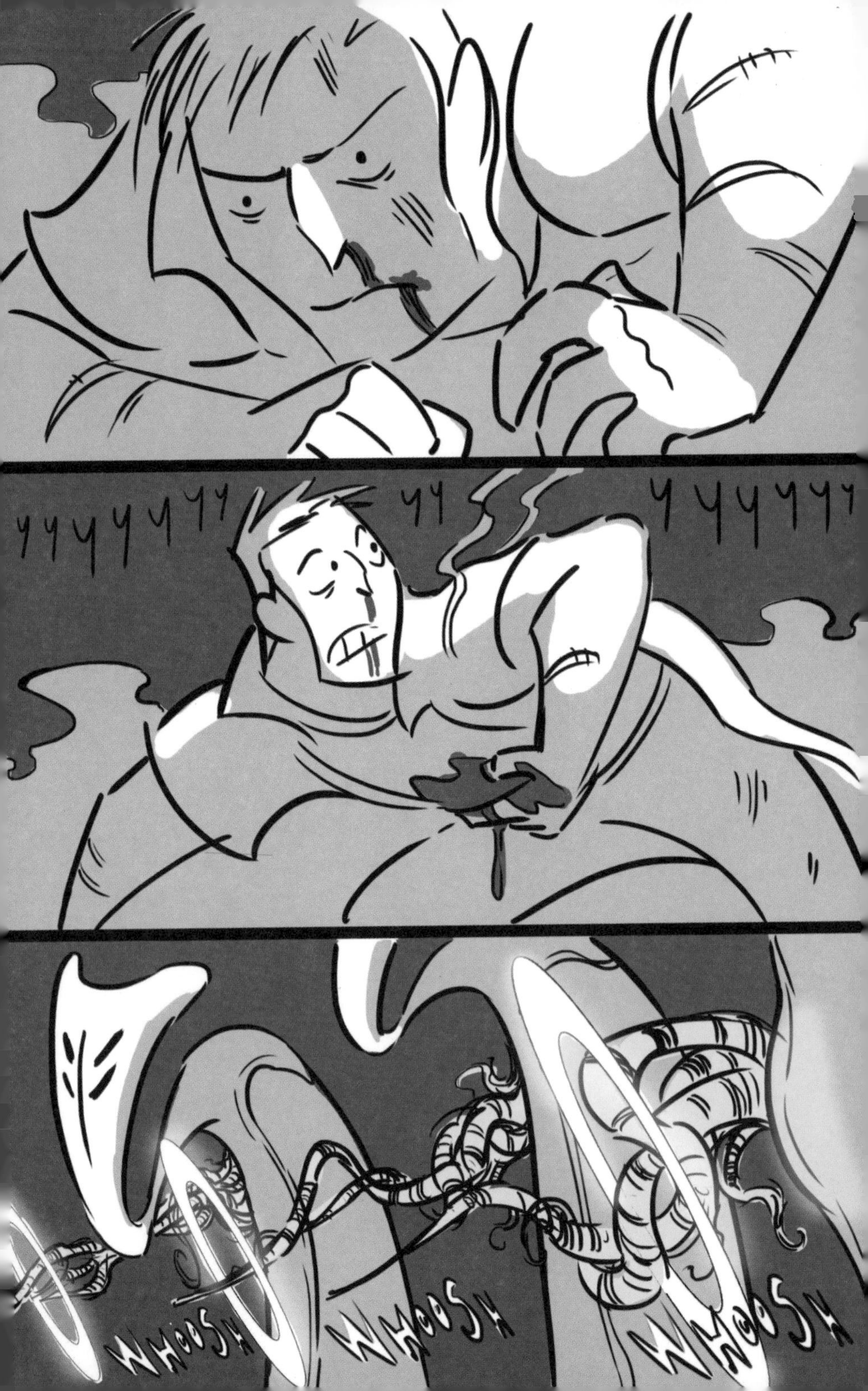

YYYYYYYY
YY
YYYYYY
WHOOSH
WHOOSH
WHOOSH

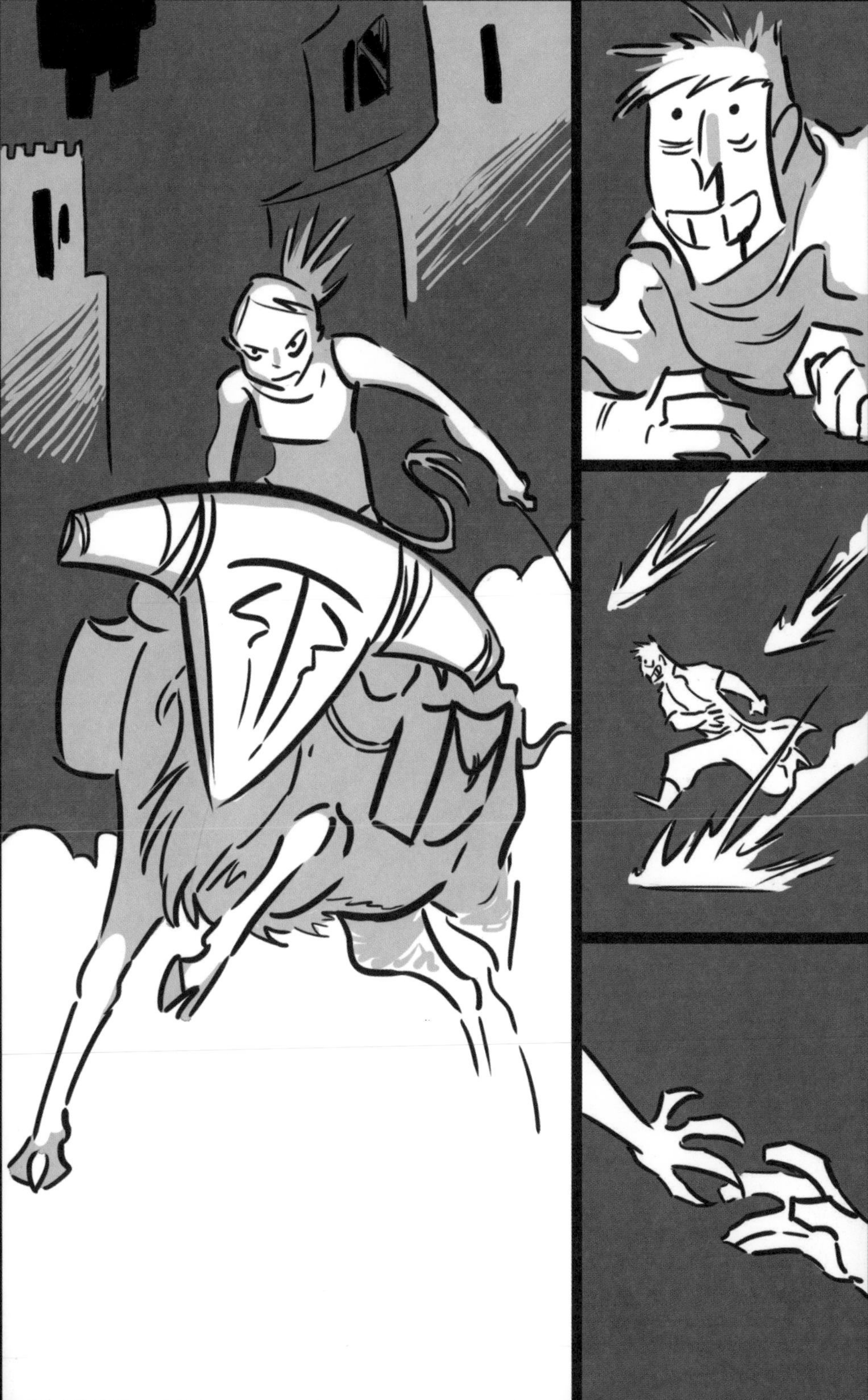

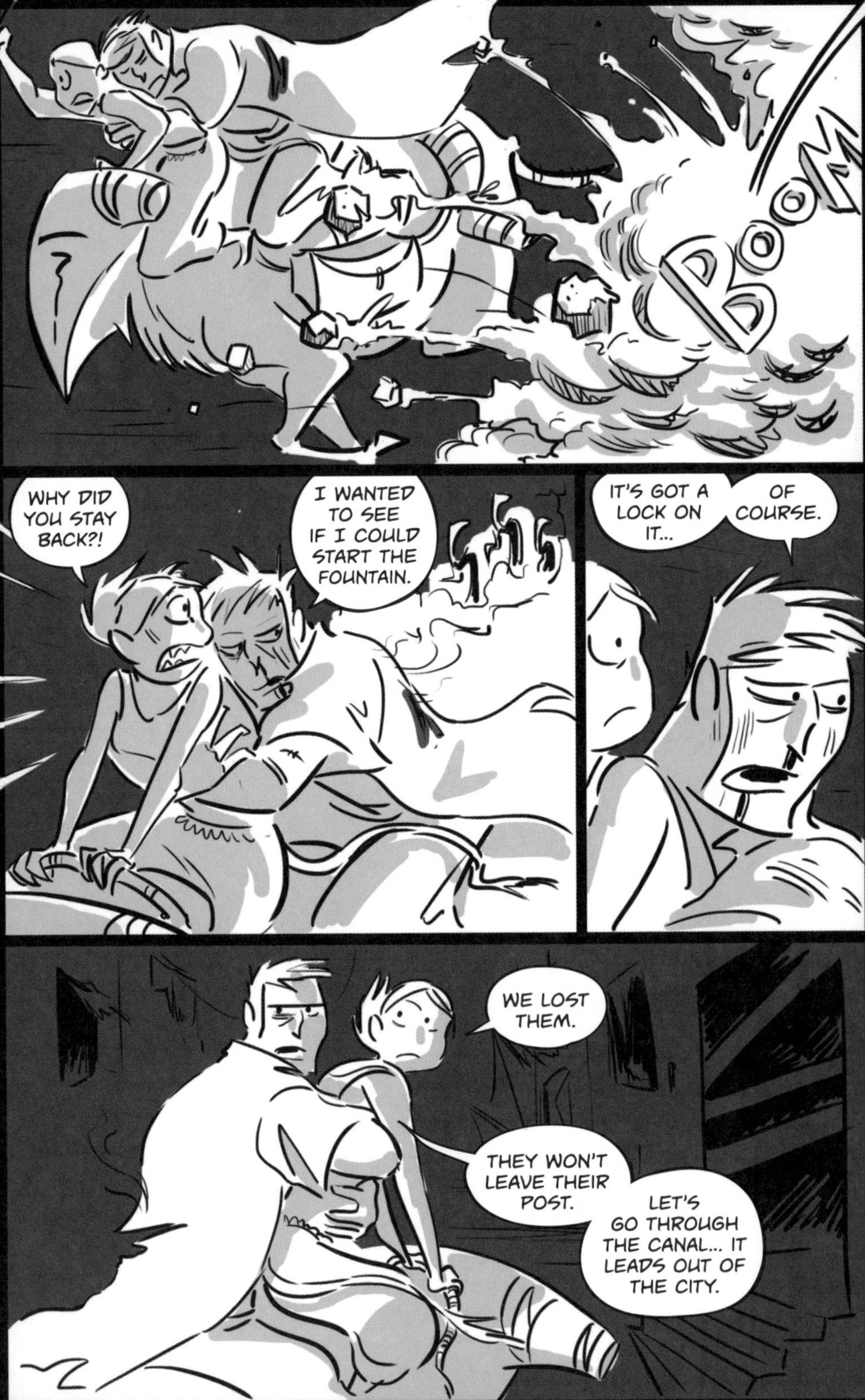
BOOM
WHY DID YOU STAY BACK?!
I WANTED TO SEE IF I COULD START THE FOUNTAIN.
IT'S GOT A LOCK ON IT...
OF COURSE.
WE LOST THEM.
THEY WON'T LEAVE THEIR POST.
LET'S GO THROUGH THE CANAL... IT LEADS OUT OF THE CITY.

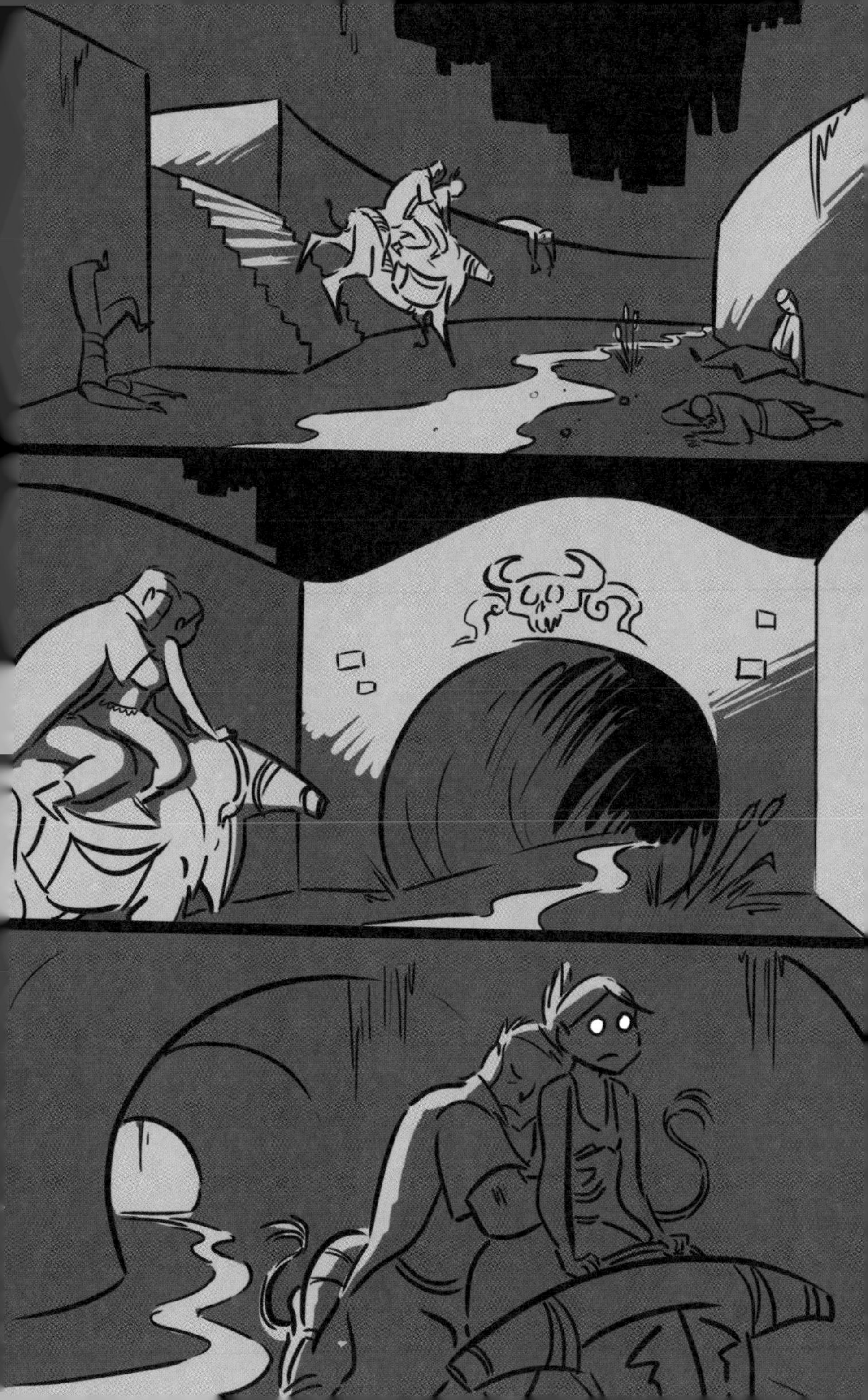

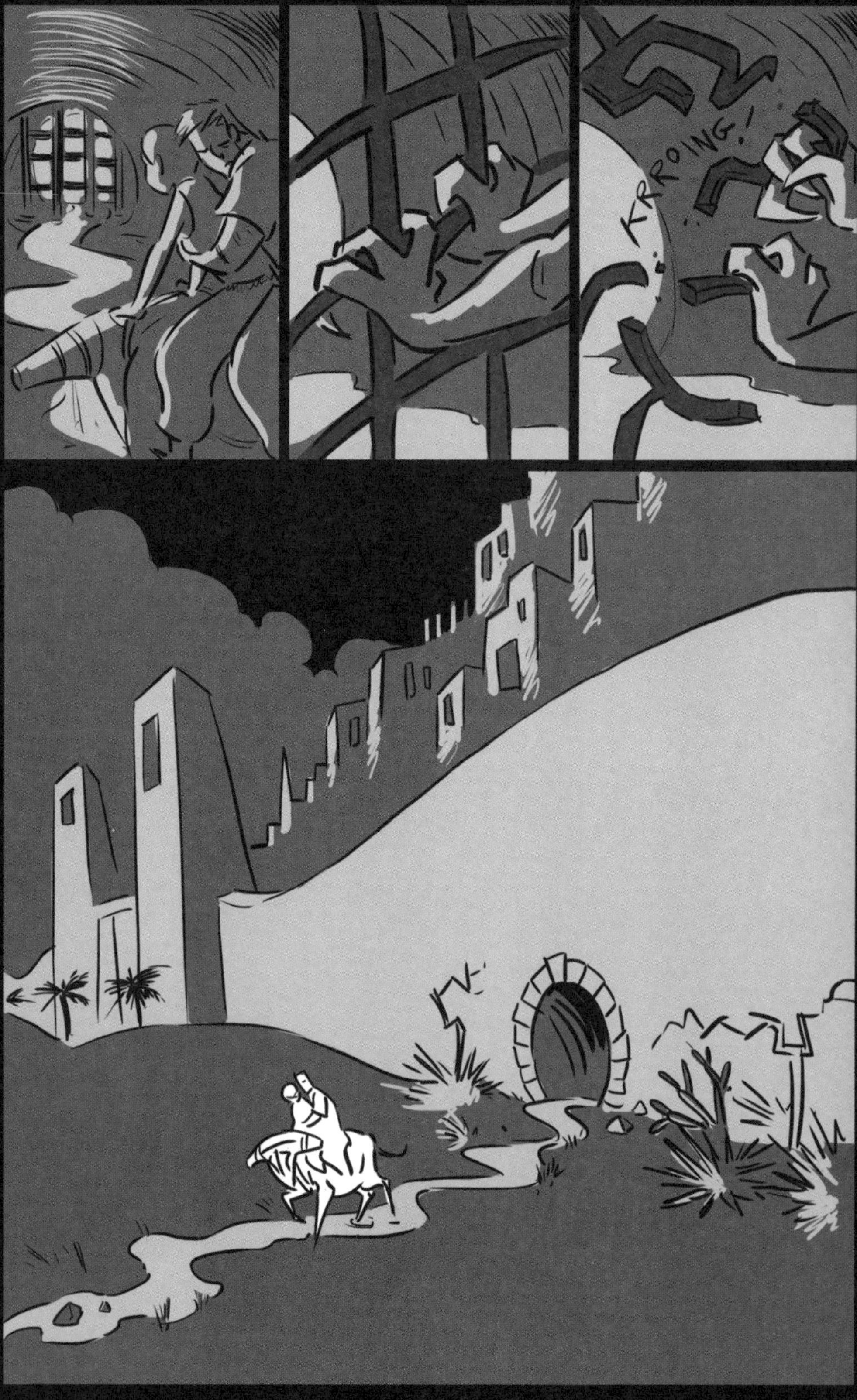
KRROING!

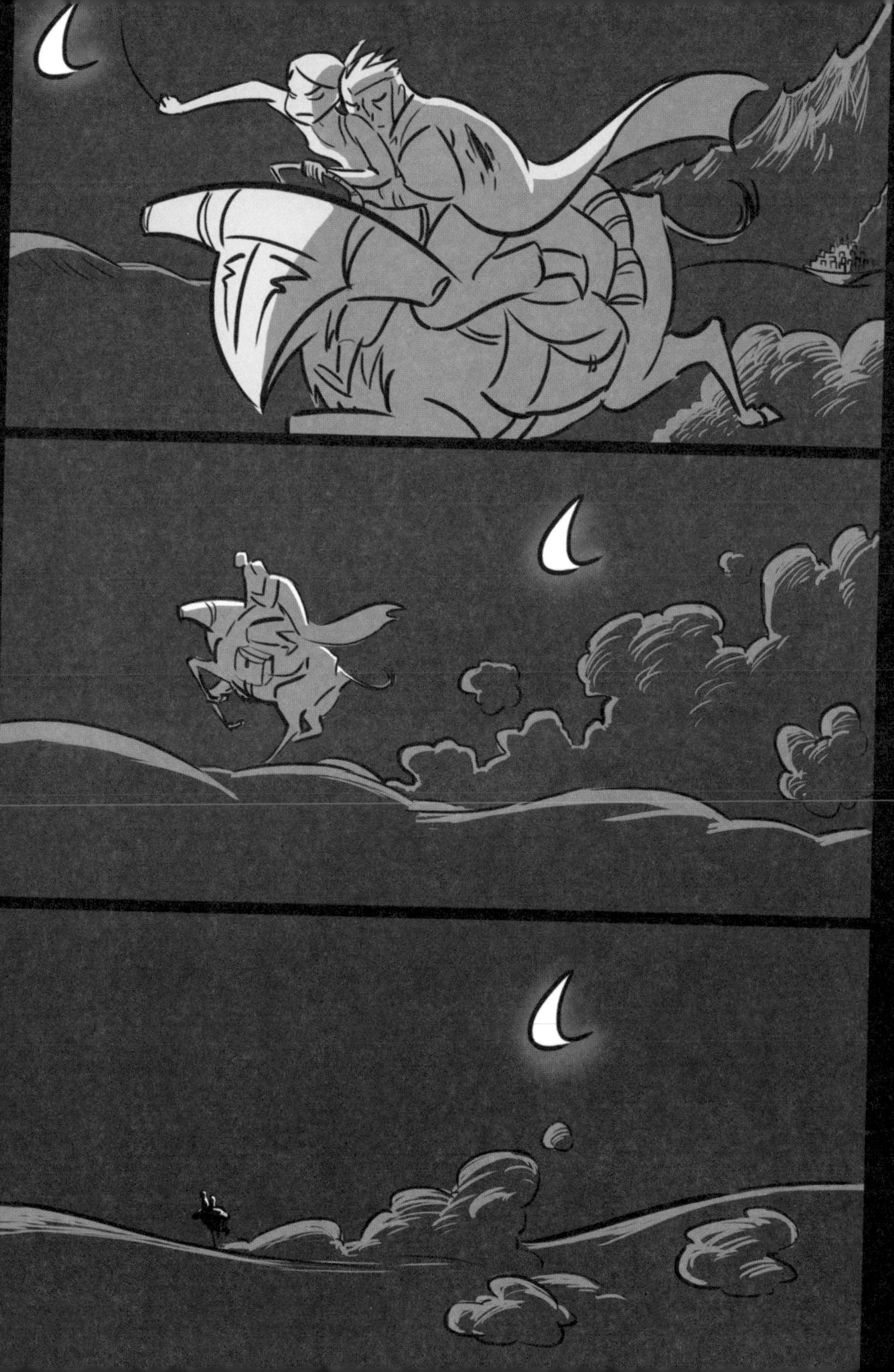

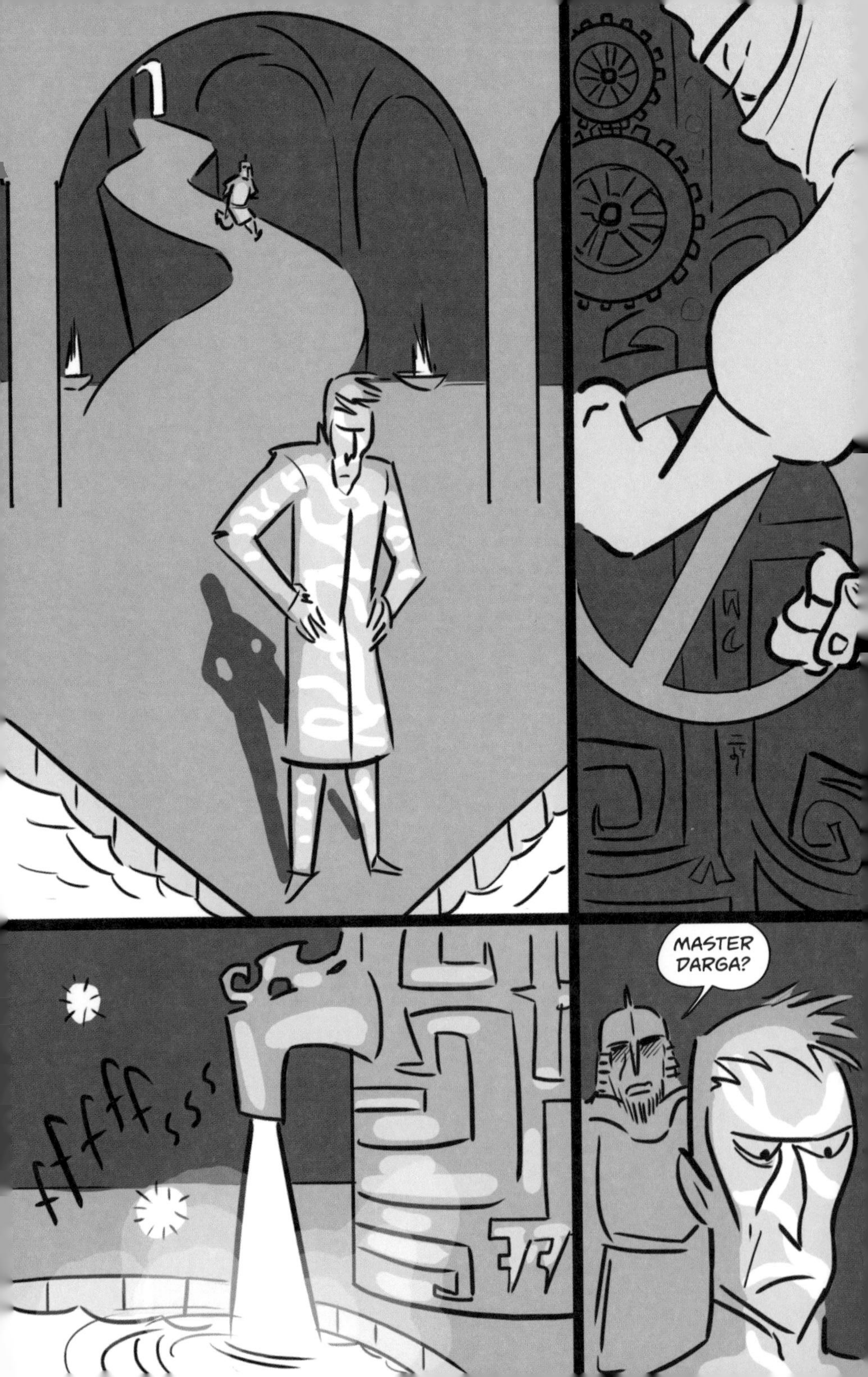
ffffsss
MASTER DARGA?

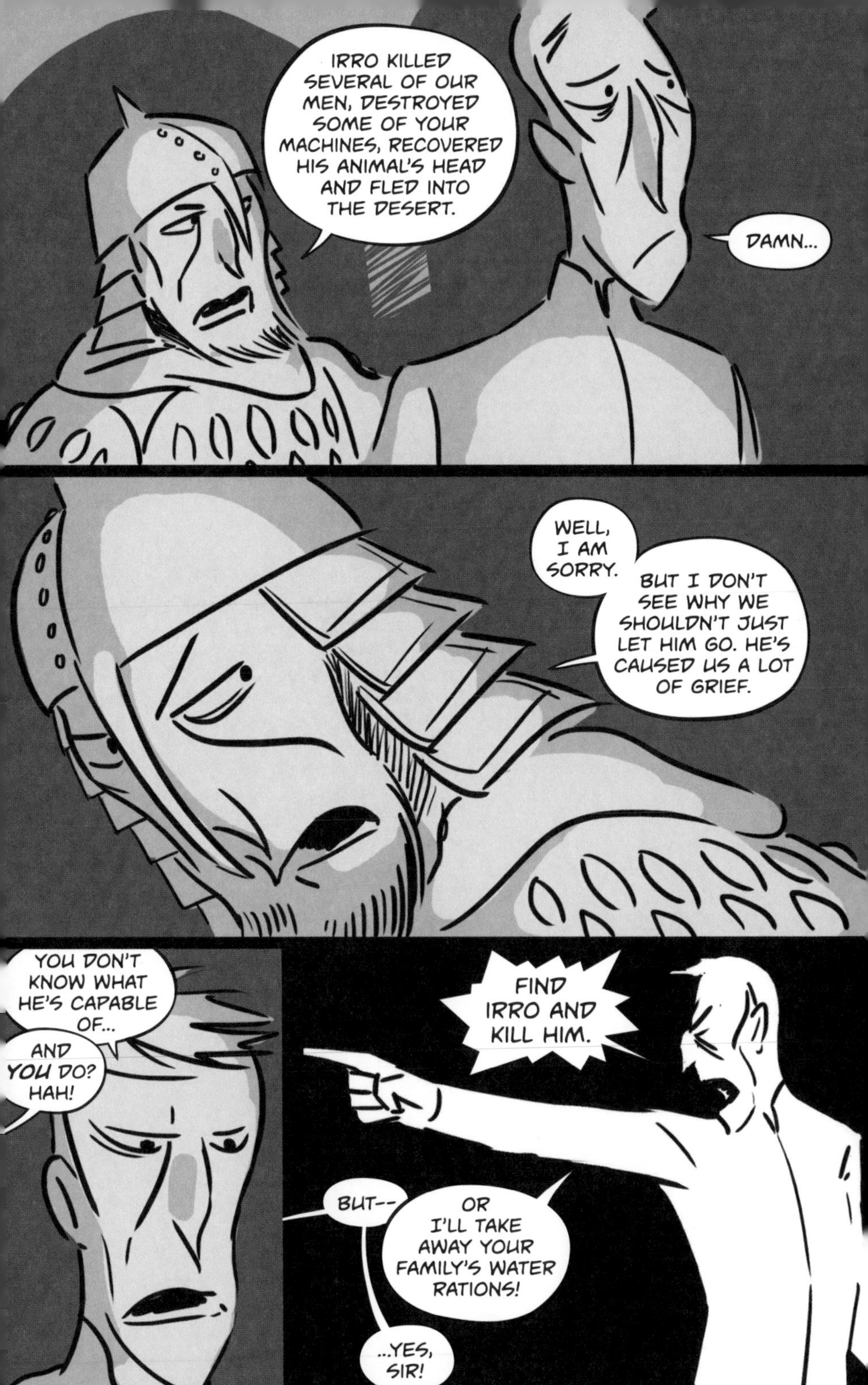
IRRO KILLED SEVERAL OF OUR MEN, DESTROYED SOME OF YOUR MACHINES, RECOVERED HIS ANIMAL'S HEAD AND FLED INTO THE DESERT.
DAMN...
WELL, I AM SORRY.
BUT I DON'T SEE WHY WE SHOULDN'T JUST LET HIM GO. HE'S CAUSED US A LOT OF GRIEF.
YOU DON'T KNOW WHAT HE'S CAPABLE OF...
AND *YOU* DO? HAH!
FIND IRRO AND KILL HIM.
BUT--
OR I'LL TAKE AWAY YOUR FAMILY'S WATER RATIONS!
...YES, SIR!

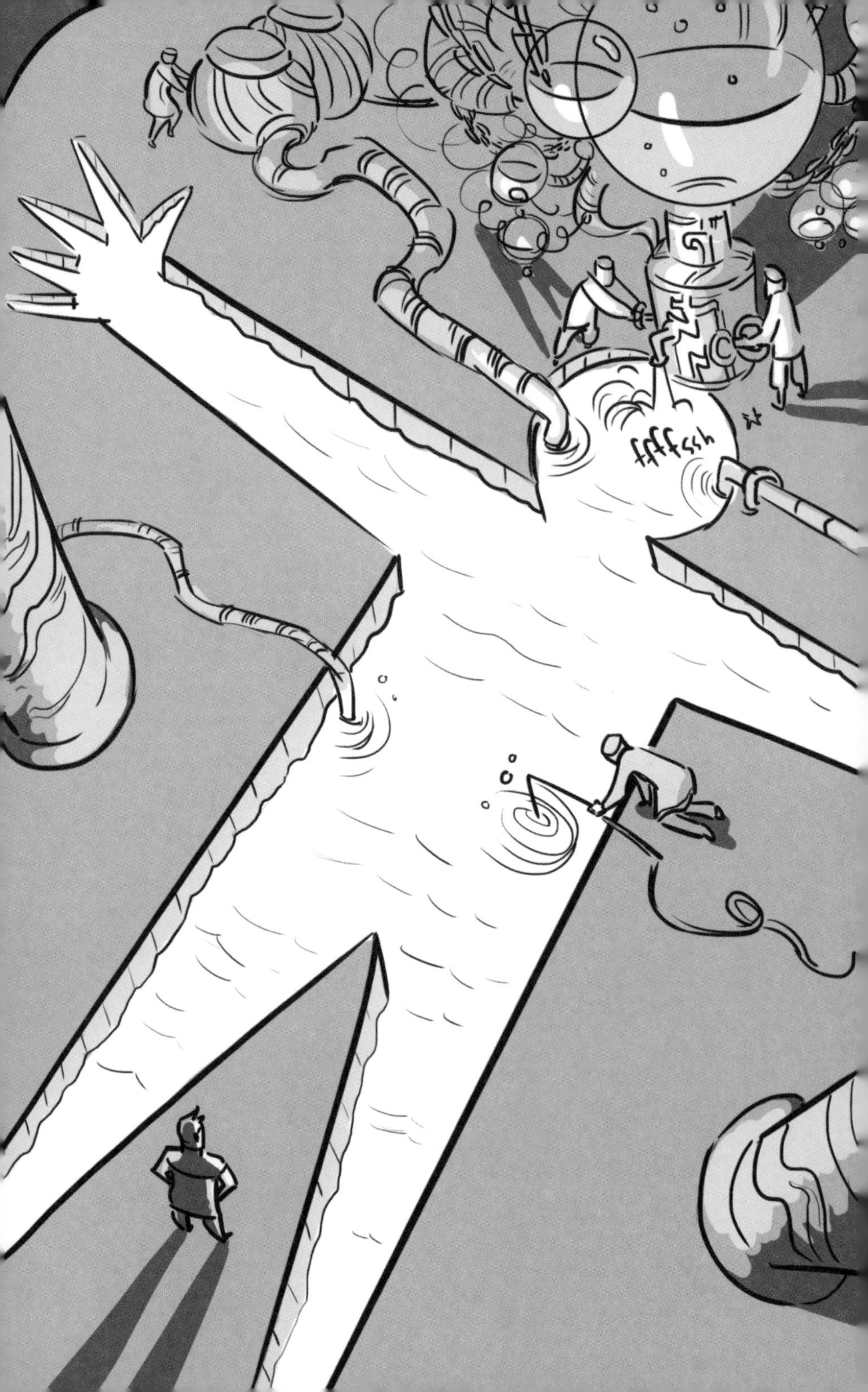
ffffssh

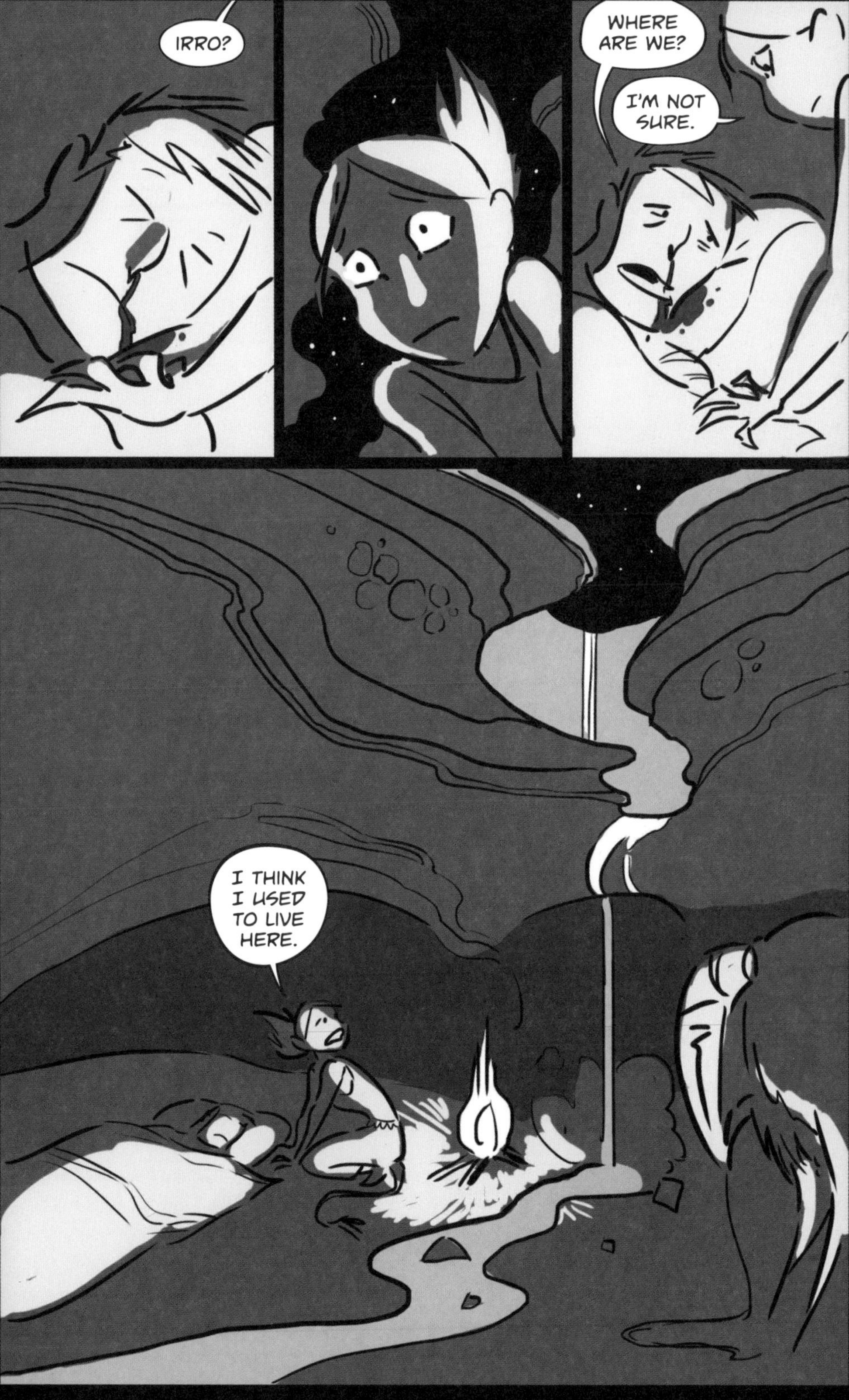
IRRO?
WHERE ARE WE?
I'M NOT SURE.
I THINK I USED TO LIVE HERE.

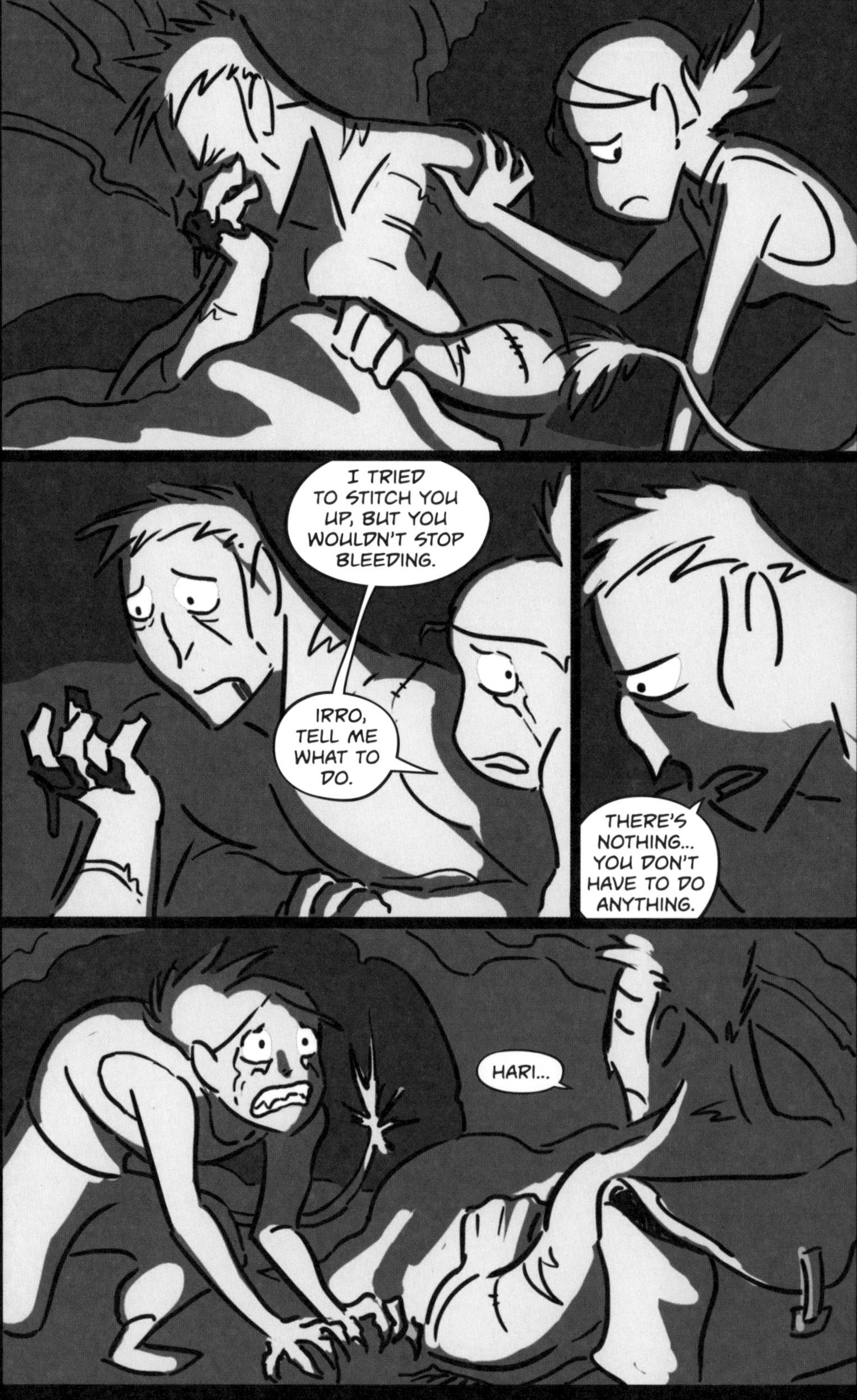
I TRIED TO STITCH YOU UP, BUT YOU WOULDN'T STOP BLEEDING.
IRRO, TELL ME WHAT TO DO.
THERE'S NOTHING... YOU DON'T HAVE TO DO ANYTHING.
HARI...

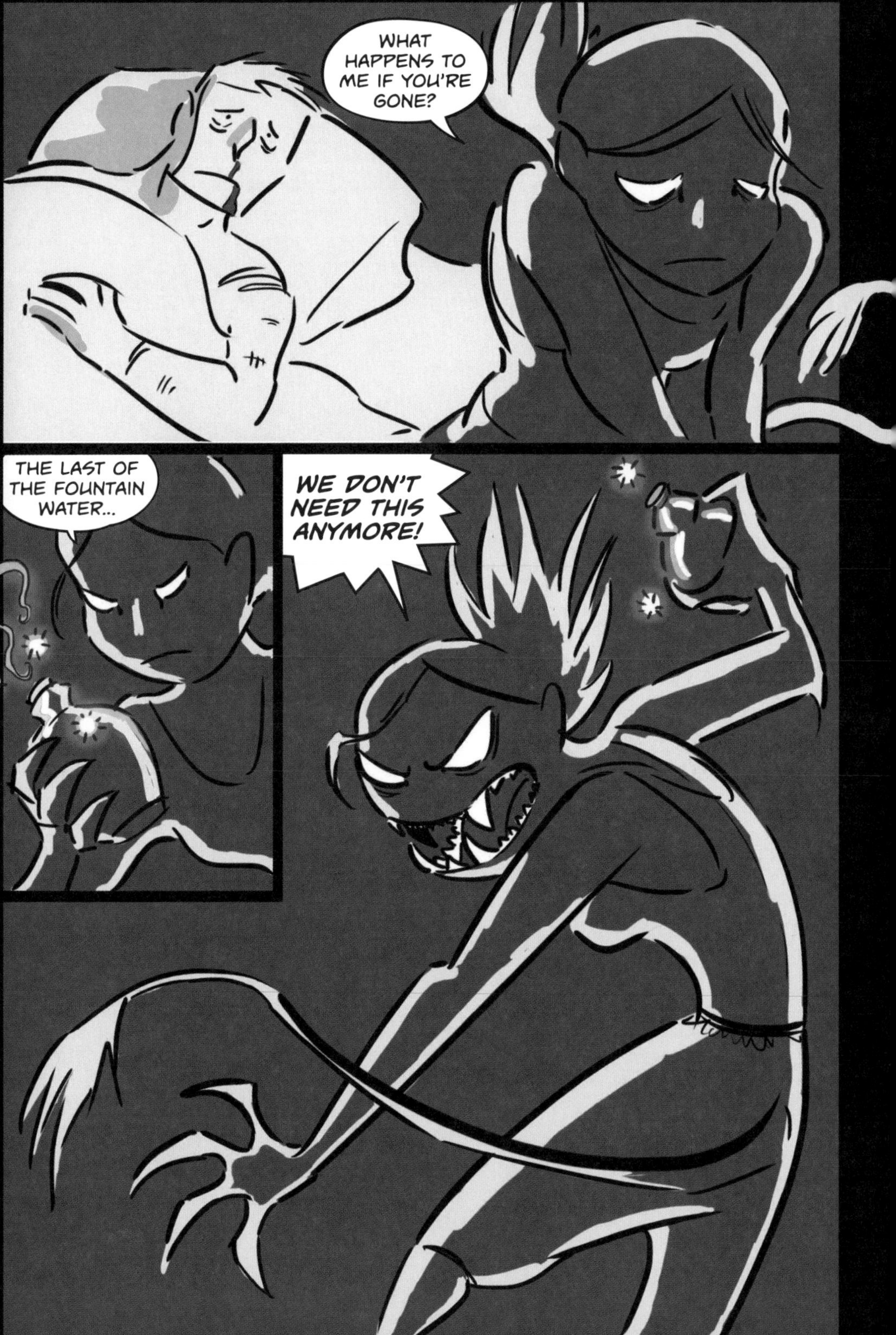
WHAT HAPPENS TO ME IF YOU'RE GONE?
THE LAST OF THE FOUNTAIN WATER...
WE DON'T NEED THIS ANYMORE!

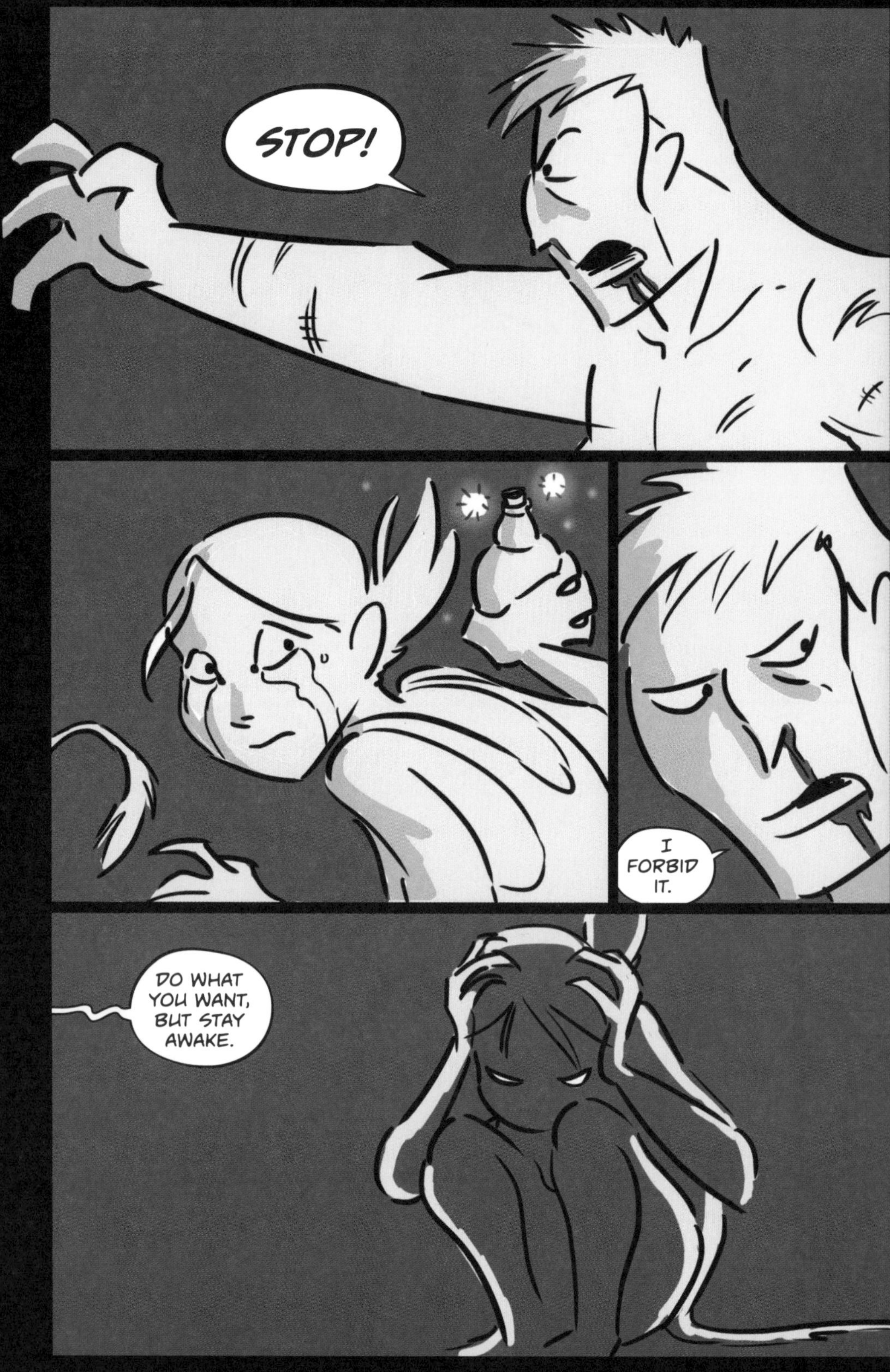
STOP!
I FORBID IT.
DO WHAT YOU WANT, BUT STAY AWAKE.

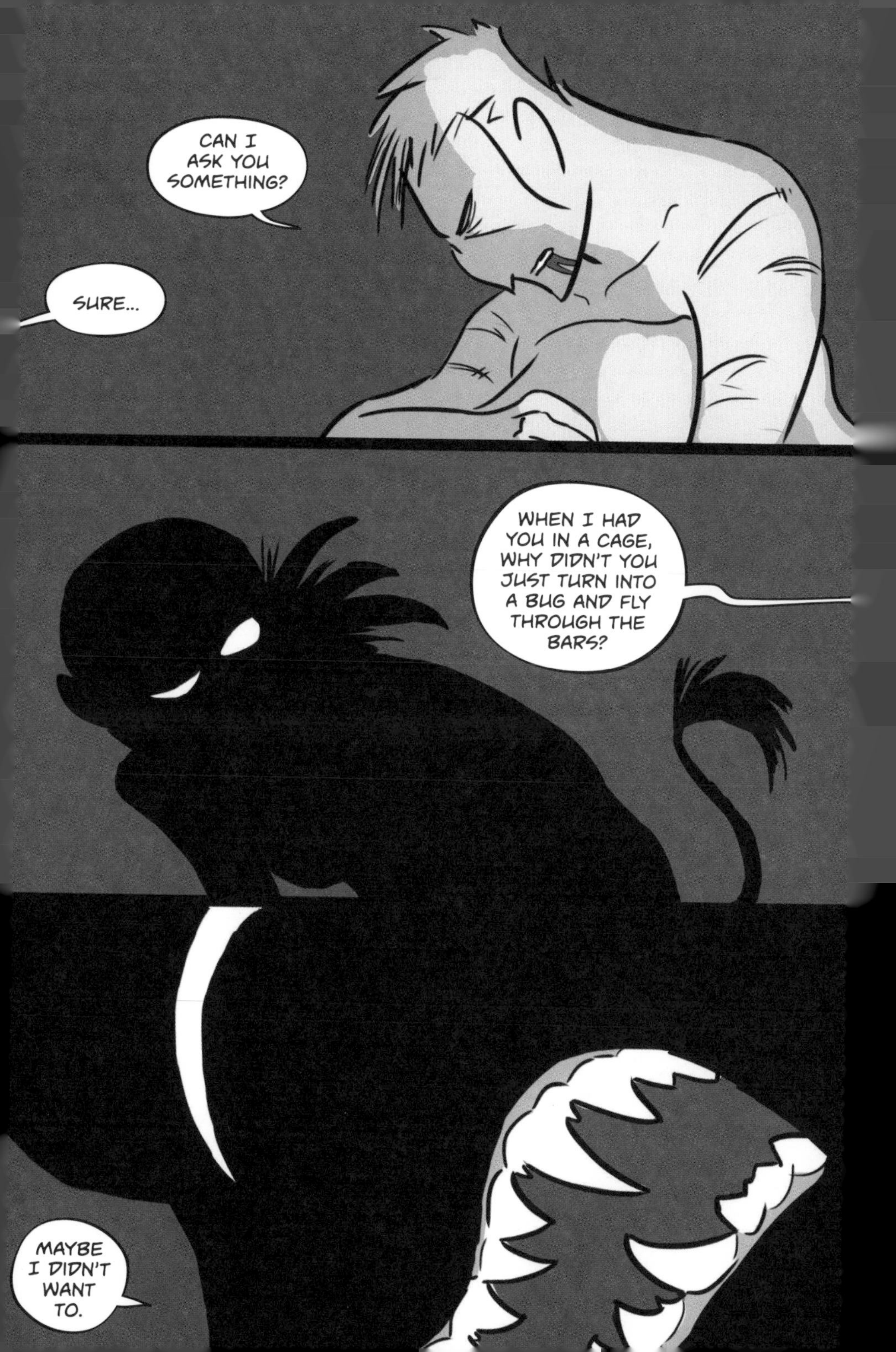
CAN I ASK YOU SOMETHING?
SURE...
WHEN I HAD YOU IN A CAGE, WHY DIDN'T YOU JUST TURN INTO A BUG AND FLY THROUGH THE BARS?
MAYBE I DIDN'T WANT TO.

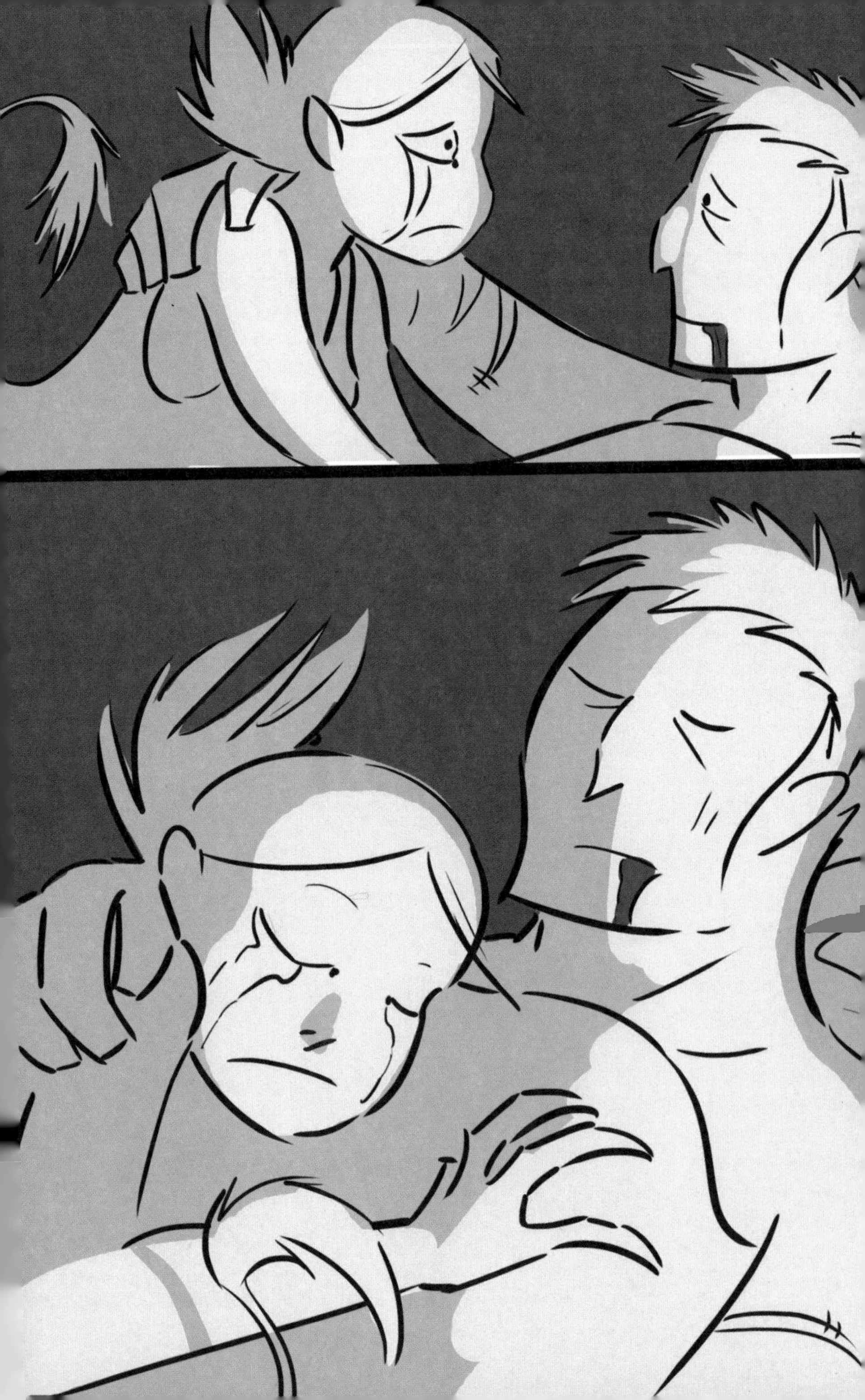

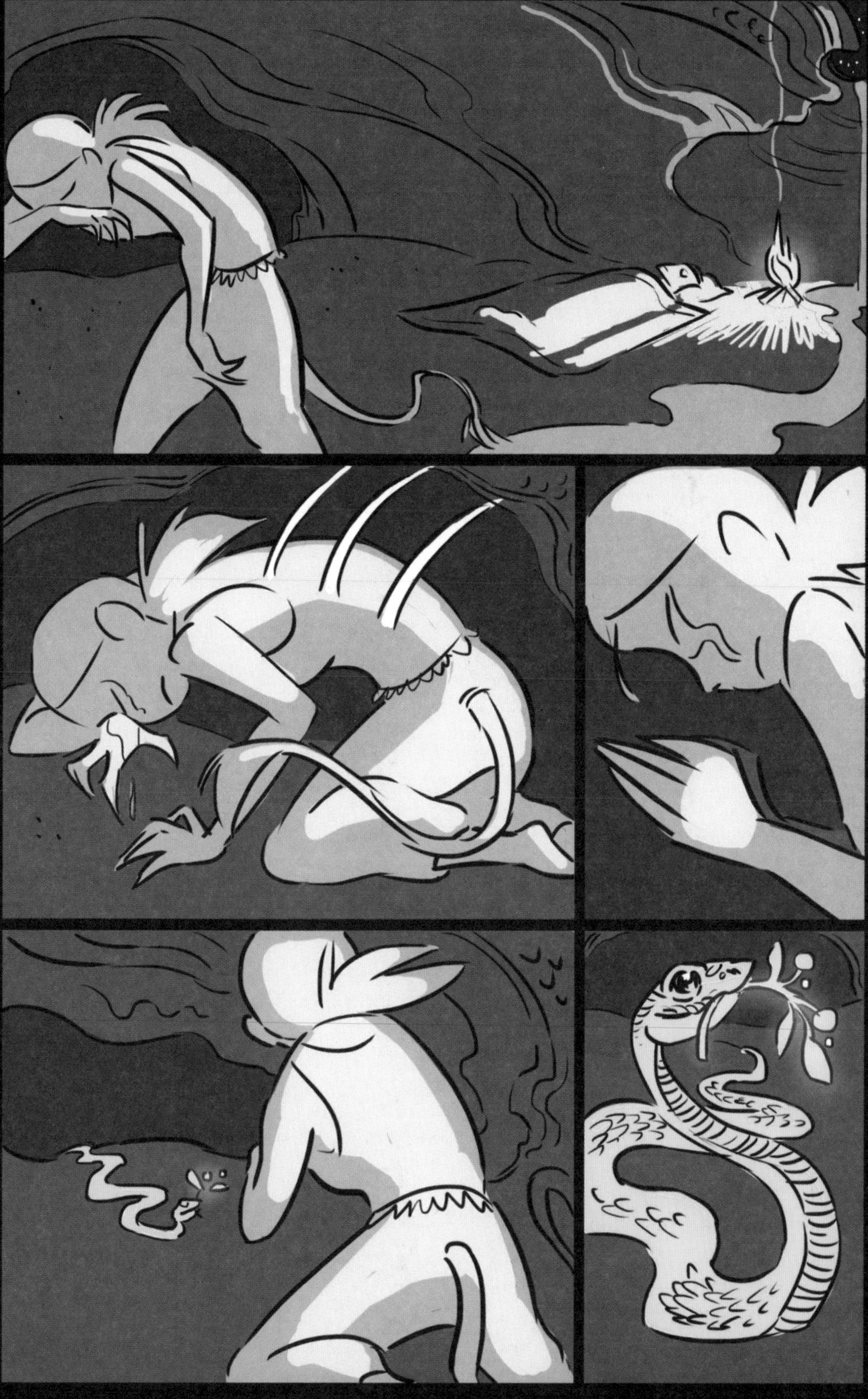

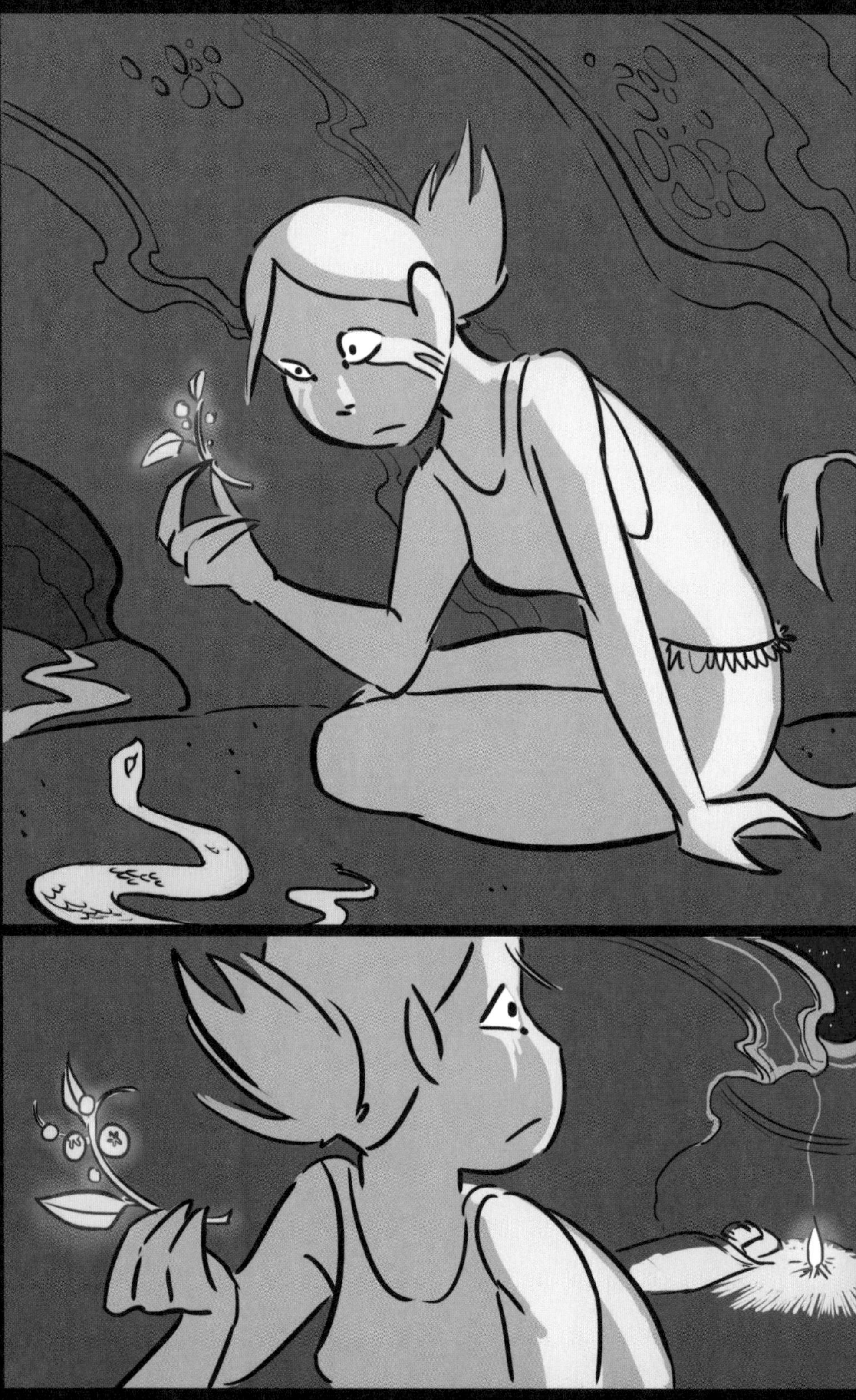

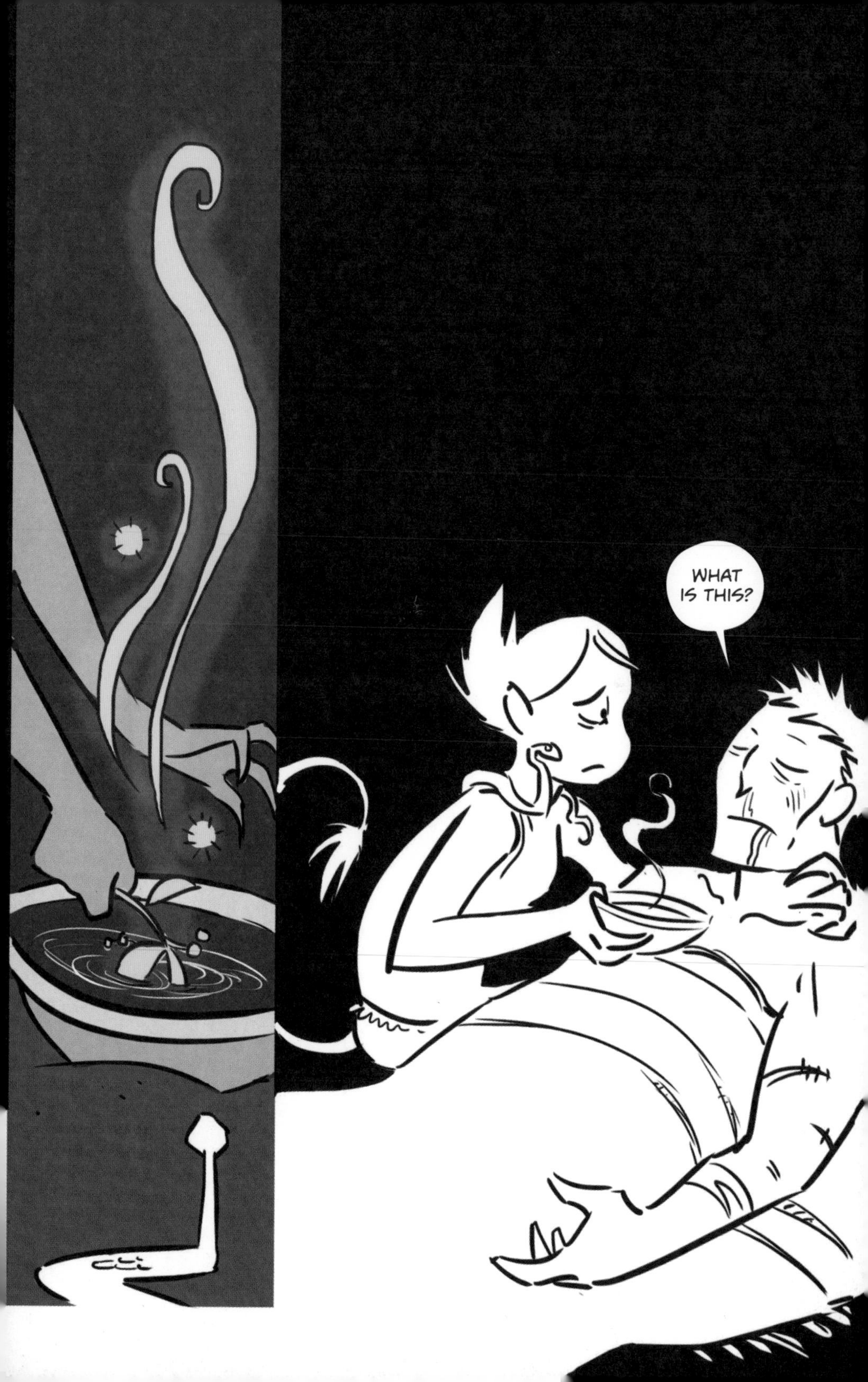
WHAT IS THIS?

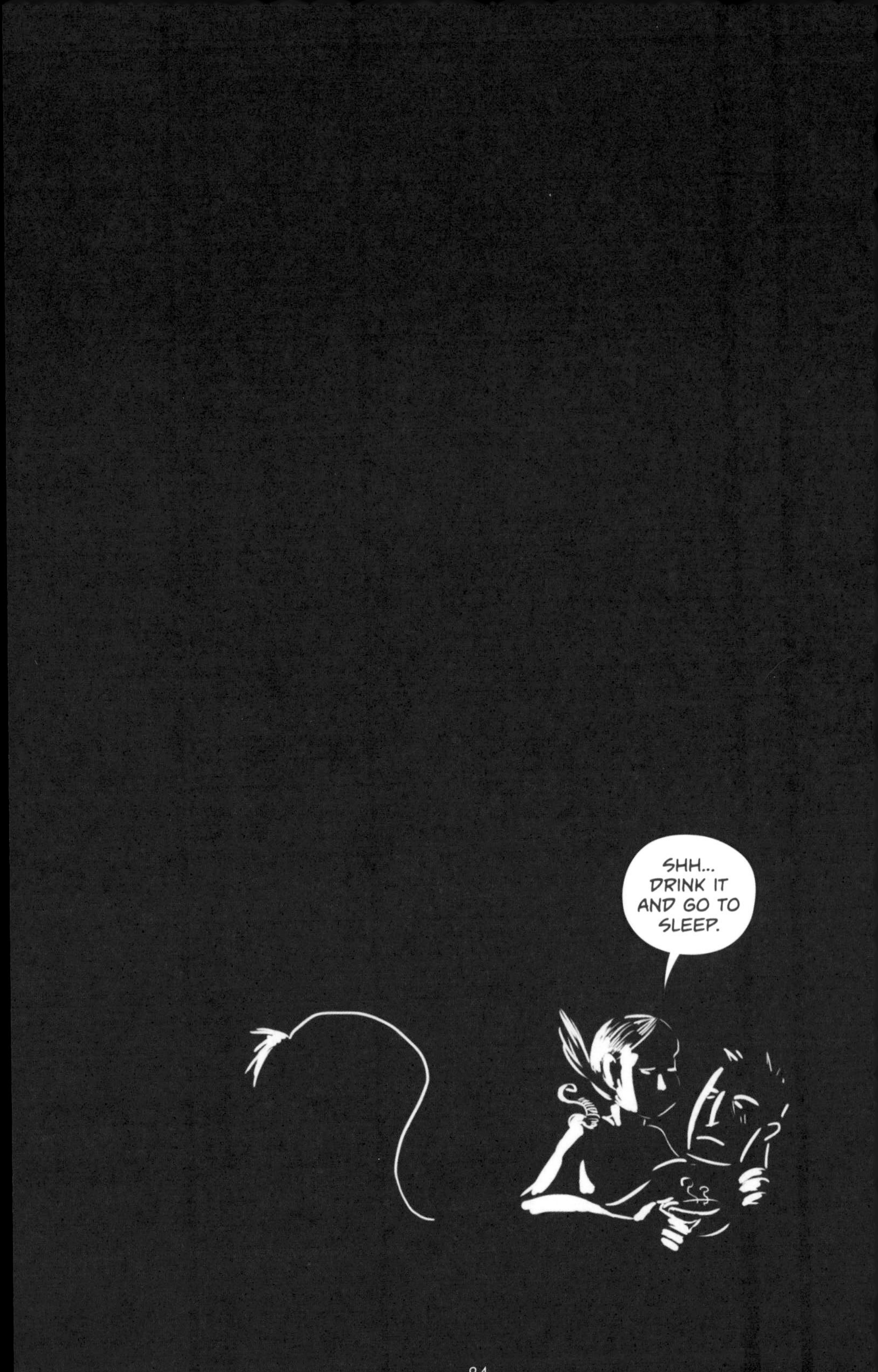
SHH... DRINK IT AND GO TO SLEEP.

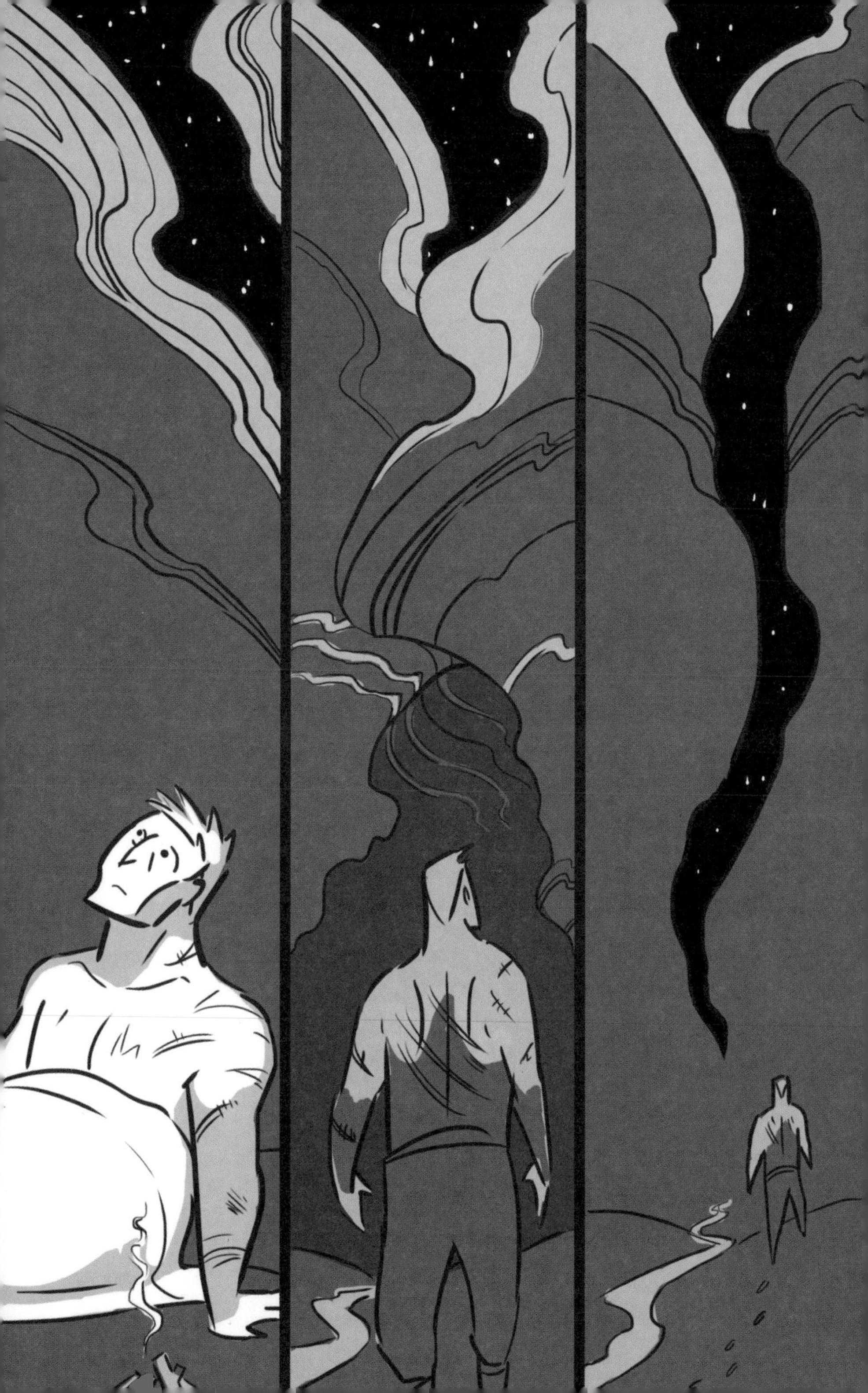

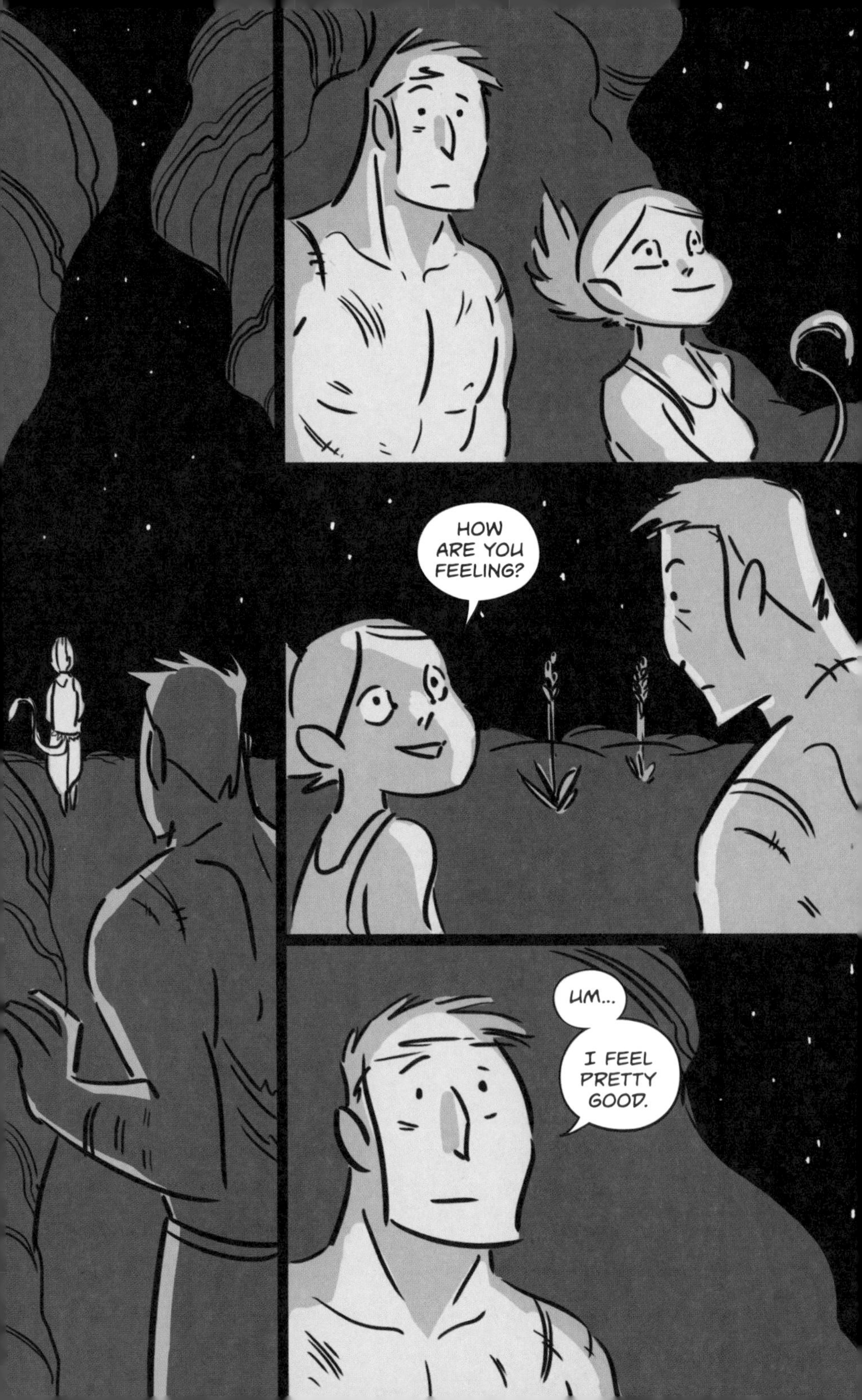
HOW ARE YOU FEELING?
UM...
I FEEL PRETTY GOOD.

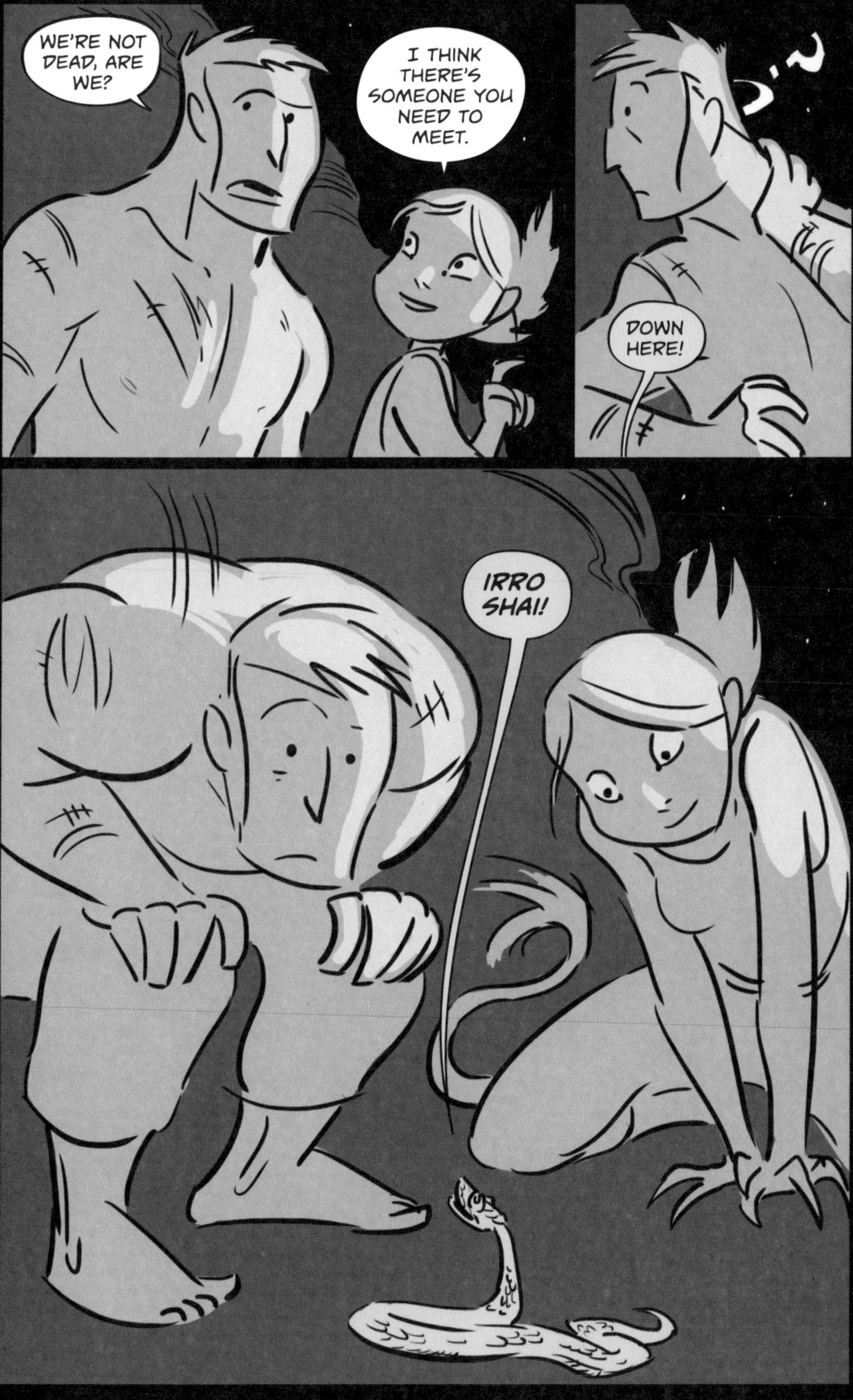
WE'RE NOT DEAD, ARE WE?
I THINK THERE'S SOMEONE YOU NEED TO MEET.
DOWN HERE!
IRRO SHAI!

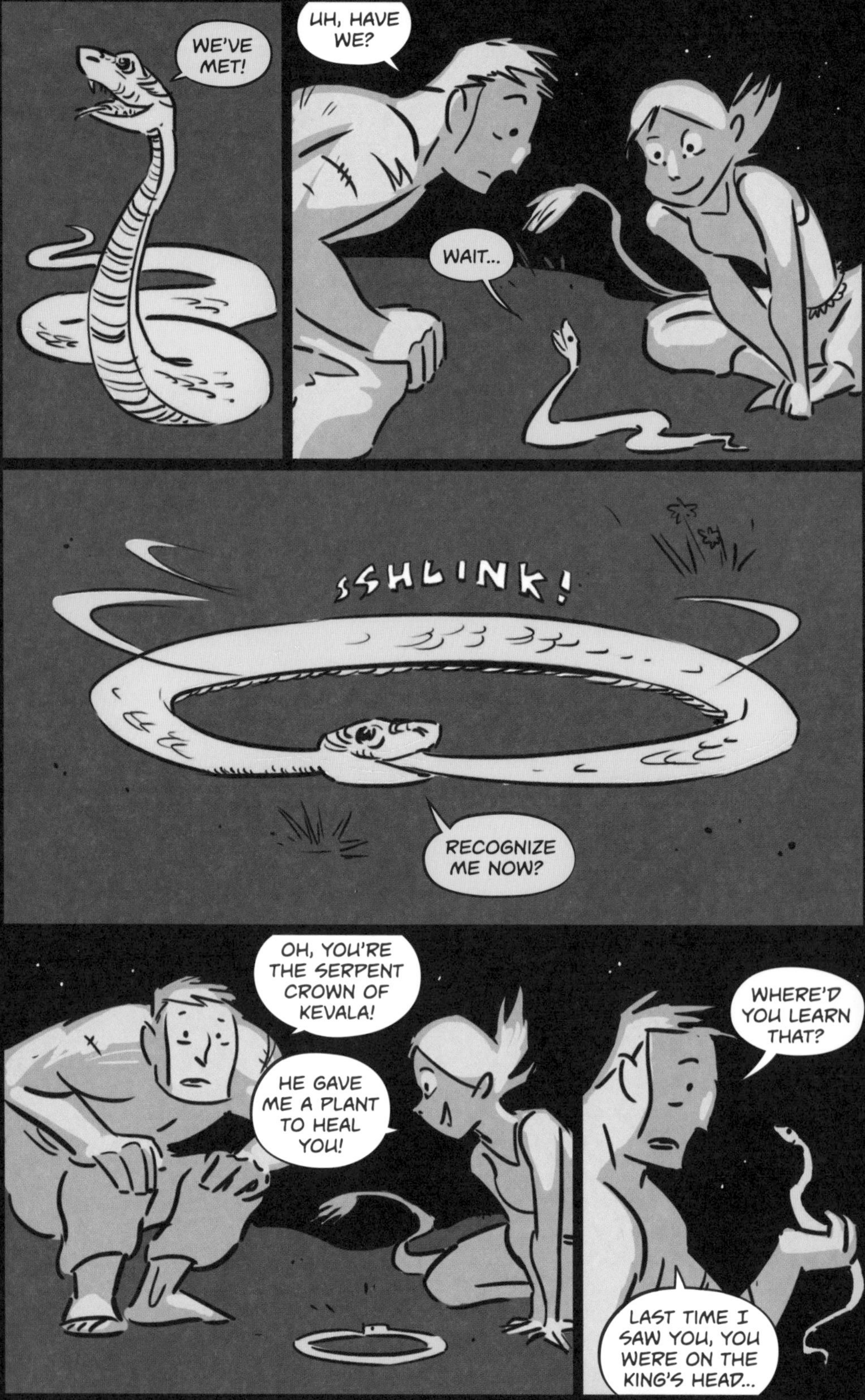
WE'VE MET!
UH, HAVE WE?
WAIT...
SSHLINK!
RECOGNIZE ME NOW?
OH, YOU'RE THE SERPENT CROWN OF KEVALA!
HE GAVE ME A PLANT TO HEAL YOU!
WHERE'D YOU LEARN THAT?
LAST TIME I SAW YOU, YOU WERE ON THE KING'S HEAD...

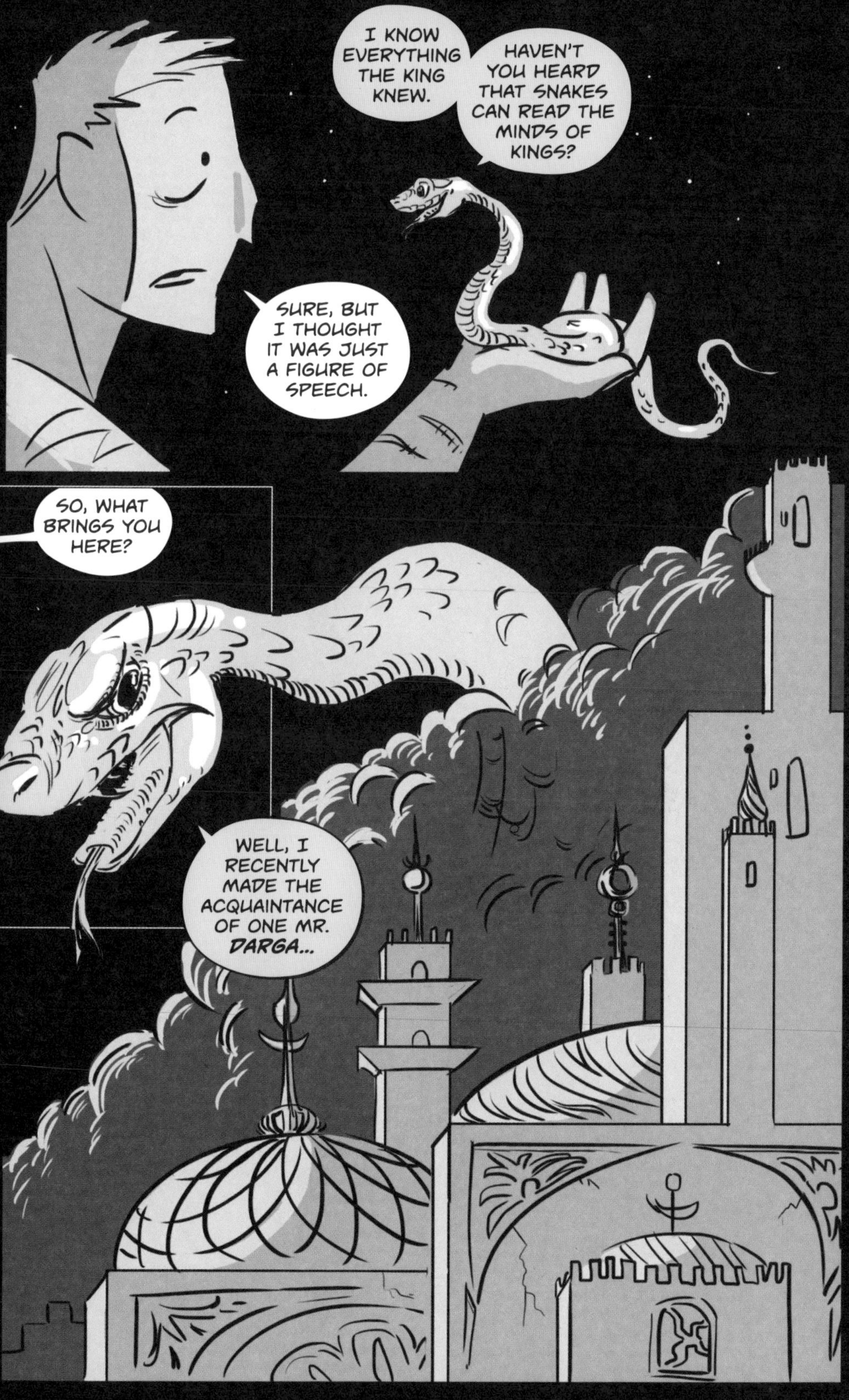
I KNOW EVERYTHING THE KING KNEW.
HAVEN'T YOU HEARD THAT SNAKES CAN READ THE MINDS OF KINGS?
SURE, BUT I THOUGHT IT WAS JUST A FIGURE OF SPEECH.
SO, WHAT BRINGS YOU HERE?
WELL, I RECENTLY MADE THE ACQUAINTANCE OF ONE MR. DARGA...

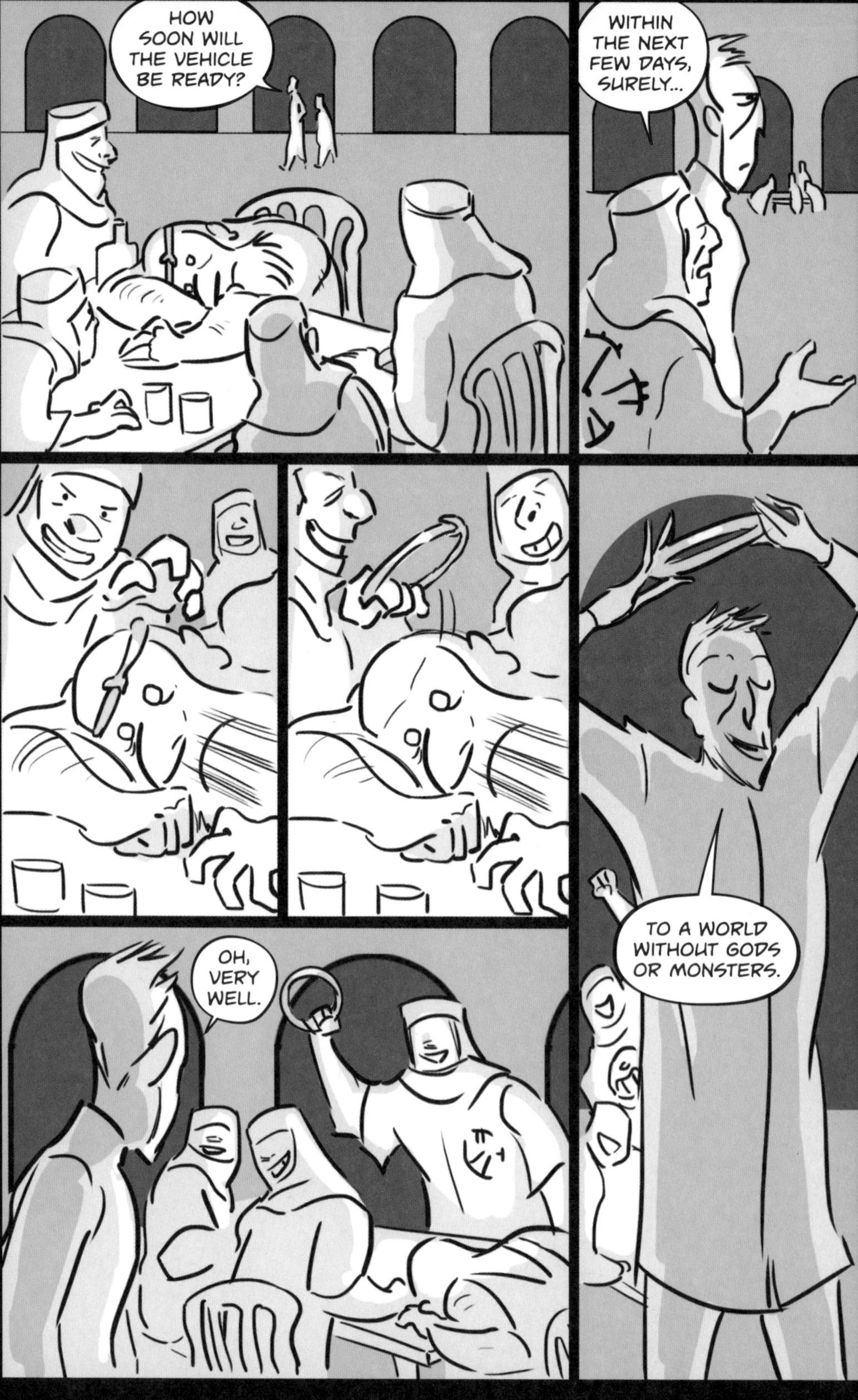
HOW SOON WILL THE VEHICLE BE READY?
WITHIN THE NEXT FEW DAYS, SURELY...
OH, VERY WELL.
TO A WORLD WITHOUT GODS OR MONSTERS.

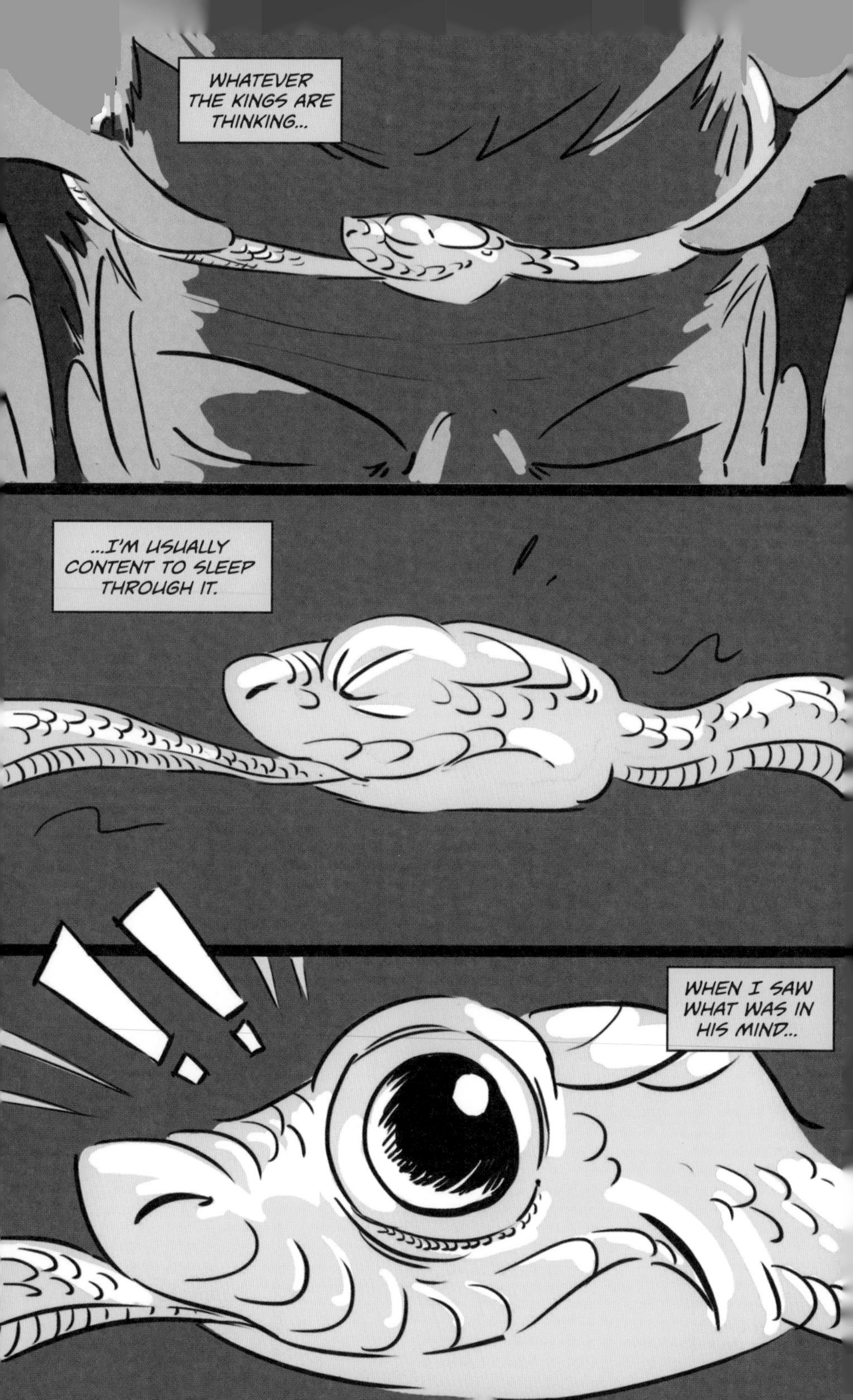
WHATEVER THE KINGS ARE THINKING...
...I'M USUALLY CONTENT TO SLEEP THROUGH IT.
WHEN I SAW WHAT WAS IN HIS MIND...

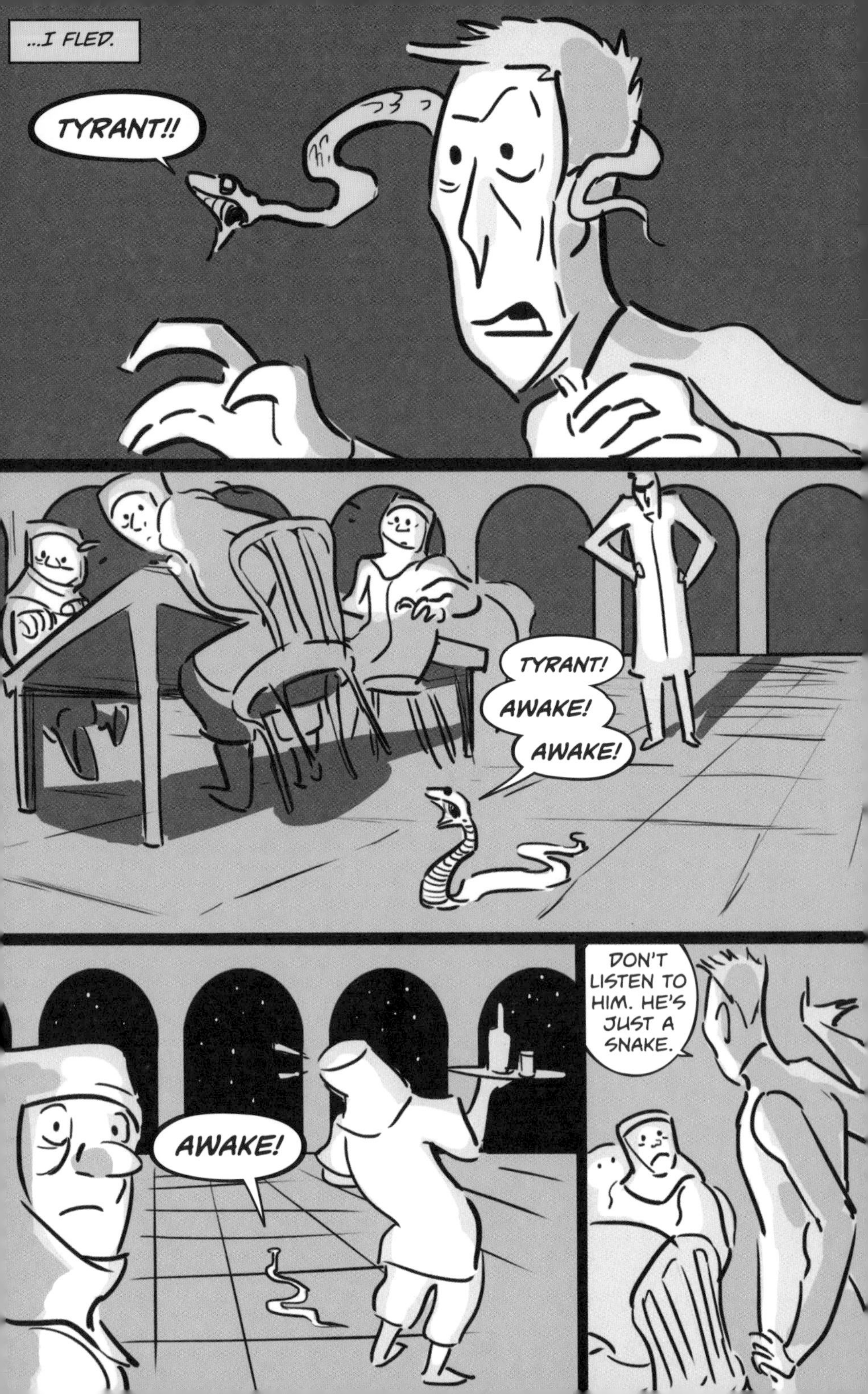
...I FLED.
TYRANT!!
TYRANT!
AWAKE!
AWAKE!
AWAKE!
DON'T LISTEN TO HIM. HE'S JUST A SNAKE.

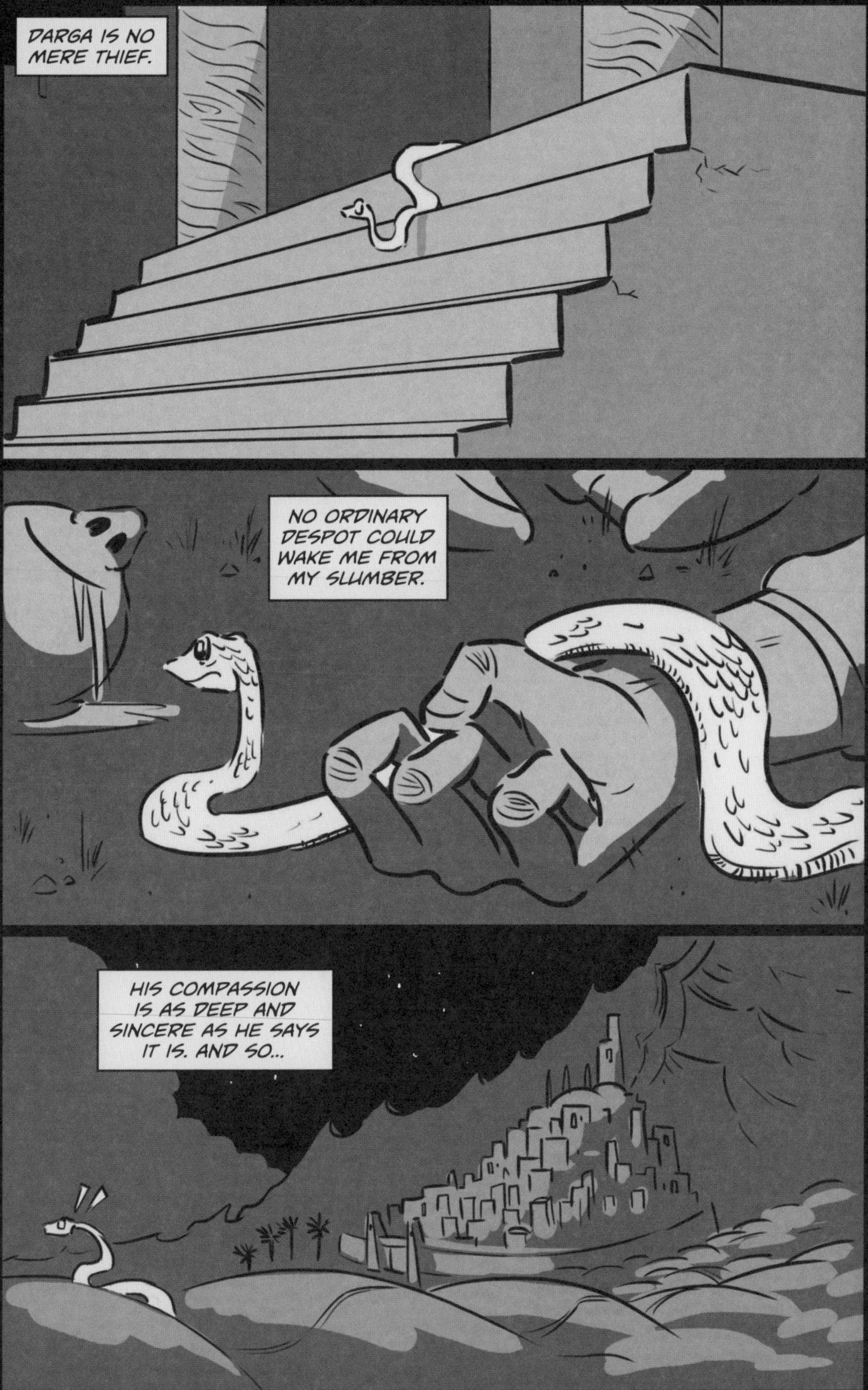
DARGA IS NO MERE THIEF.
NO ORDINARY DESPOT COULD WAKE ME FROM MY SLUMBER.
HIS COMPASSION IS AS DEEP AND SINCERE AS HE SAYS IT IS. AND SO...

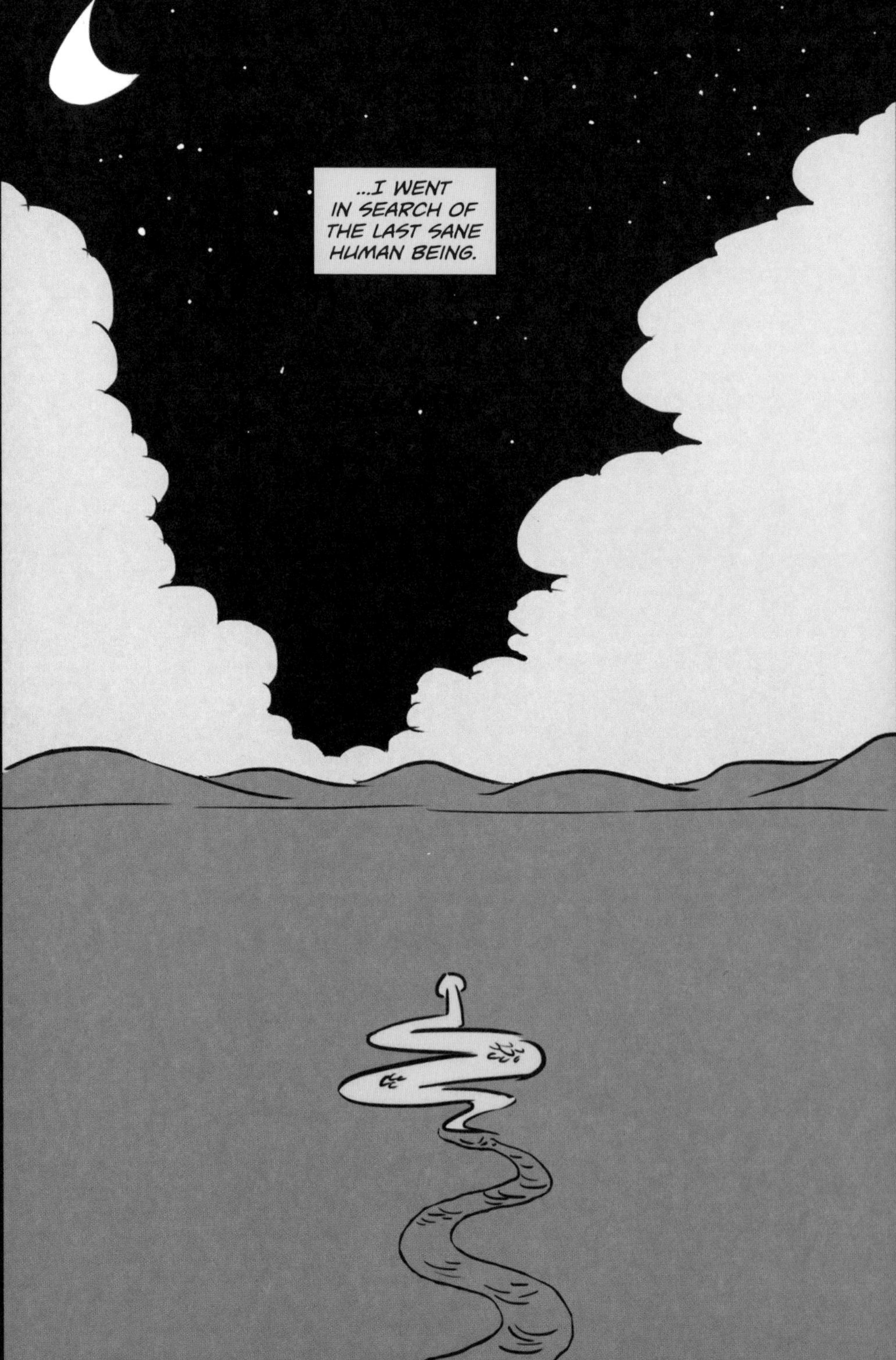
...I WENT IN SEARCH OF THE LAST SANE HUMAN BEING.

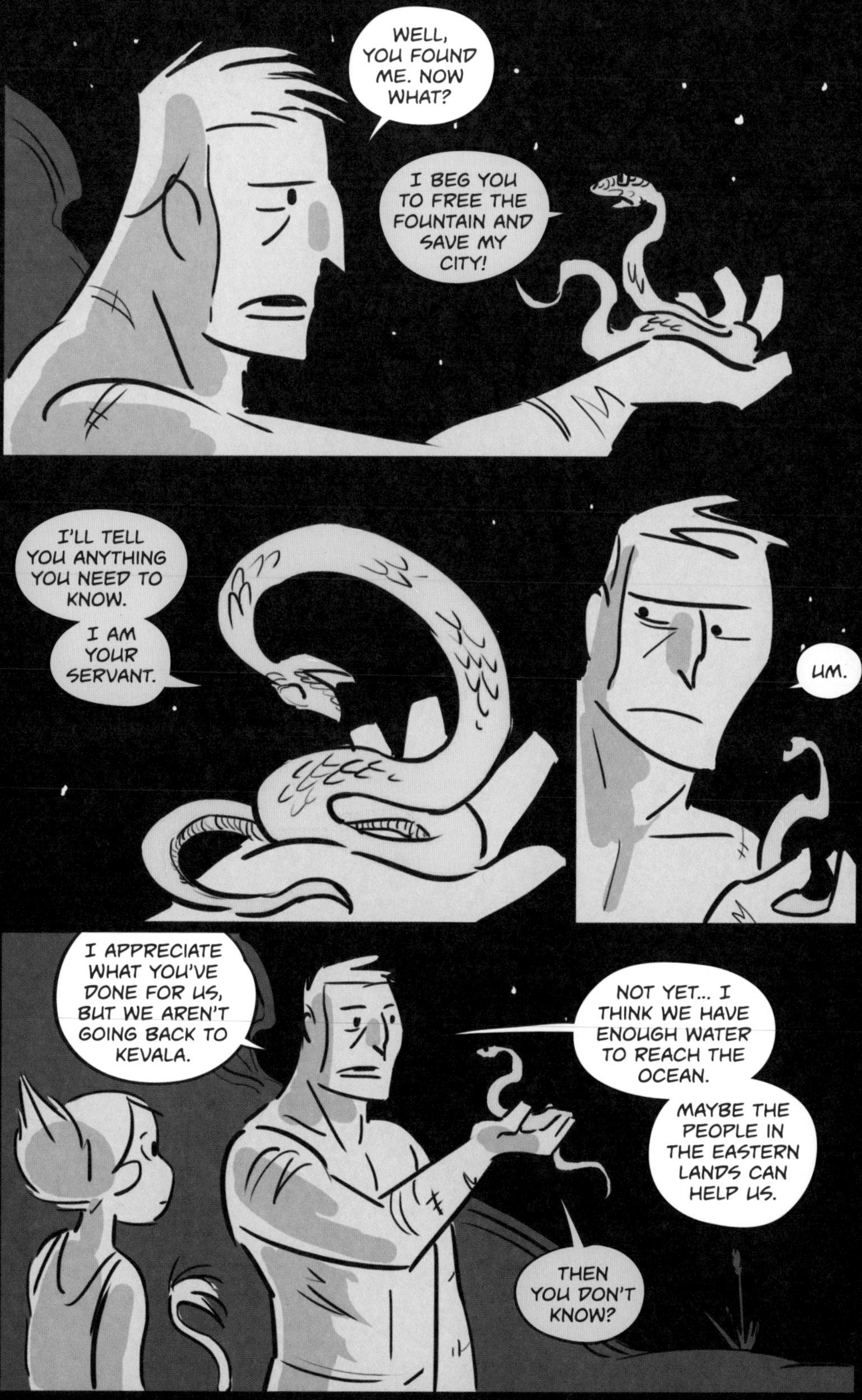
WELL, YOU FOUND ME. NOW WHAT?
I BEG YOU TO FREE THE FOUNTAIN AND SAVE MY CITY!
I'LL TELL YOU ANYTHING YOU NEED TO KNOW.
I AM YOUR SERVANT.
UM.
I APPRECIATE WHAT YOU'VE DONE FOR US, BUT WE AREN'T GOING BACK TO KEVALA.
NOT YET... I THINK WE HAVE ENOUGH WATER TO REACH THE OCEAN.
MAYBE THE PEOPLE IN THE EASTERN LANDS CAN HELP US.
THEN YOU DON'T KNOW?

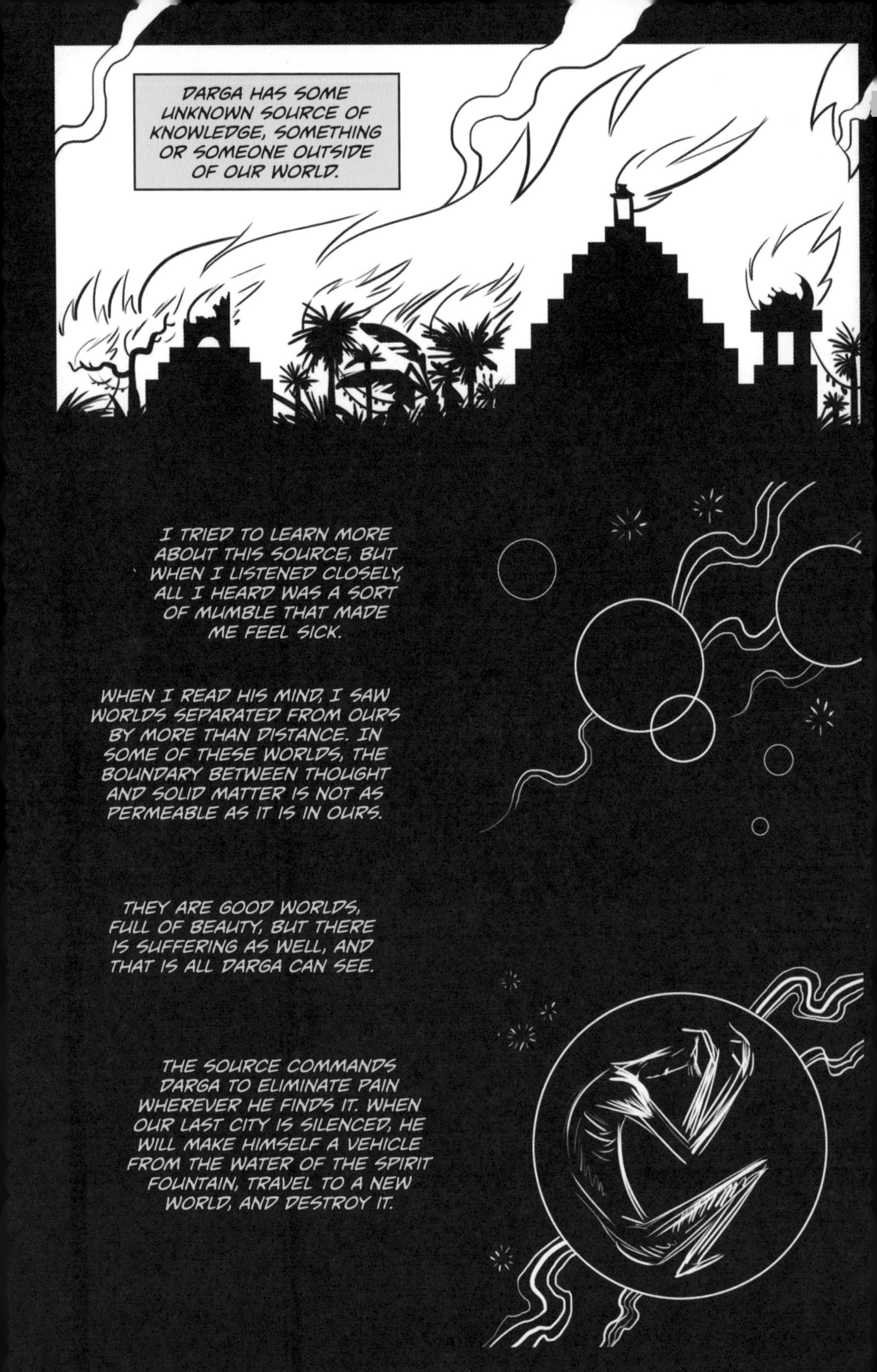
DARGA HAS SOME UNKNOWN SOURCE OF KNOWLEDGE, SOMETHING OR SOMEONE OUTSIDE OF OUR WORLD.
I TRIED TO LEARN MORE ABOUT THIS SOURCE, BUT WHEN I LISTENED CLOSELY, ALL I HEARD WAS A SORT OF MUMBLE THAT MADE ME FEEL SICK.
WHEN I READ HIS MIND, I SAW WORLDS SEPARATED FROM OURS BY MORE THAN DISTANCE. IN SOME OF THESE WORLDS, THE BOUNDARY BETWEEN THOUGHT AND SOLID MATTER IS NOT AS PERMEABLE AS IT IS IN OURS.
THEY ARE GOOD WORLDS, FULL OF BEAUTY, BUT THERE IS SUFFERING AS WELL, AND THAT IS ALL DARGA CAN SEE.
THE SOURCE COMMANDS DARGA TO ELIMINATE PAIN WHEREVER HE FINDS IT. WHEN OUR LAST CITY IS SILENCED, HE WILL MAKE HIMSELF A VEHICLE FROM THE WATER OF THE SPIRIT FOUNTAIN, TRAVEL TO A NEW WORLD, AND DESTROY IT.

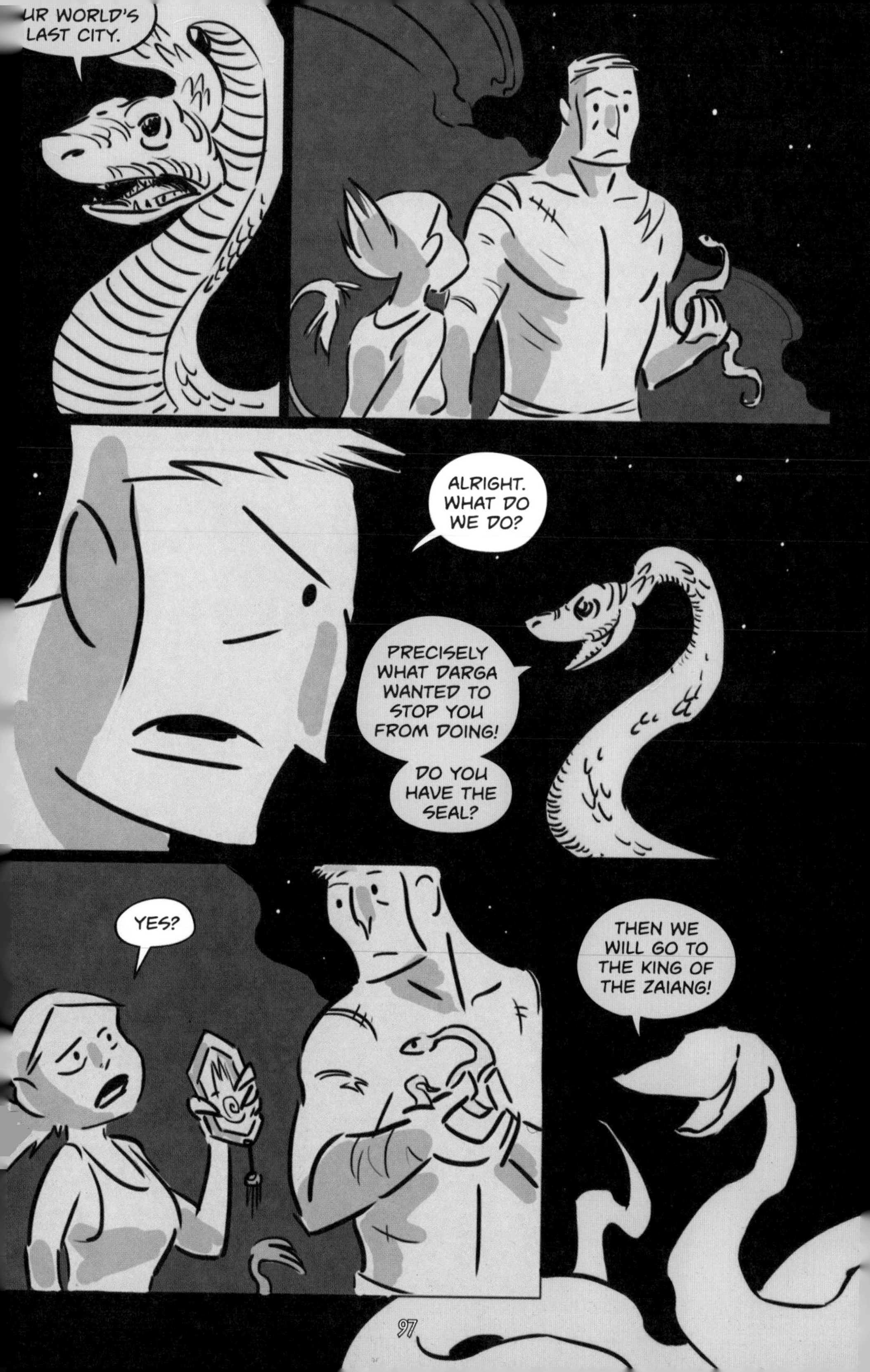
UR WORLD'S LAST CITY.
ALRIGHT. WHAT DO WE DO?
PRECISELY WHAT DARGA WANTED TO STOP YOU FROM DOING!
DO YOU HAVE THE SEAL?
YES?
THEN WE WILL GO TO THE KING OF THE ZAIANG!

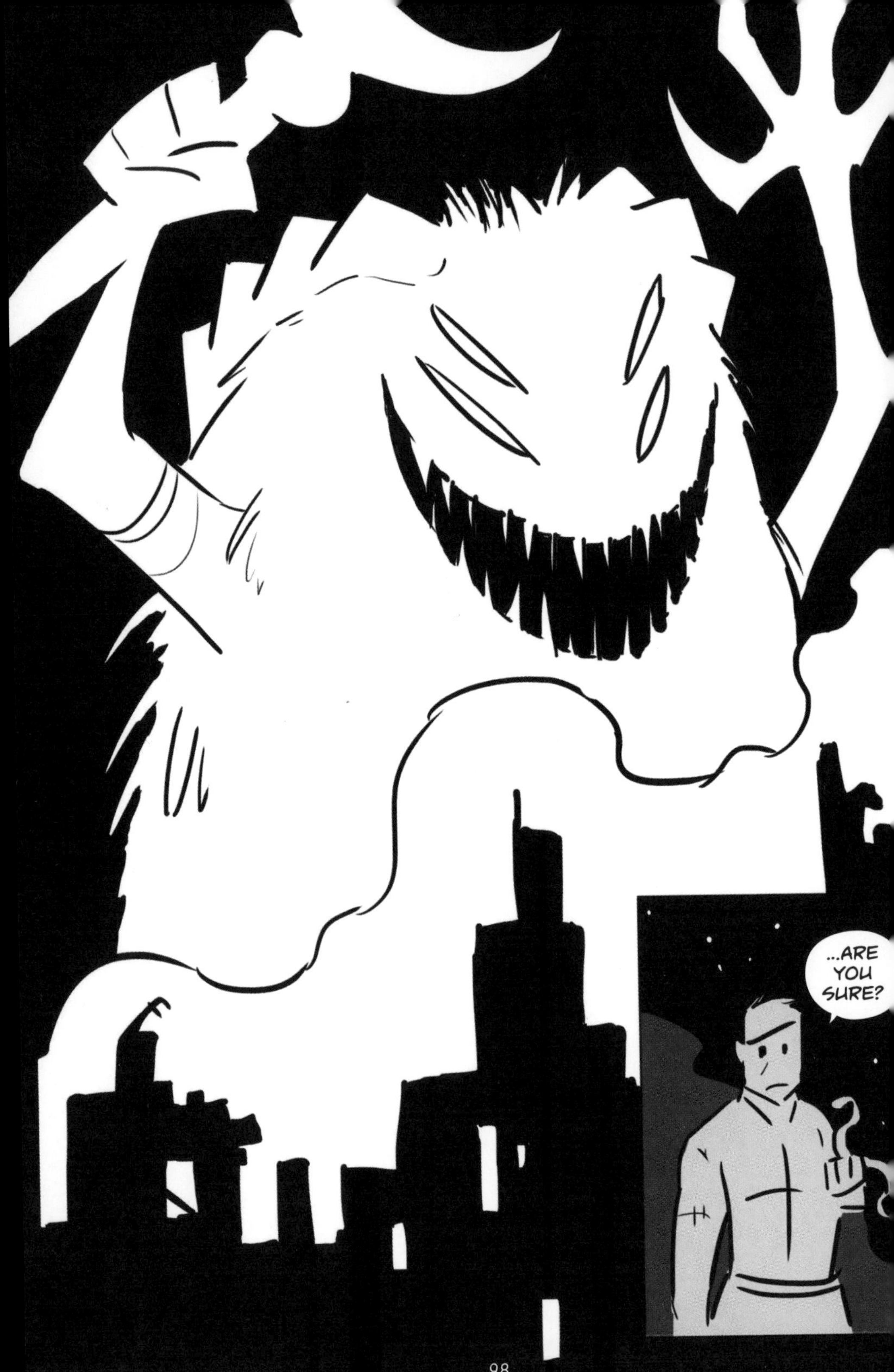
...ARE YOU SURE?

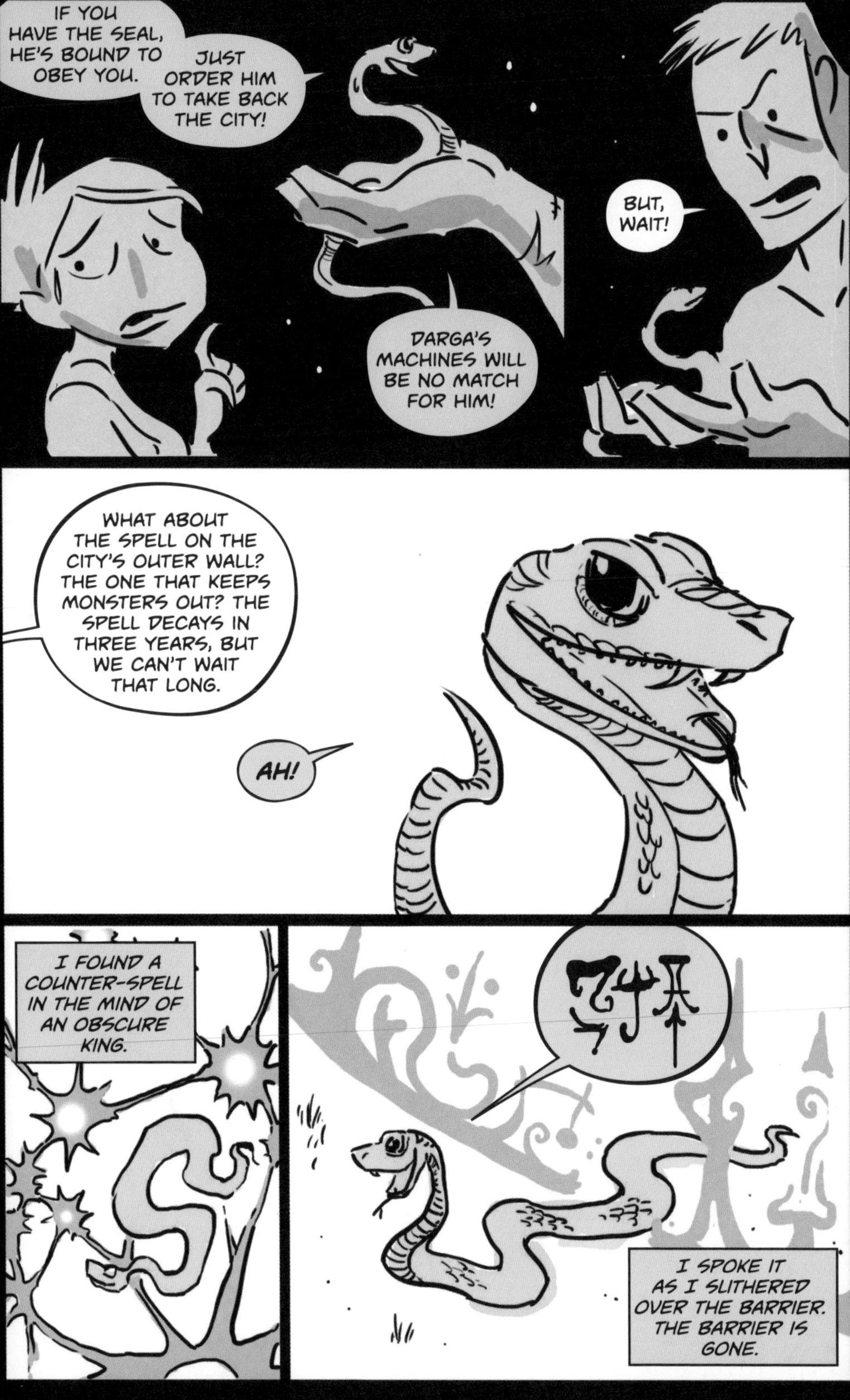
IF YOU HAVE THE SEAL, HE'S BOUND TO OBEY YOU.
JUST ORDER HIM TO TAKE BACK THE CITY!
BUT, WAIT!
DARGA'S MACHINES WILL BE NO MATCH FOR HIM!
WHAT ABOUT THE SPELL ON THE CITY'S OUTER WALL? THE ONE THAT KEEPS MONSTERS OUT? THE SPELL DECAYS IN THREE YEARS, BUT WE CAN'T WAIT THAT LONG.
AH!
I FOUND A COUNTER-SPELL IN THE MIND OF AN OBSCURE KING.
I SPOKE IT AS I SLITHERED OVER THE BARRIER. THE BARRIER IS GONE.

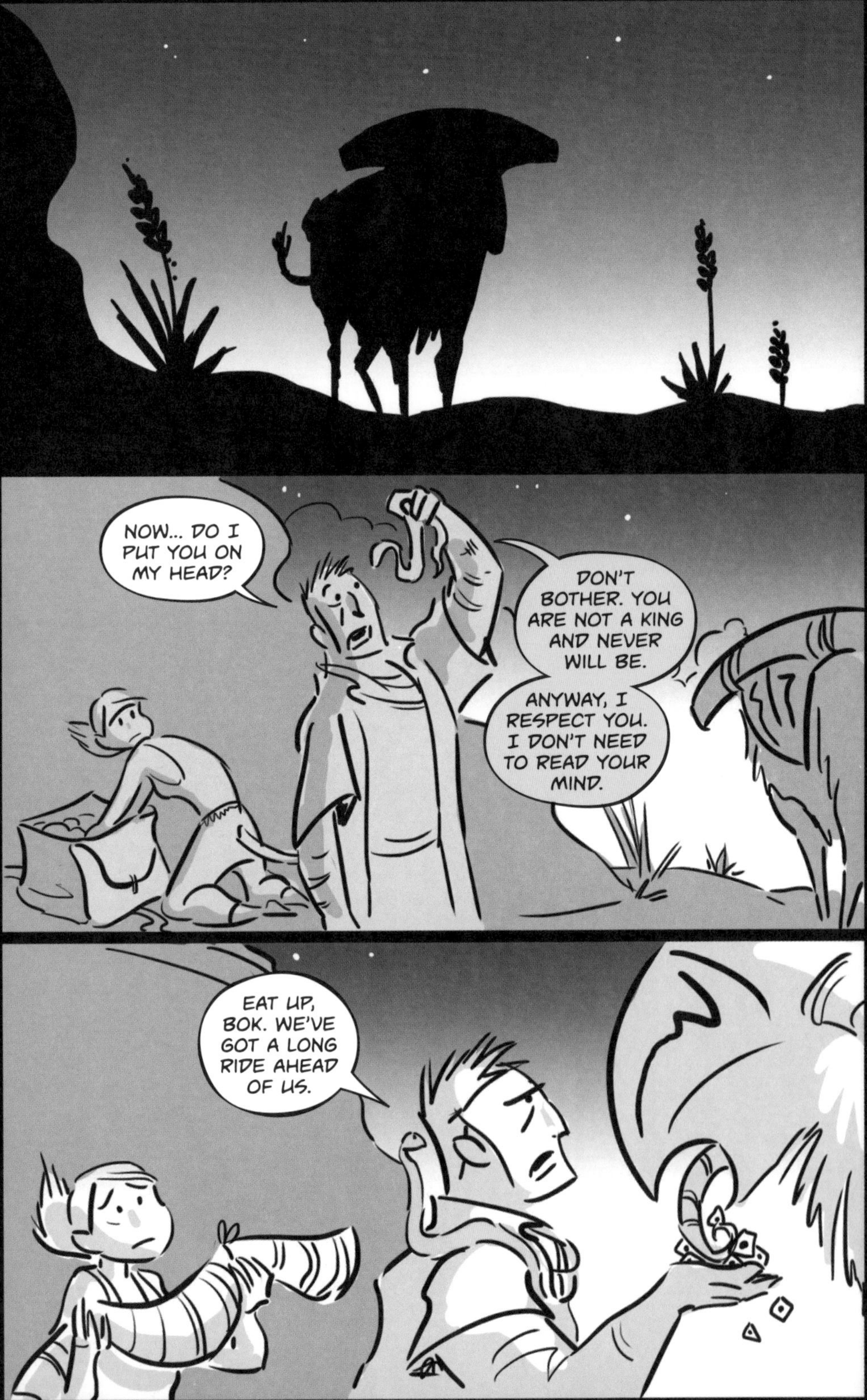
NOW... DO I PUT YOU ON MY HEAD?
DON'T BOTHER. YOU ARE NOT A KING AND NEVER WILL BE.
ANYWAY, I RESPECT YOU. I DON'T NEED TO READ YOUR MIND.
EAT UP, BOK. WE'VE GOT A LONG RIDE AHEAD OF US.

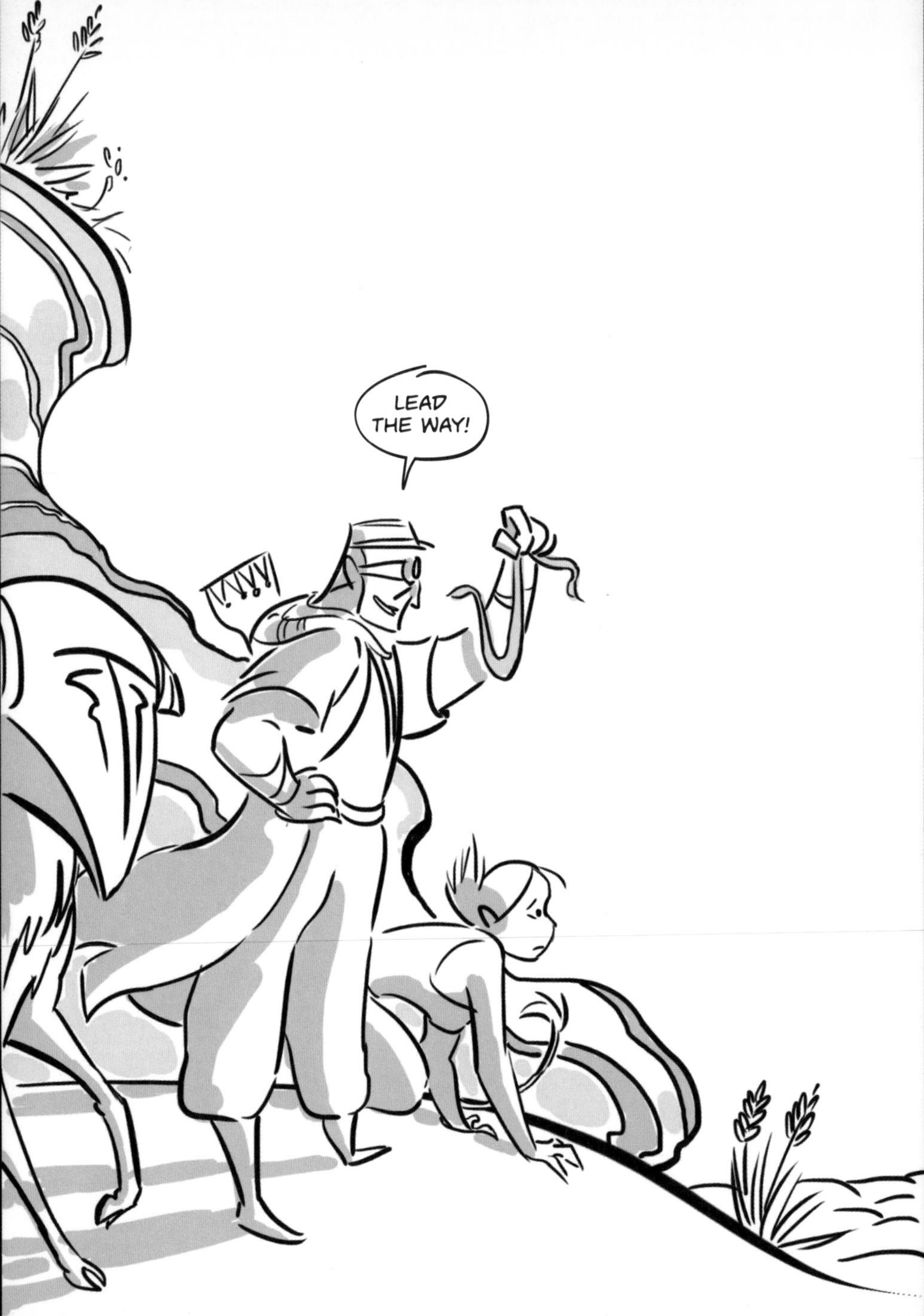
LEAD THE WAY!

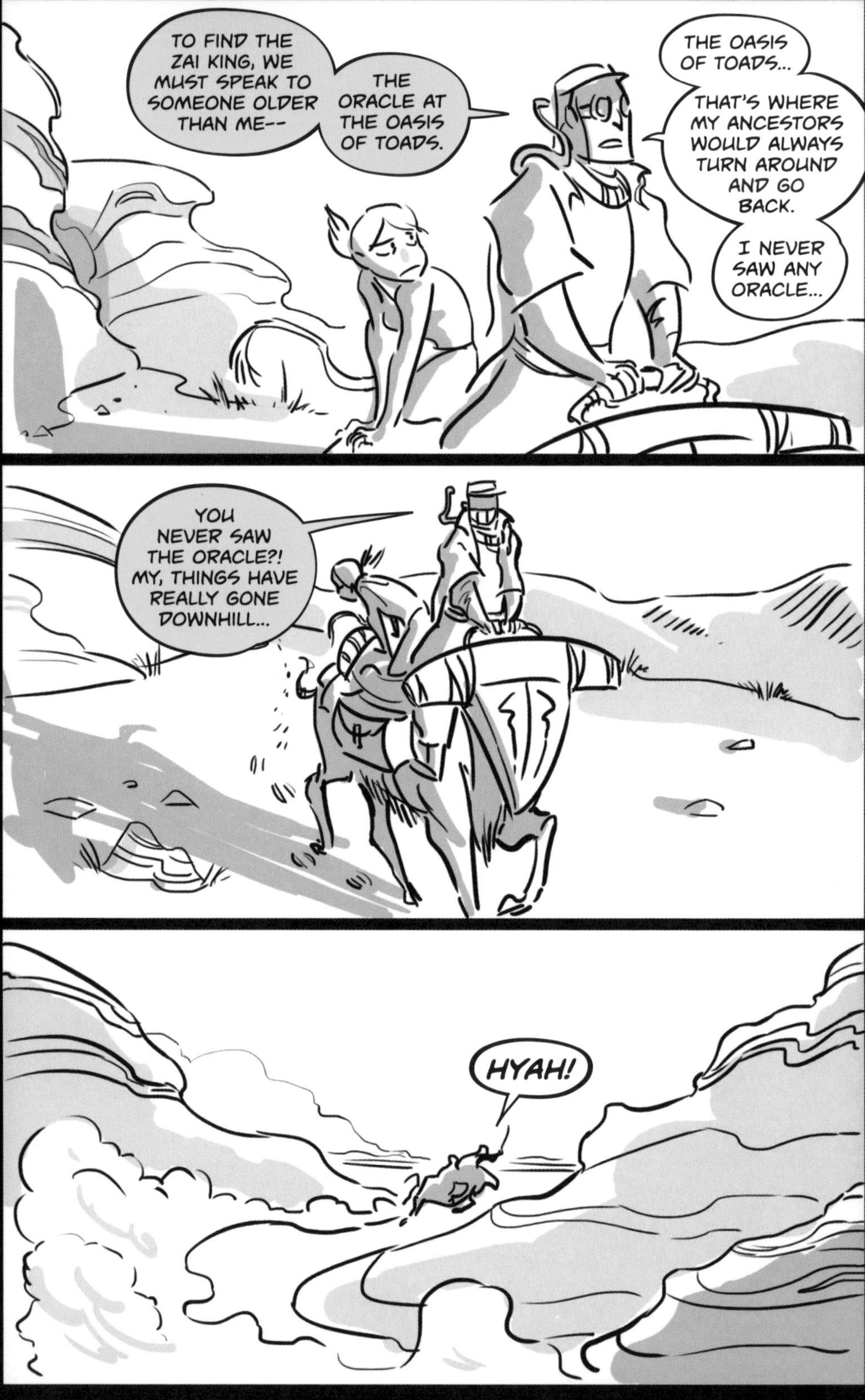
TO FIND THE ZAI KING, WE MUST SPEAK TO SOMEONE OLDER THAN ME--
THE ORACLE AT THE OASIS OF TOADS.
THE OASIS OF TOADS...
THAT'S WHERE MY ANCESTORS WOULD ALWAYS TURN AROUND AND GO BACK.
I NEVER SAW ANY ORACLE...
YOU NEVER SAW THE ORACLE?! MY, THINGS HAVE REALLY GONE DOWNHILL...
HYAH!

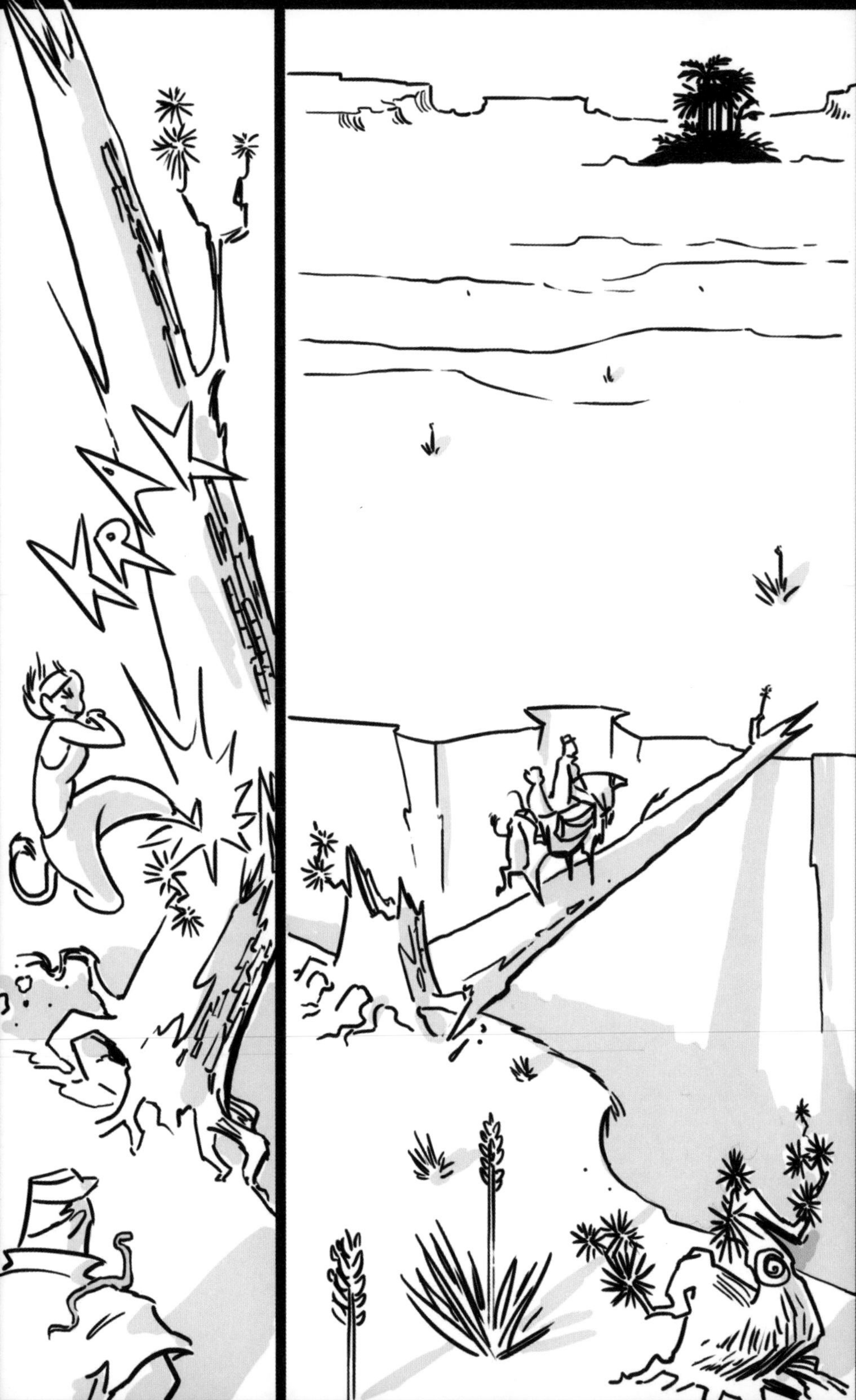
KRAK

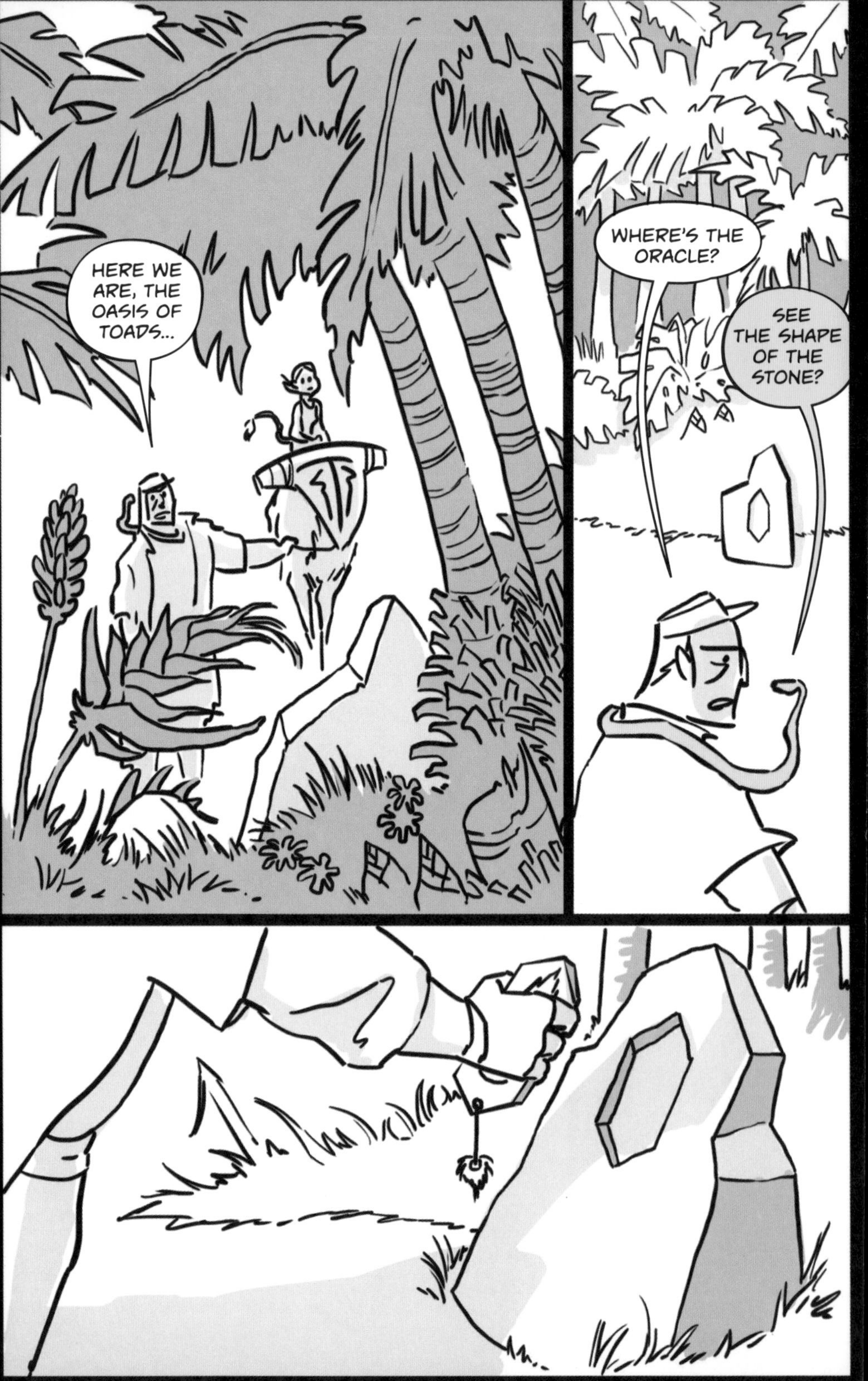
HERE WE ARE, THE OASIS OF TOADS...
WHERE'S THE ORACLE?
SEE THE SHAPE OF THE STONE?

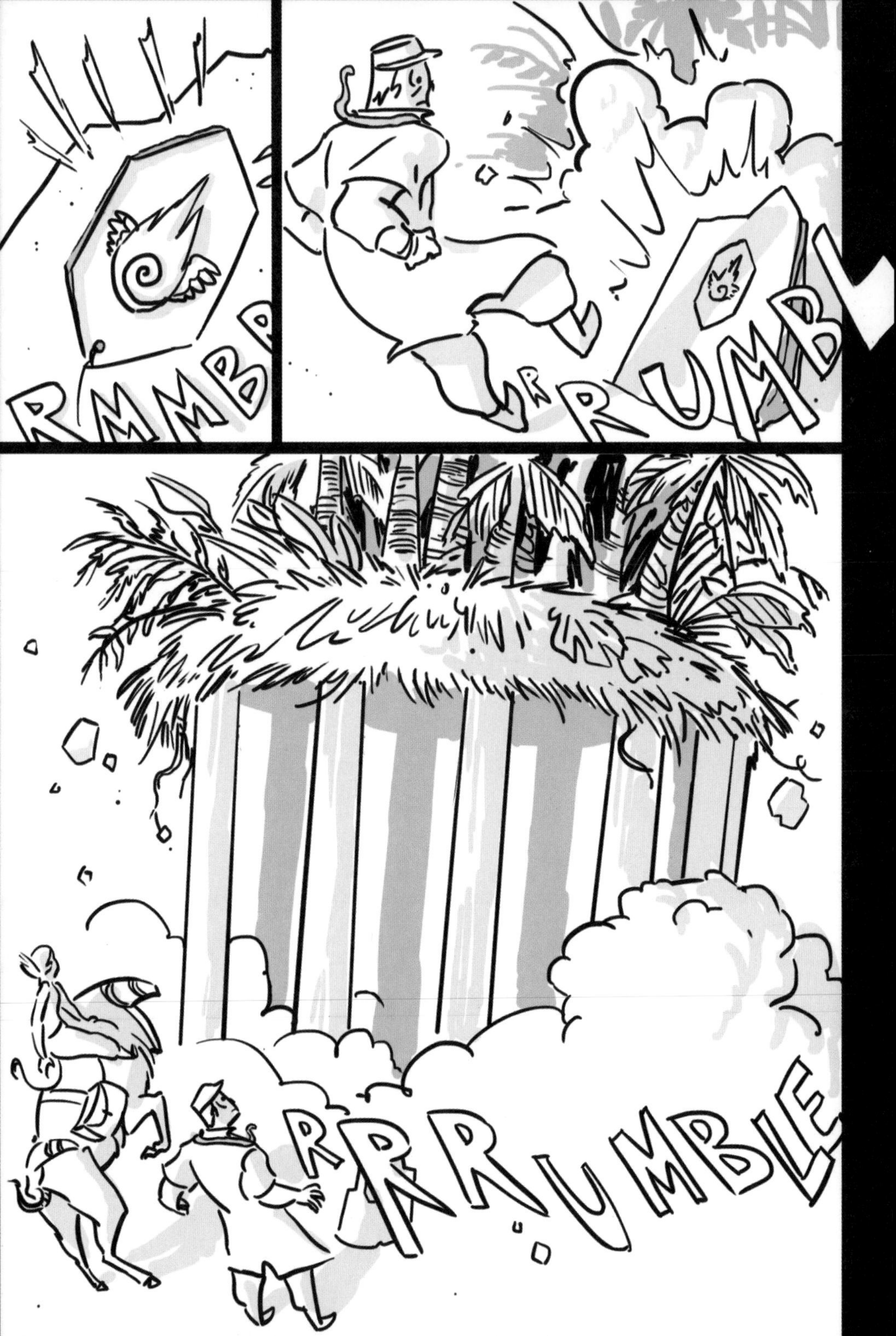
RMMB
RRUMBL
RRRUMBLE

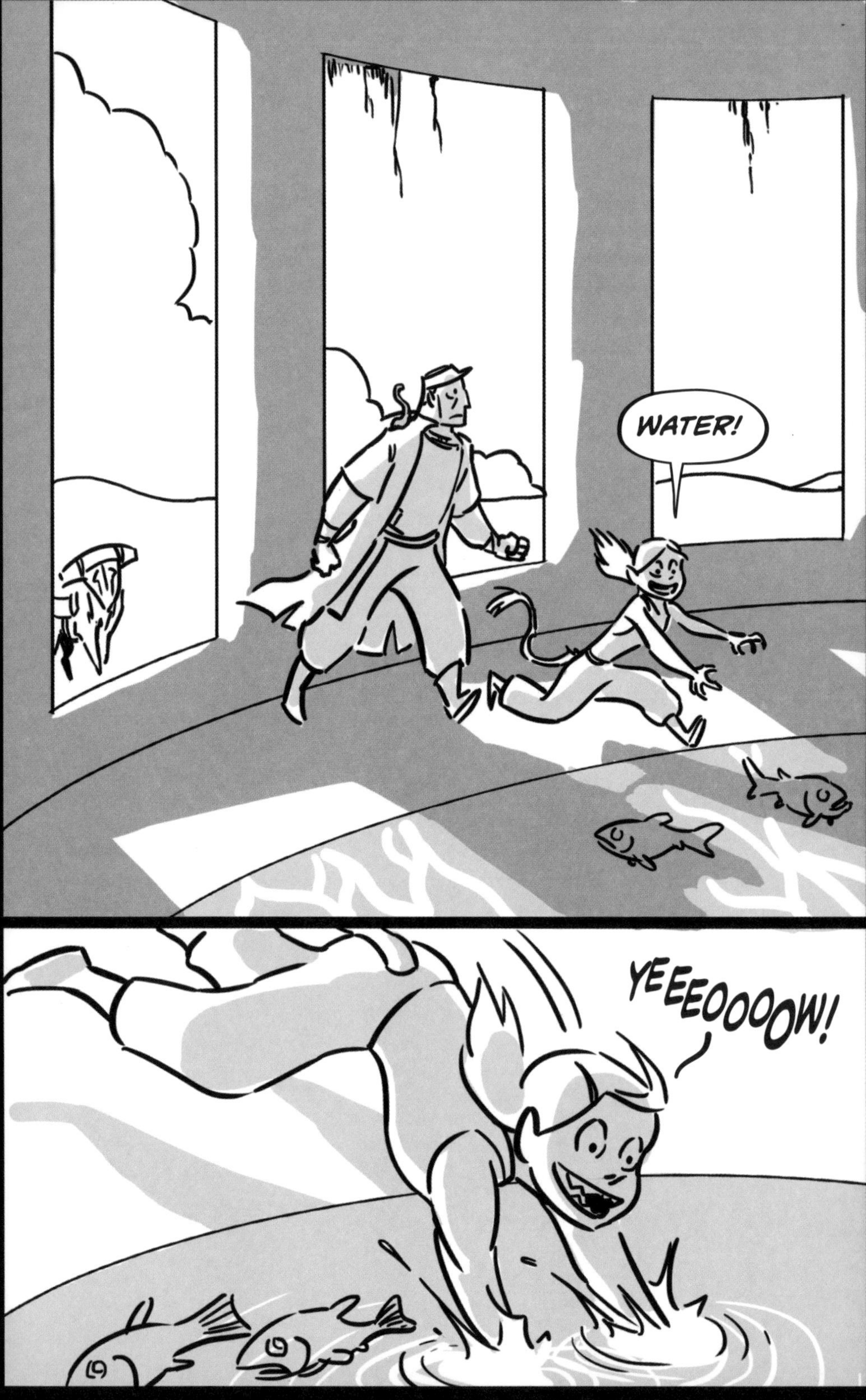
WATER!
YEEEOOOOW!

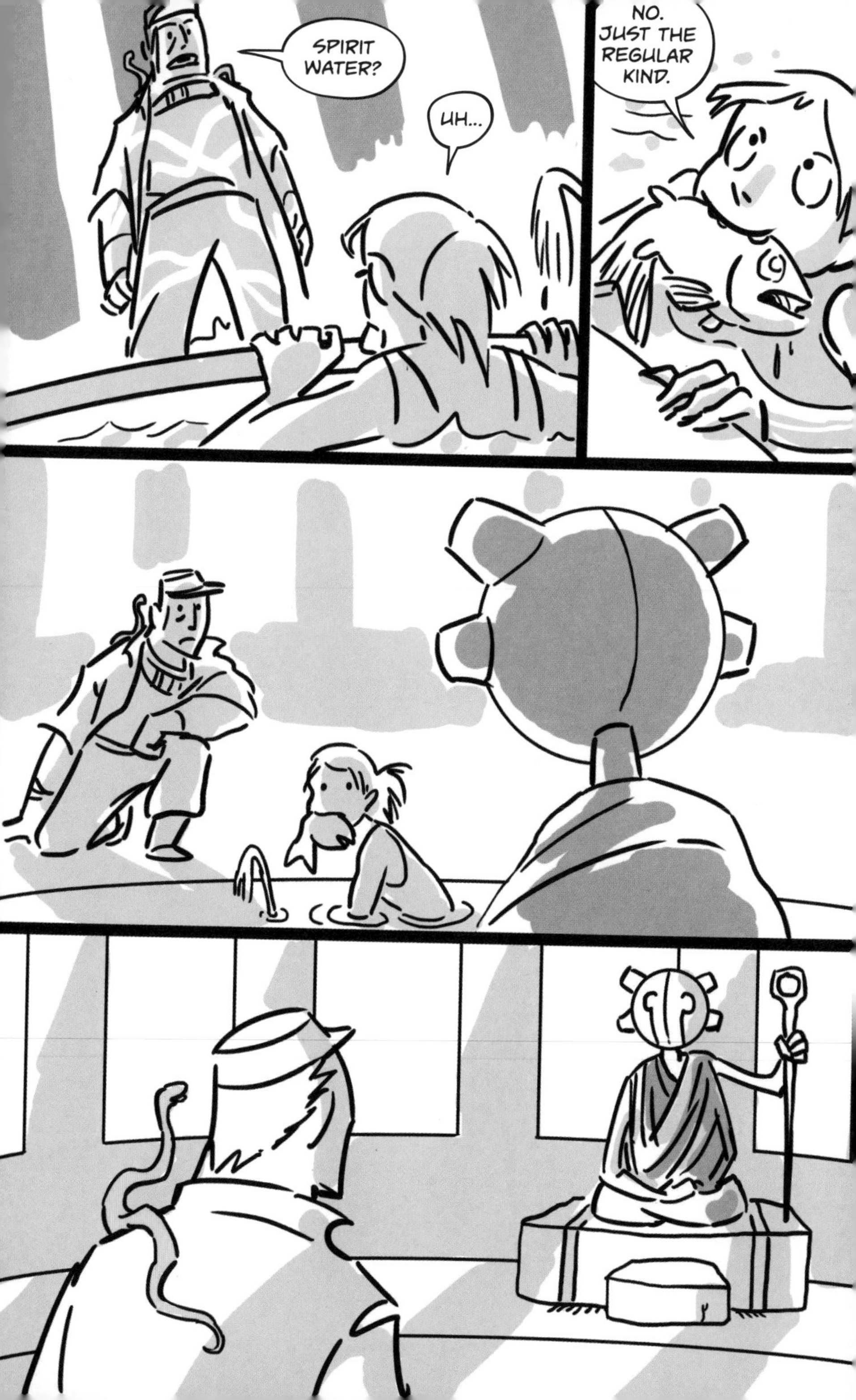
SPIRIT WATER?
UH...
NO. JUST THE REGULAR KIND.

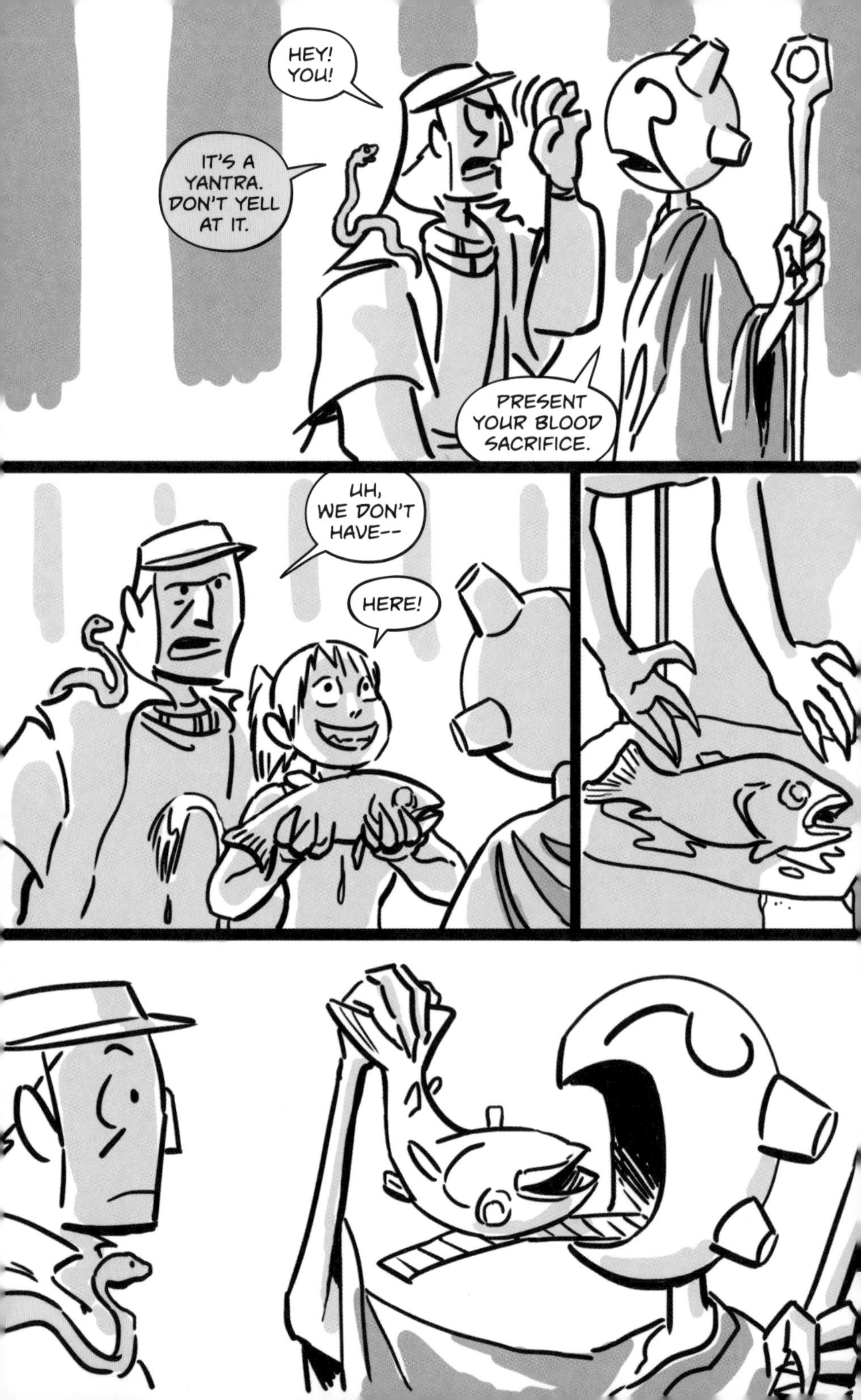
HEY! YOU!
IT'S A YANTRA. DON'T YELL AT IT.
PRESENT YOUR BLOOD SACRIFICE.
UH, WE DON'T HAVE--
HERE!

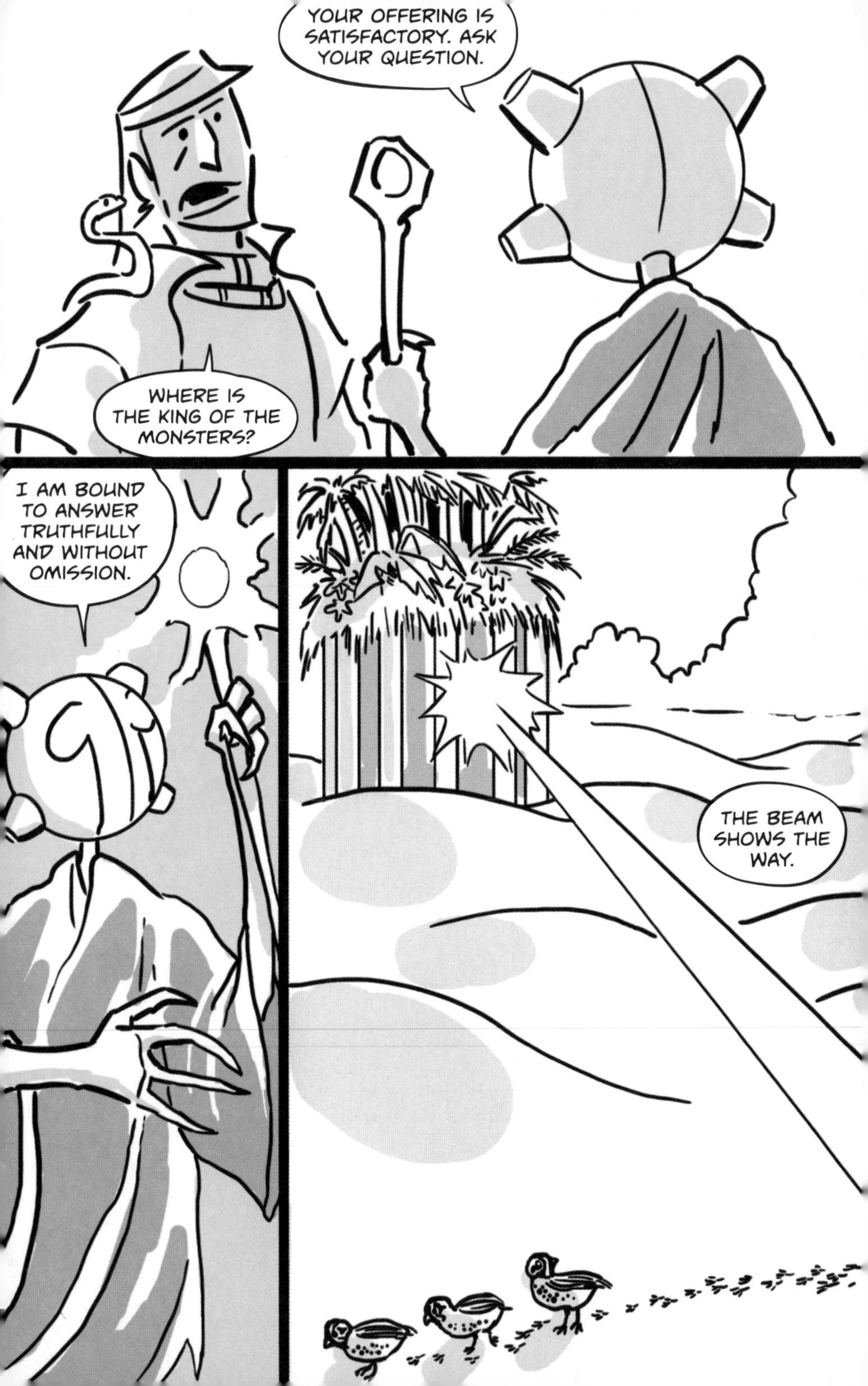
YOUR OFFERING IS SATISFACTORY. ASK YOUR QUESTION.
WHERE IS THE KING OF THE MONSTERS?
I AM BOUND TO ANSWER TRUTHFULLY AND WITHOUT OMISSION.
THE BEAM SHOWS THE WAY.

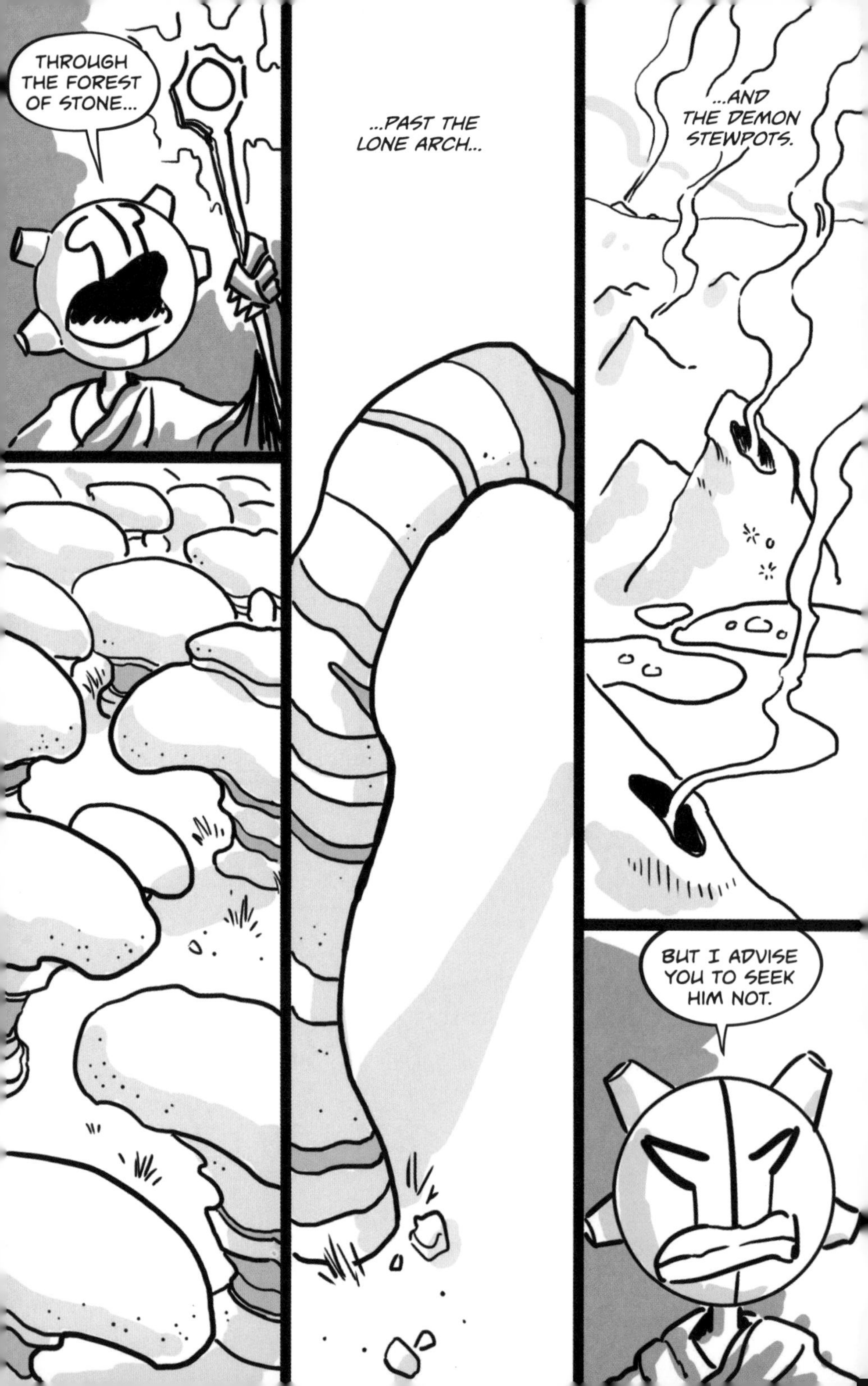
THROUGH THE FOREST OF STONE...
...PAST THE LONE ARCH...
...AND THE DEMON STEWPOTS.
BUT I ADVISE YOU TO SEEK HIM NOT.

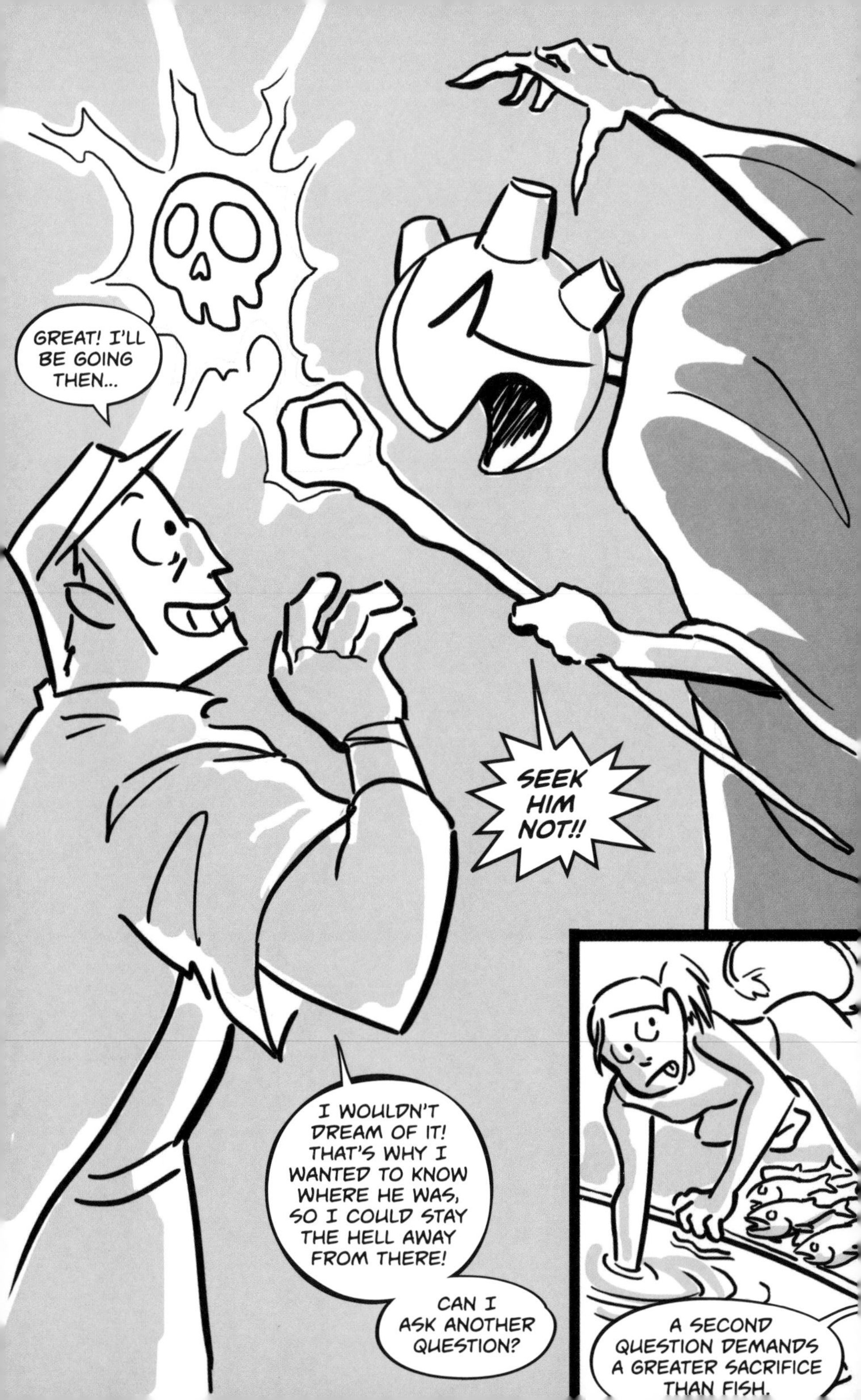
GREAT! I'LL BE GOING THEN...
SEEK HIM NOT!!
I WOULDN'T DREAM OF IT! THAT'S WHY I WANTED TO KNOW WHERE HE WAS, SO I COULD STAY THE HELL AWAY FROM THERE!
CAN I ASK ANOTHER QUESTION?
A SECOND QUESTION DEMANDS A GREATER SACRIFICE THAN FISH.

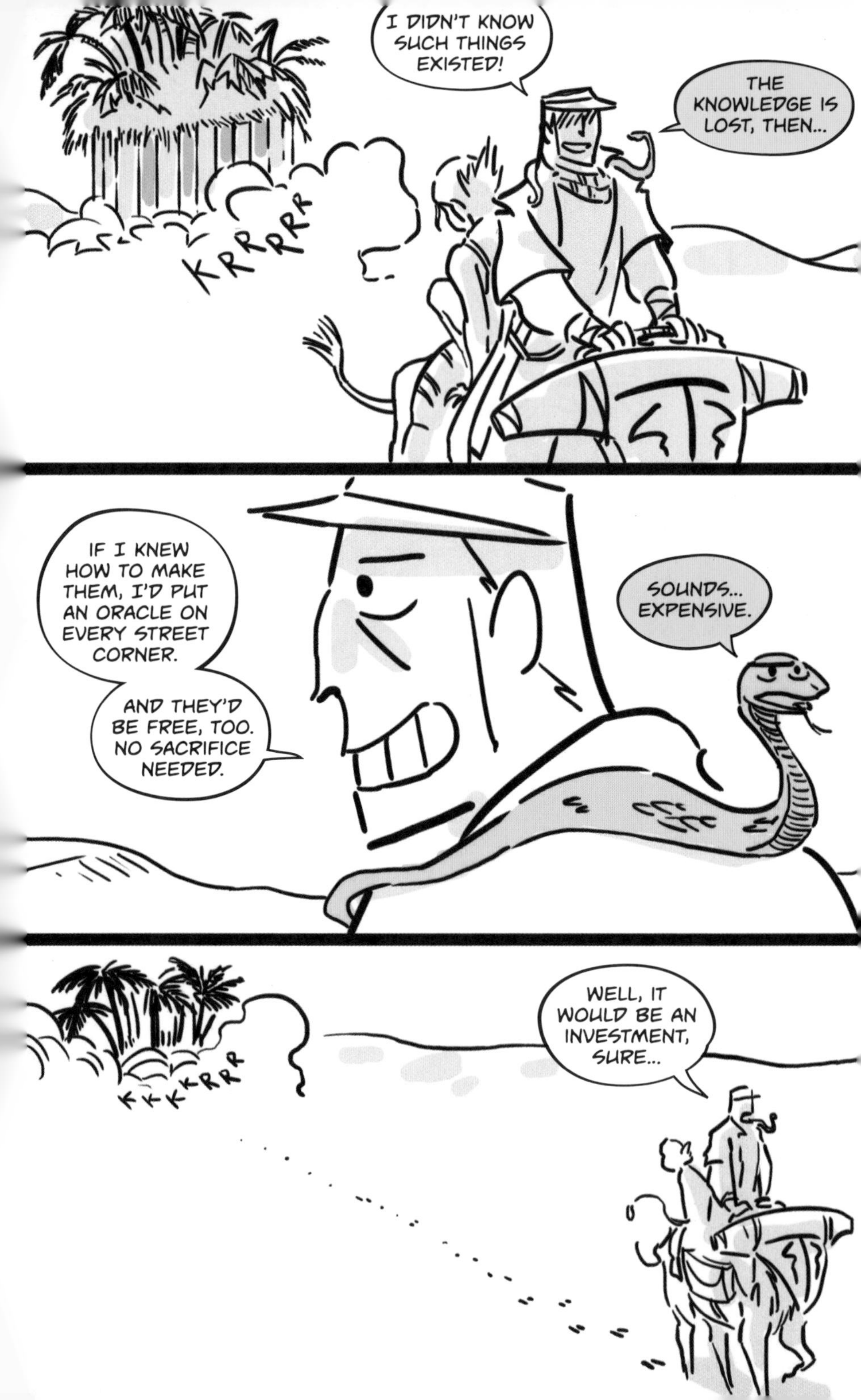
I DIDN'T KNOW SUCH THINGS EXISTED!
THE KNOWLEDGE IS LOST, THEN...
KRRRRR
IF I KNEW HOW TO MAKE THEM, I'D PUT AN ORACLE ON EVERY STREET CORNER.
AND THEY'D BE FREE, TOO. NO SACRIFICE NEEDED.
SOUNDS... EXPENSIVE.
KKKKRRR
WELL, IT WOULD BE AN INVESTMENT, SURE...

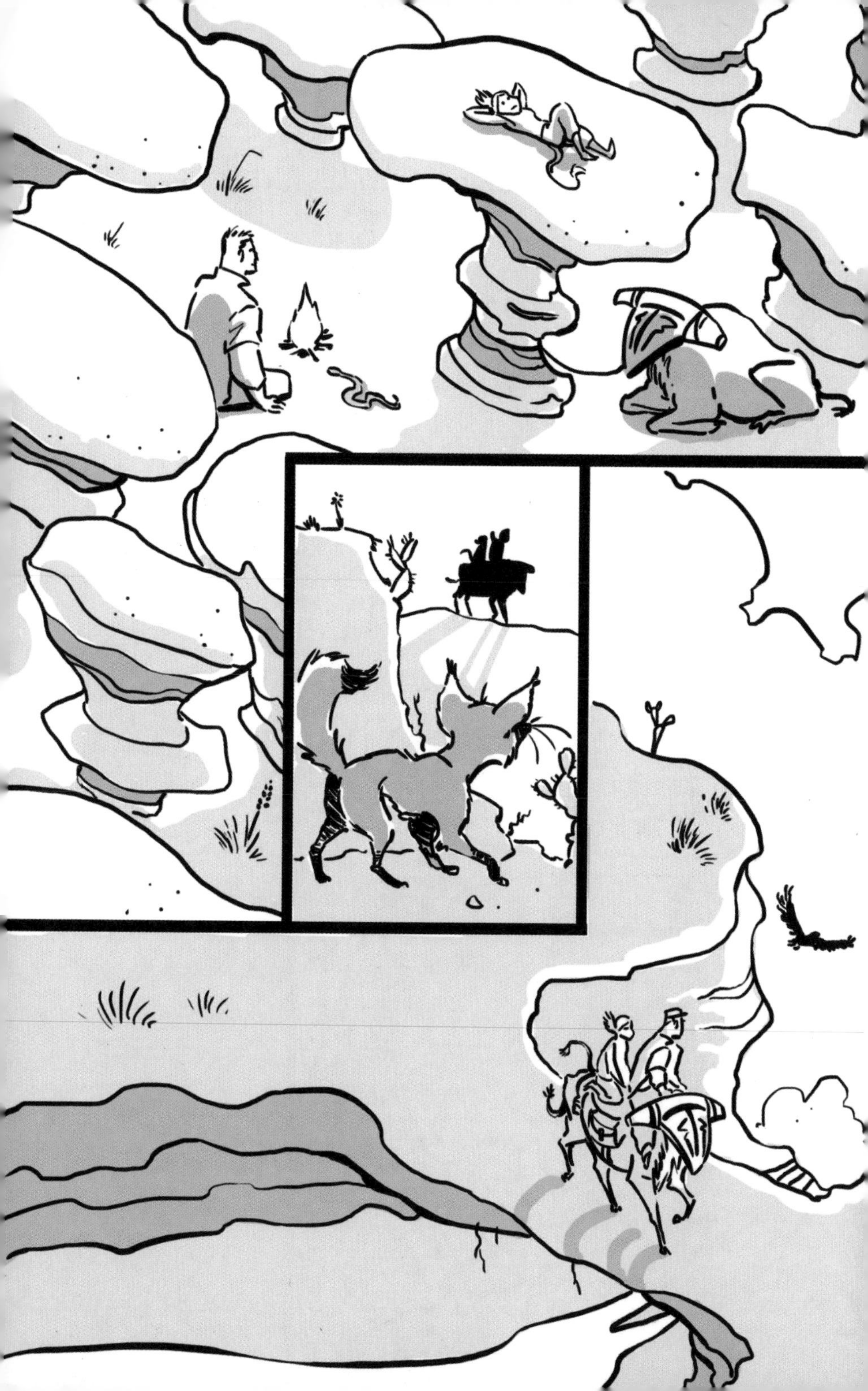

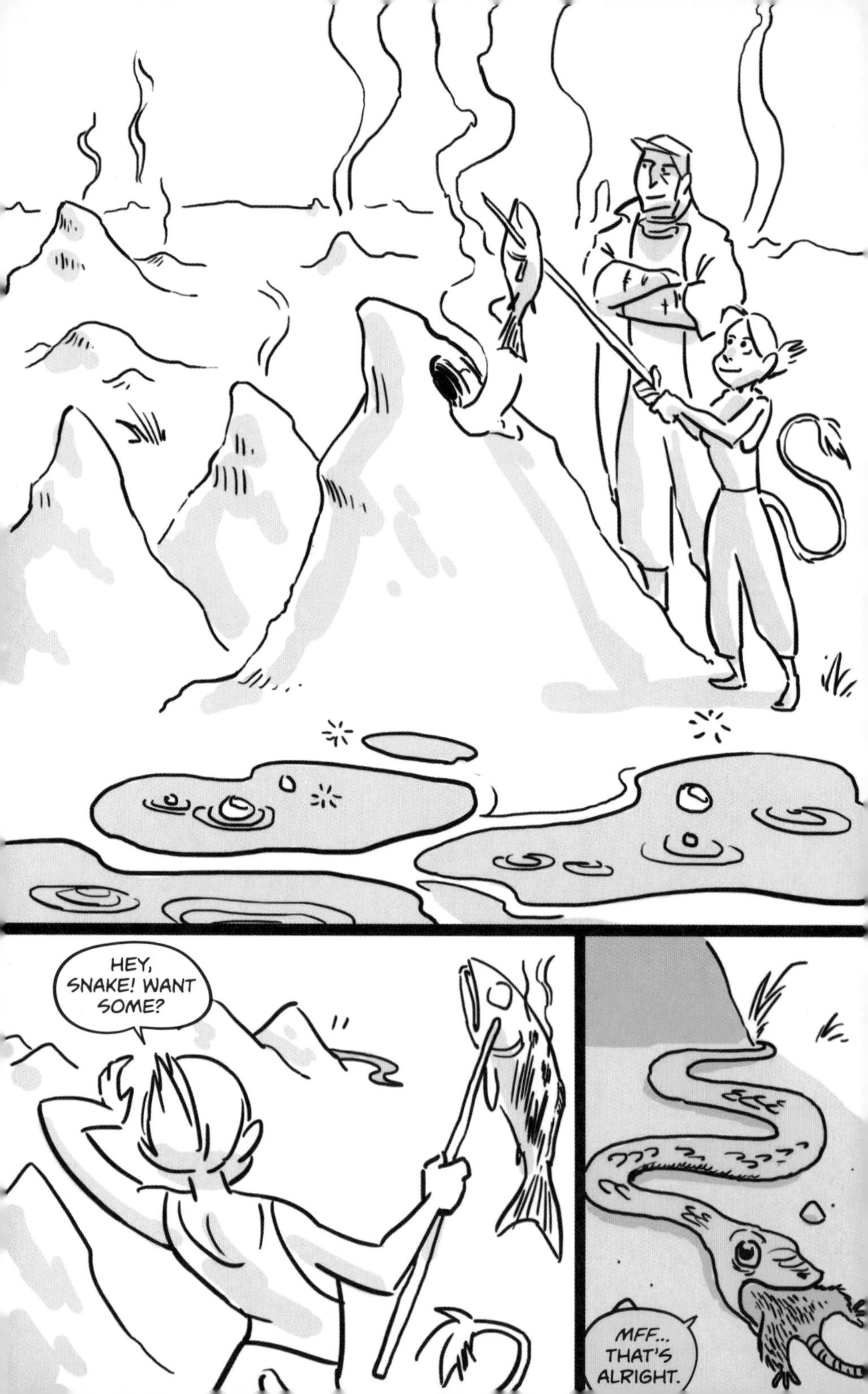
HEY, SNAKE! WANT SOME?
MFF... THAT'S ALRIGHT.

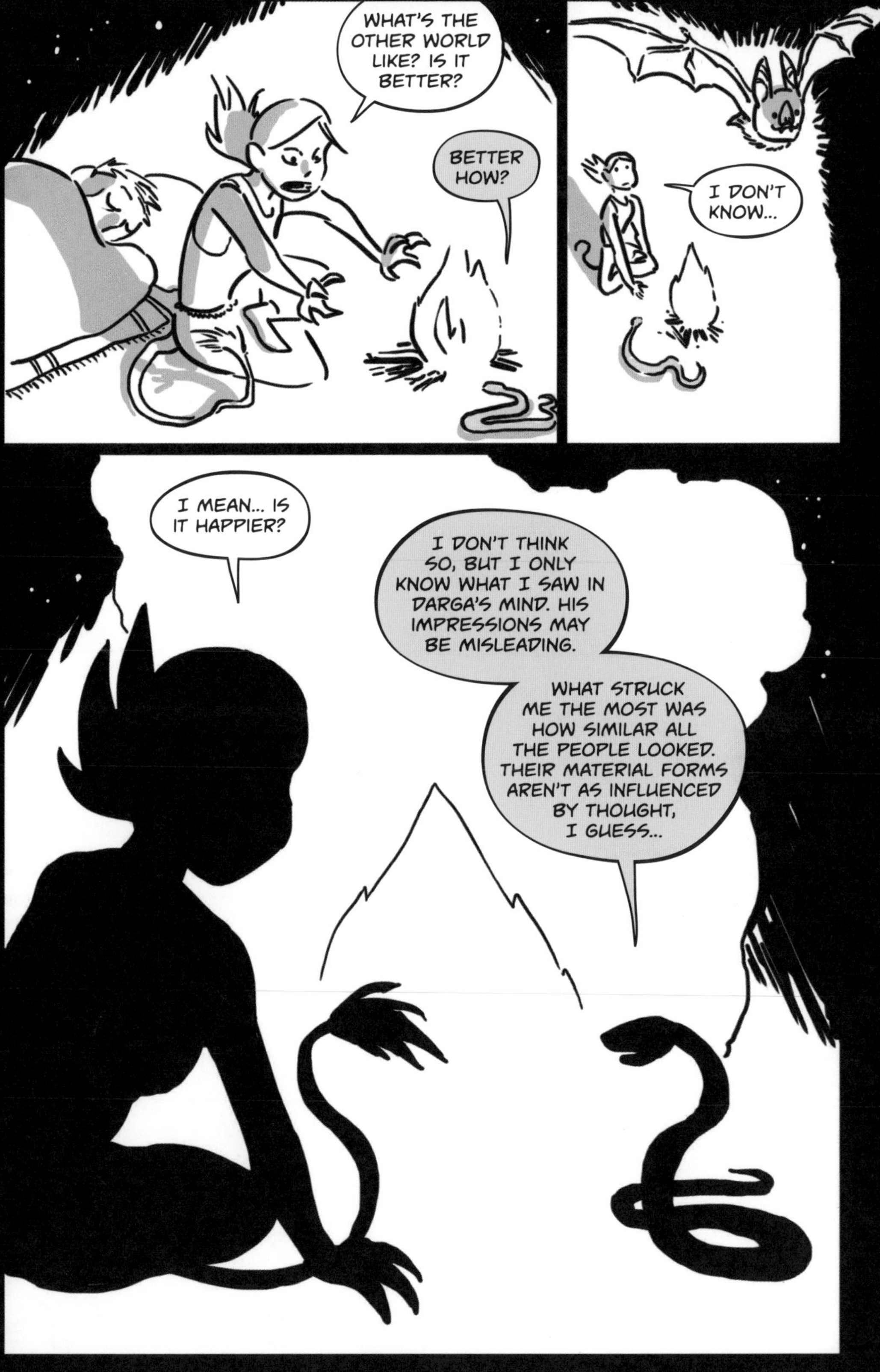
WHAT'S THE OTHER WORLD LIKE? IS IT BETTER?
BETTER HOW?
I DON'T KNOW...
I MEAN... IS IT HAPPIER?
I DON'T THINK SO, BUT I ONLY KNOW WHAT I SAW IN DARGA'S MIND. HIS IMPRESSIONS MAY BE MISLEADING.
WHAT STRUCK ME THE MOST WAS HOW SIMILAR ALL THE PEOPLE LOOKED. THEIR MATERIAL FORMS AREN'T AS INFLUENCED BY THOUGHT, I GUESS...

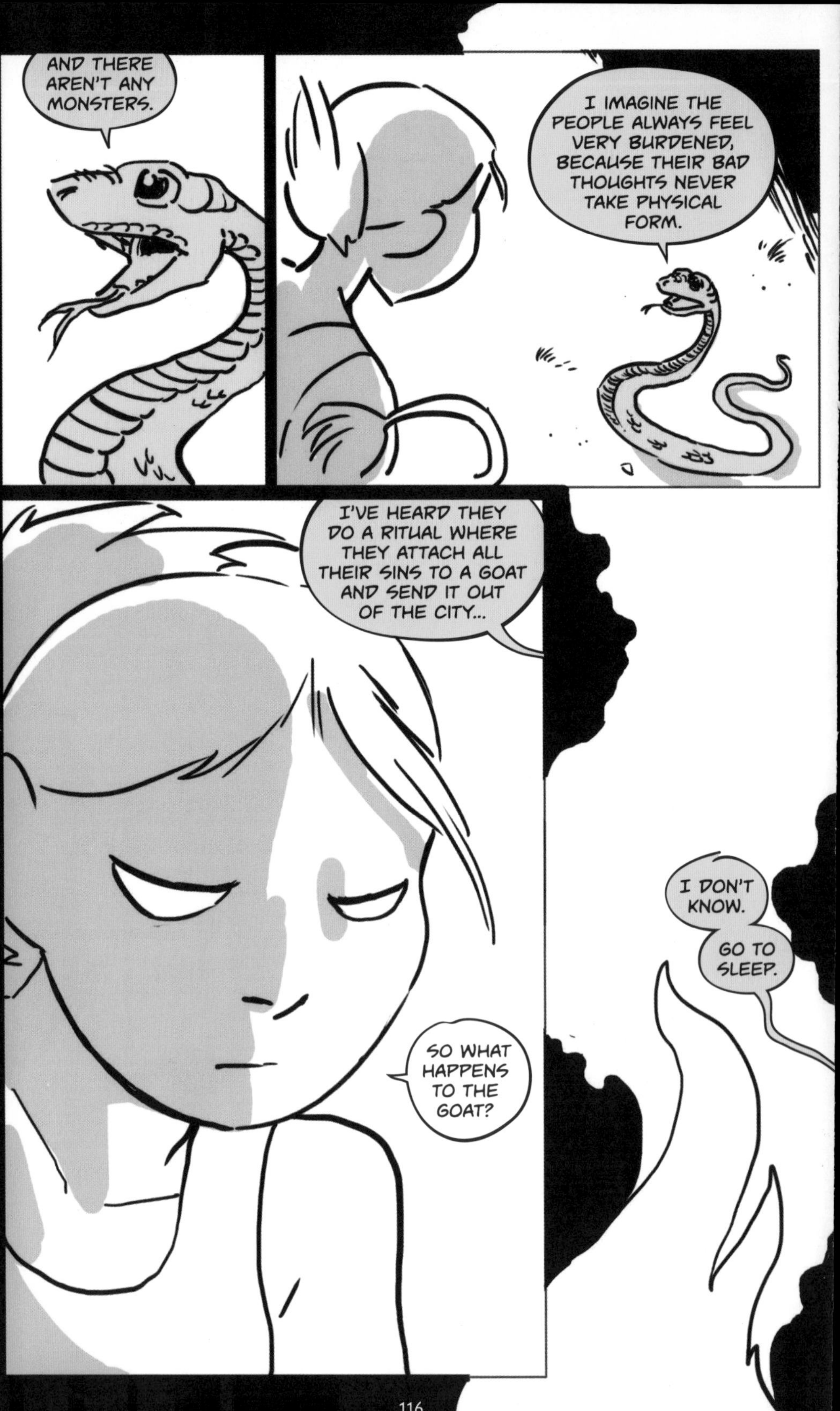
AND THERE AREN'T ANY MONSTERS.
I IMAGINE THE PEOPLE ALWAYS FEEL VERY BURDENED, BECAUSE THEIR BAD THOUGHTS NEVER TAKE PHYSICAL FORM.
I'VE HEARD THEY DO A RITUAL WHERE THEY ATTACH ALL THEIR SINS TO A GOAT AND SEND IT OUT OF THE CITY...
SO WHAT HAPPENS TO THE GOAT?
I DON'T KNOW.
GO TO SLEEP.

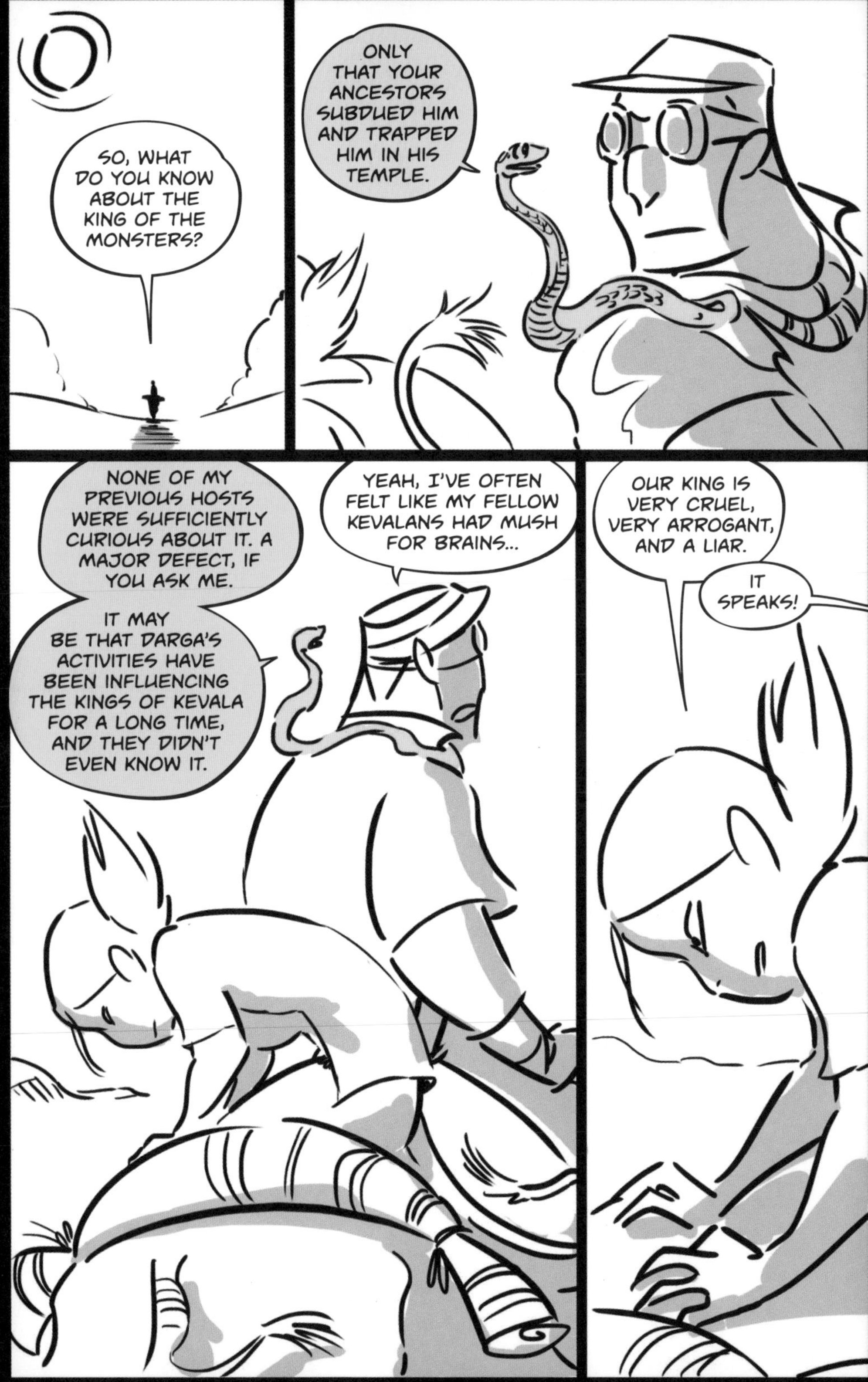
SO, WHAT DO YOU KNOW ABOUT THE KING OF THE MONSTERS?
ONLY THAT YOUR ANCESTORS SUBDUED HIM AND TRAPPED HIM IN HIS TEMPLE.
NONE OF MY PREVIOUS HOSTS WERE SUFFICIENTLY CURIOUS ABOUT IT. A MAJOR DEFECT, IF YOU ASK ME.
IT MAY BE THAT DARGA'S ACTIVITIES HAVE BEEN INFLUENCING THE KINGS OF KEVALA FOR A LONG TIME, AND THEY DIDN'T EVEN KNOW IT.
YEAH, I'VE OFTEN FELT LIKE MY FELLOW KEVALANS HAD MUSH FOR BRAINS...
OUR KING IS VERY CRUEL, VERY ARROGANT, AND A LIAR.
IT SPEAKS!

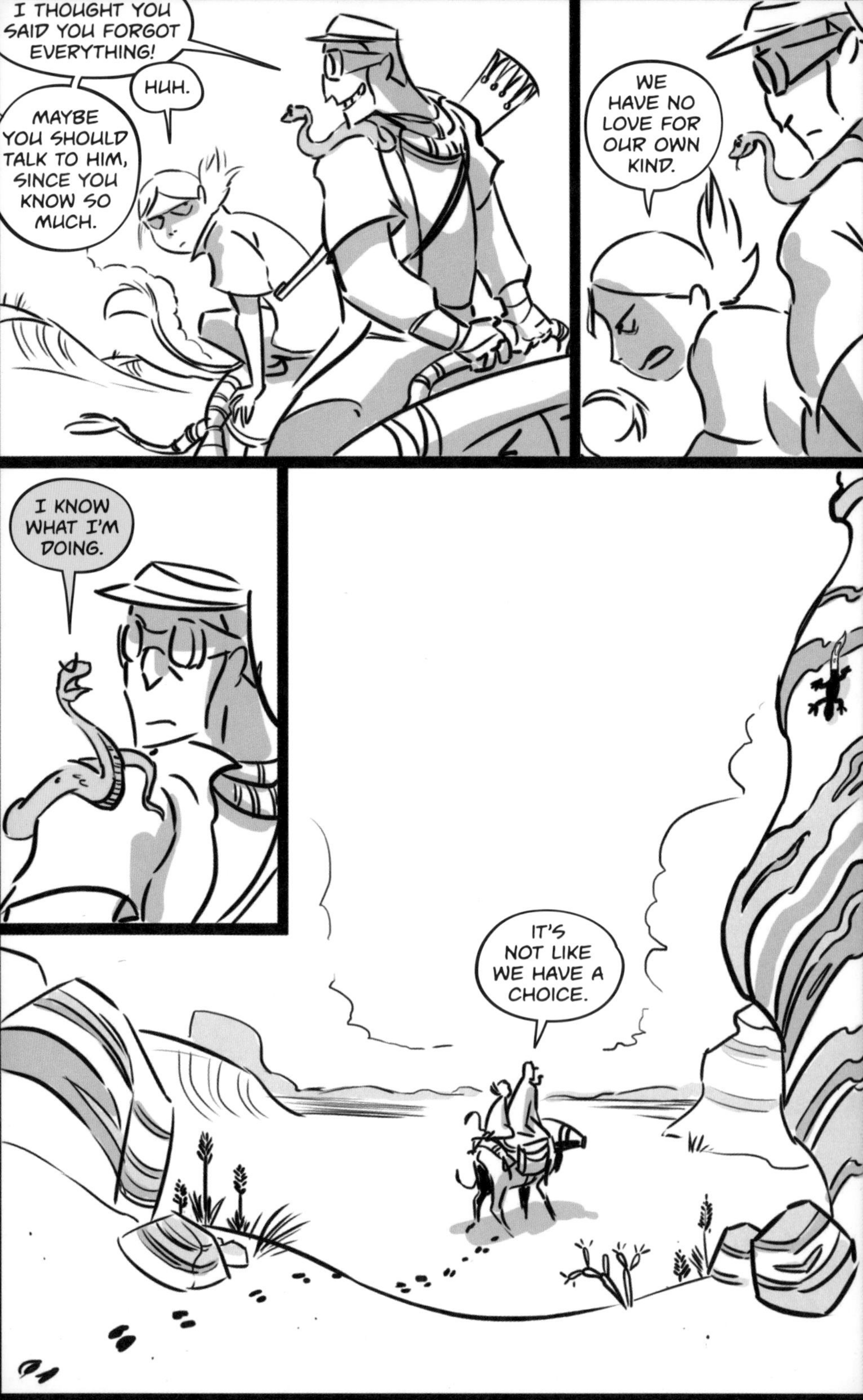
I THOUGHT YOU SAID YOU FORGOT EVERYTHING!
HUH.
MAYBE YOU SHOULD TALK TO HIM, SINCE YOU KNOW SO MUCH.
WE HAVE NO LOVE FOR OUR OWN KIND.
I KNOW WHAT I'M DOING.
IT'S NOT LIKE WE HAVE A CHOICE.

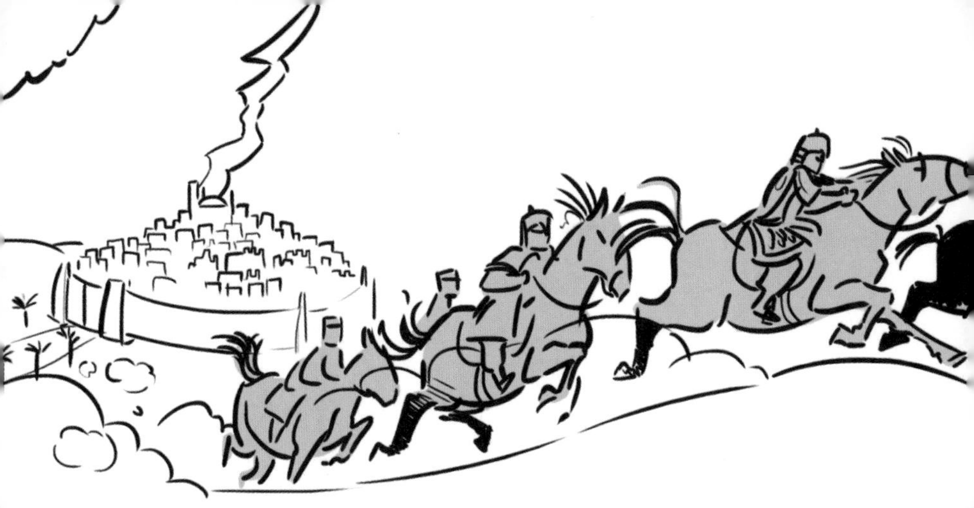
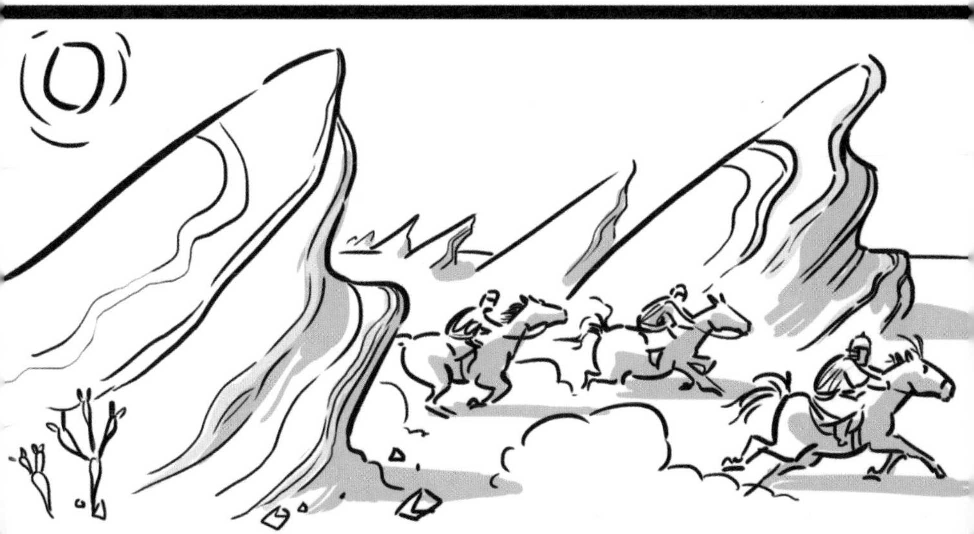
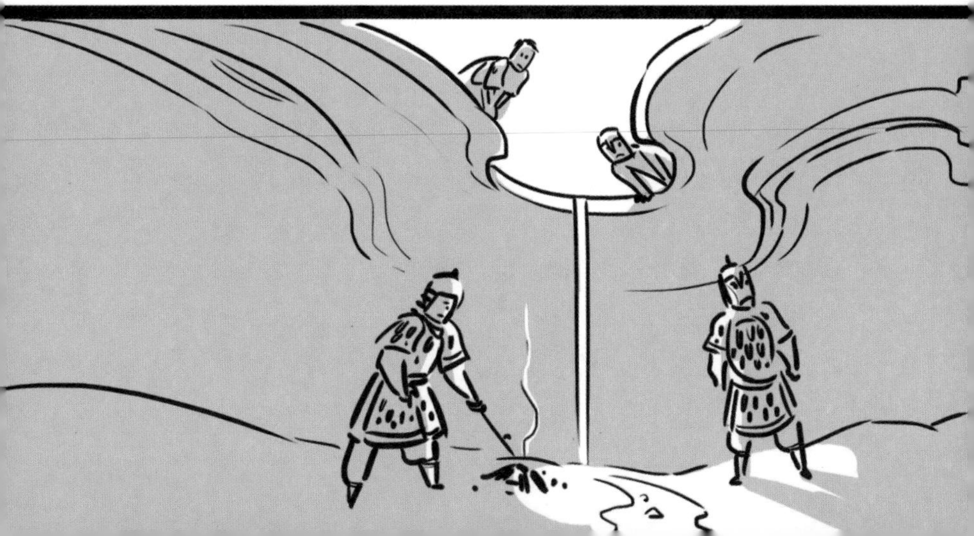

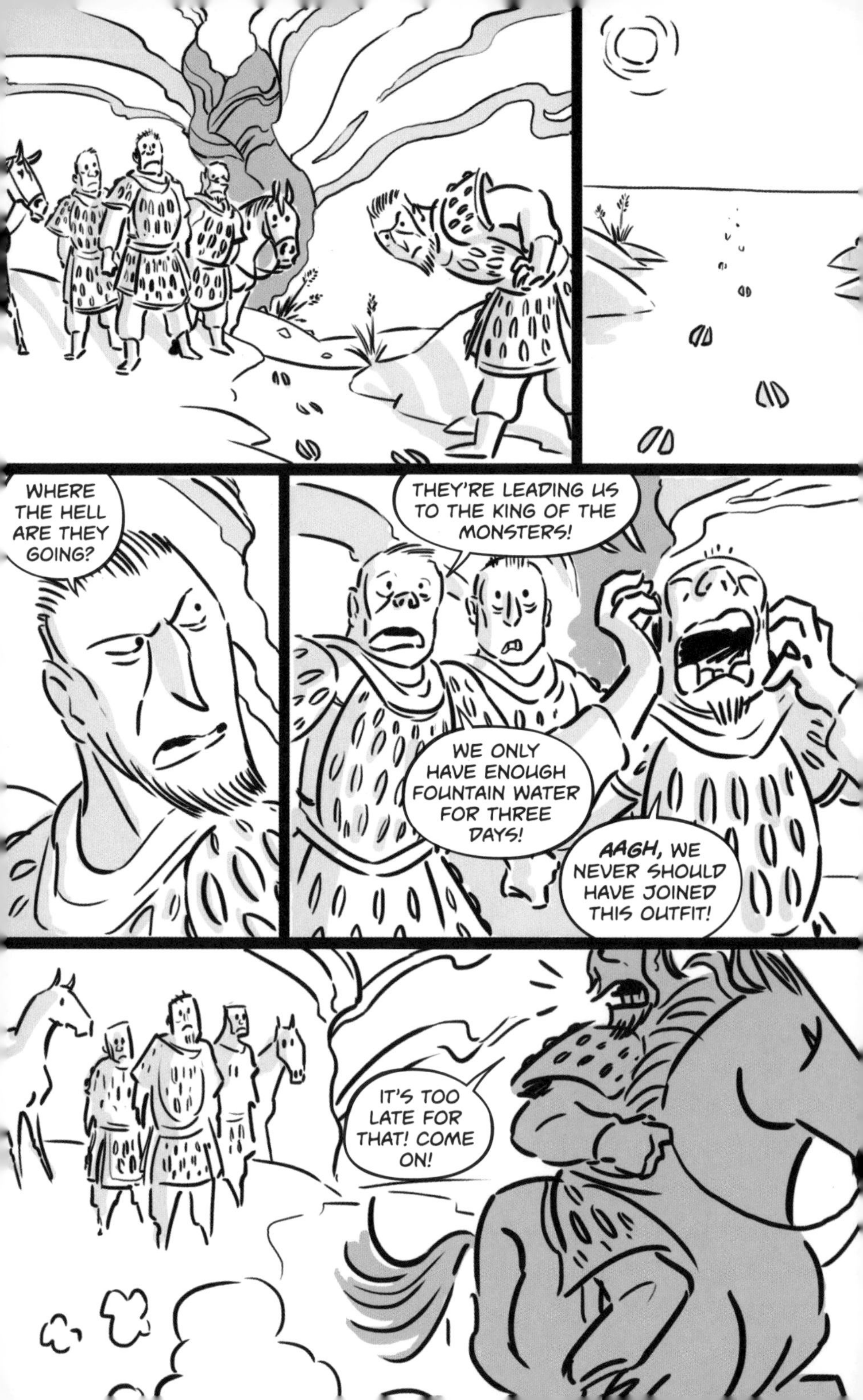
WHERE THE HELL ARE THEY GOING?
THEY'RE LEADING US TO THE KING OF THE MONSTERS!
WE ONLY HAVE ENOUGH FOUNTAIN WATER FOR THREE DAYS!
AAGH, WE NEVER SHOULD HAVE JOINED THIS OUTFIT!
IT'S TOO LATE FOR THAT! COME ON!

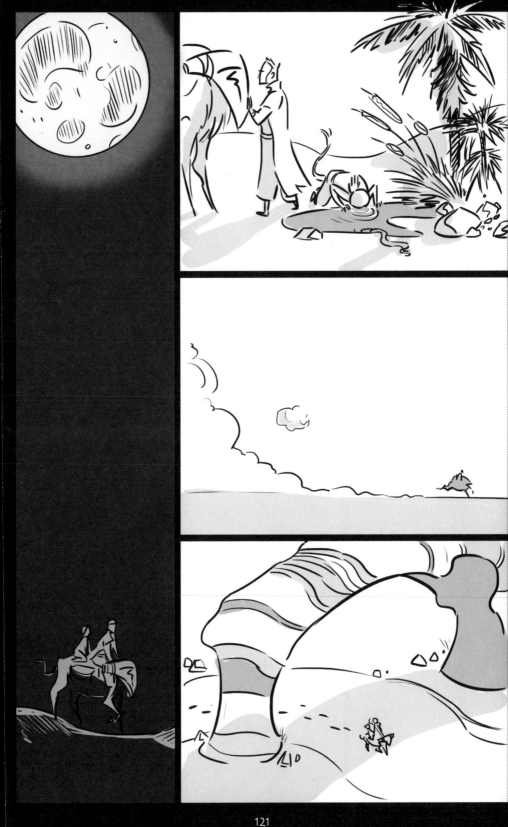

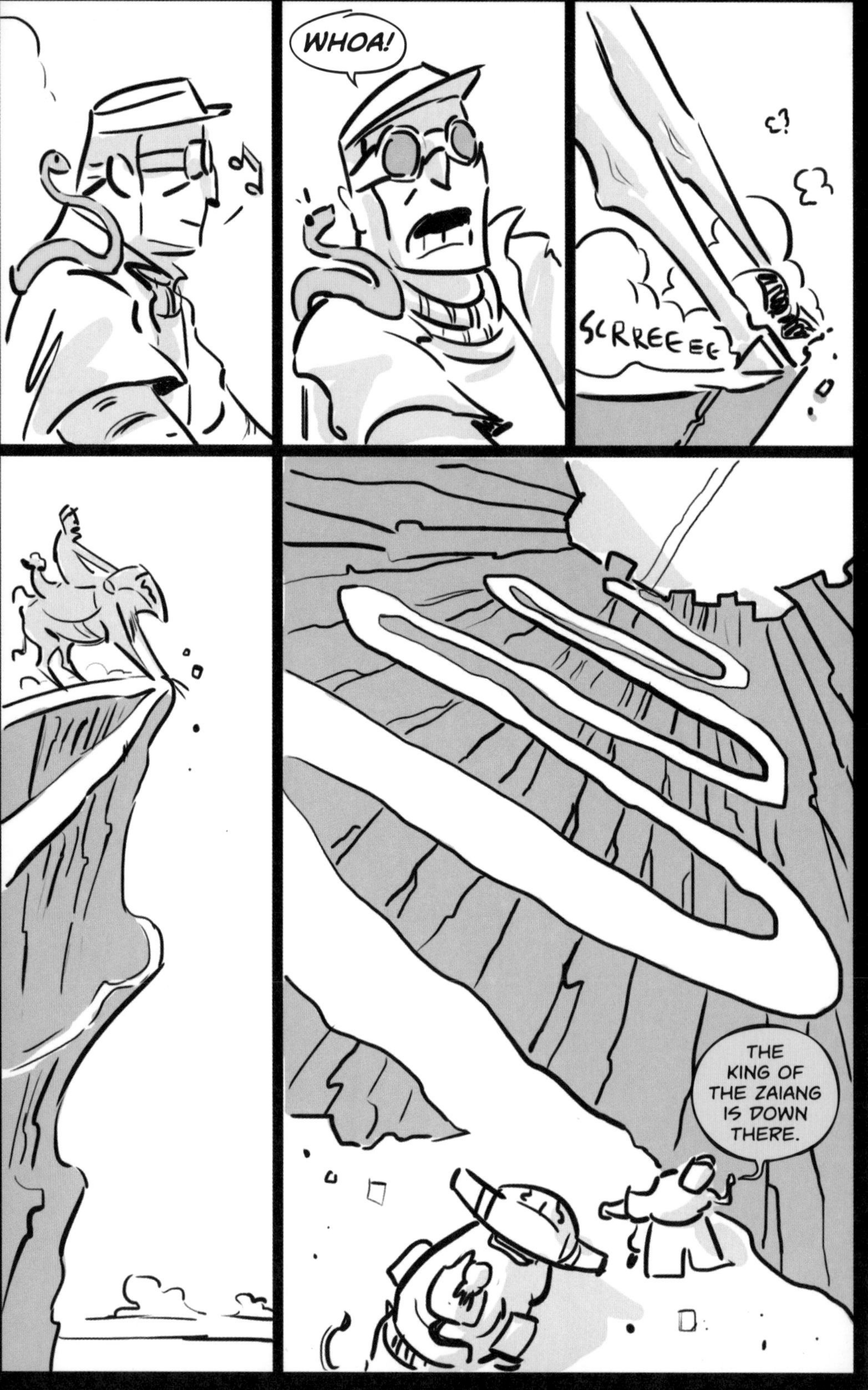
WHOA!
SCRREEEEE
THE KING OF THE ZAIANG IS DOWN THERE.

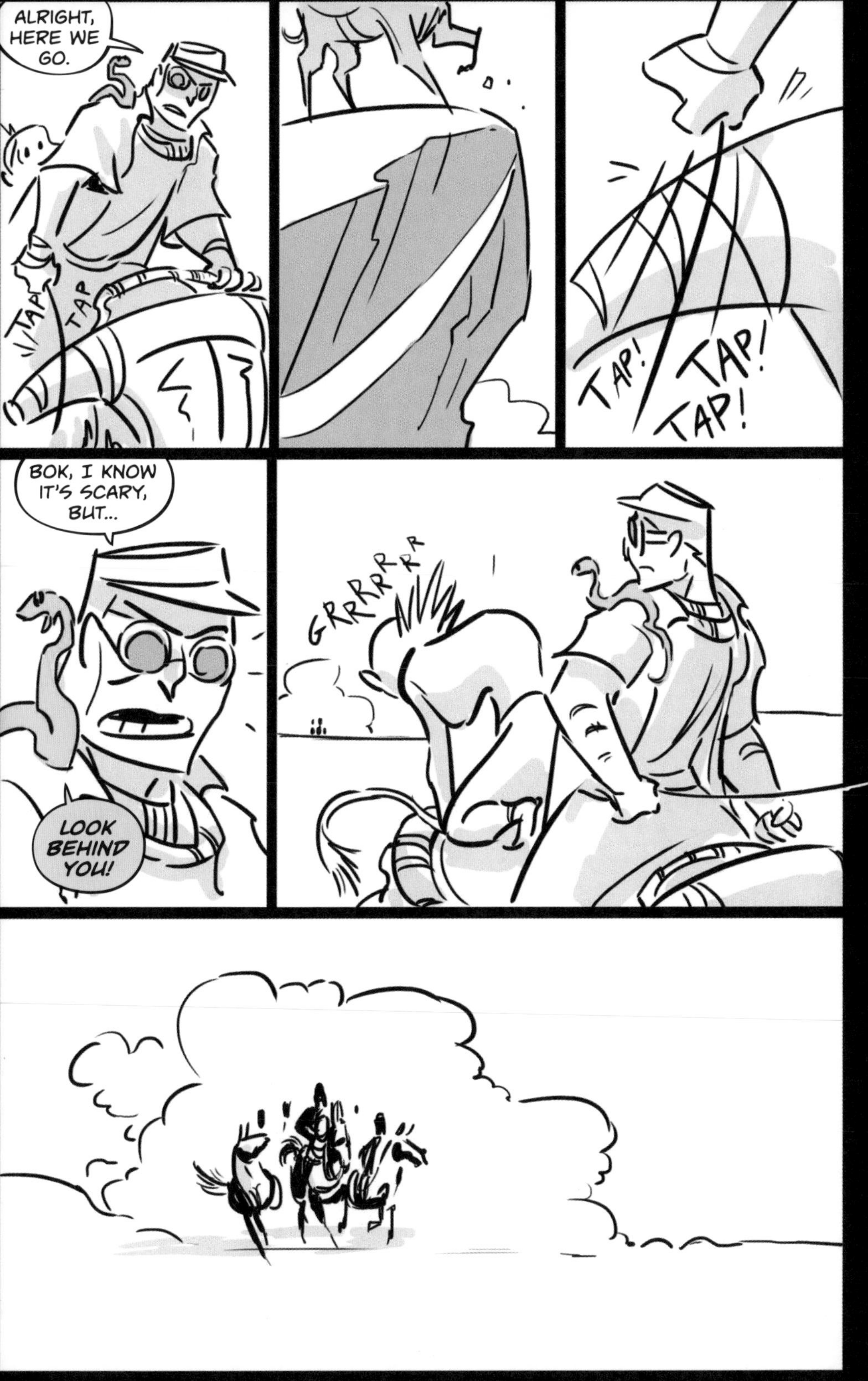
ALRIGHT, HERE WE GO.
TAP
TAP
TAP! TAP! TAP!
BOK, I KNOW IT'S SCARY, BUT...
LOOK BEHIND YOU!
GRRRRRRR

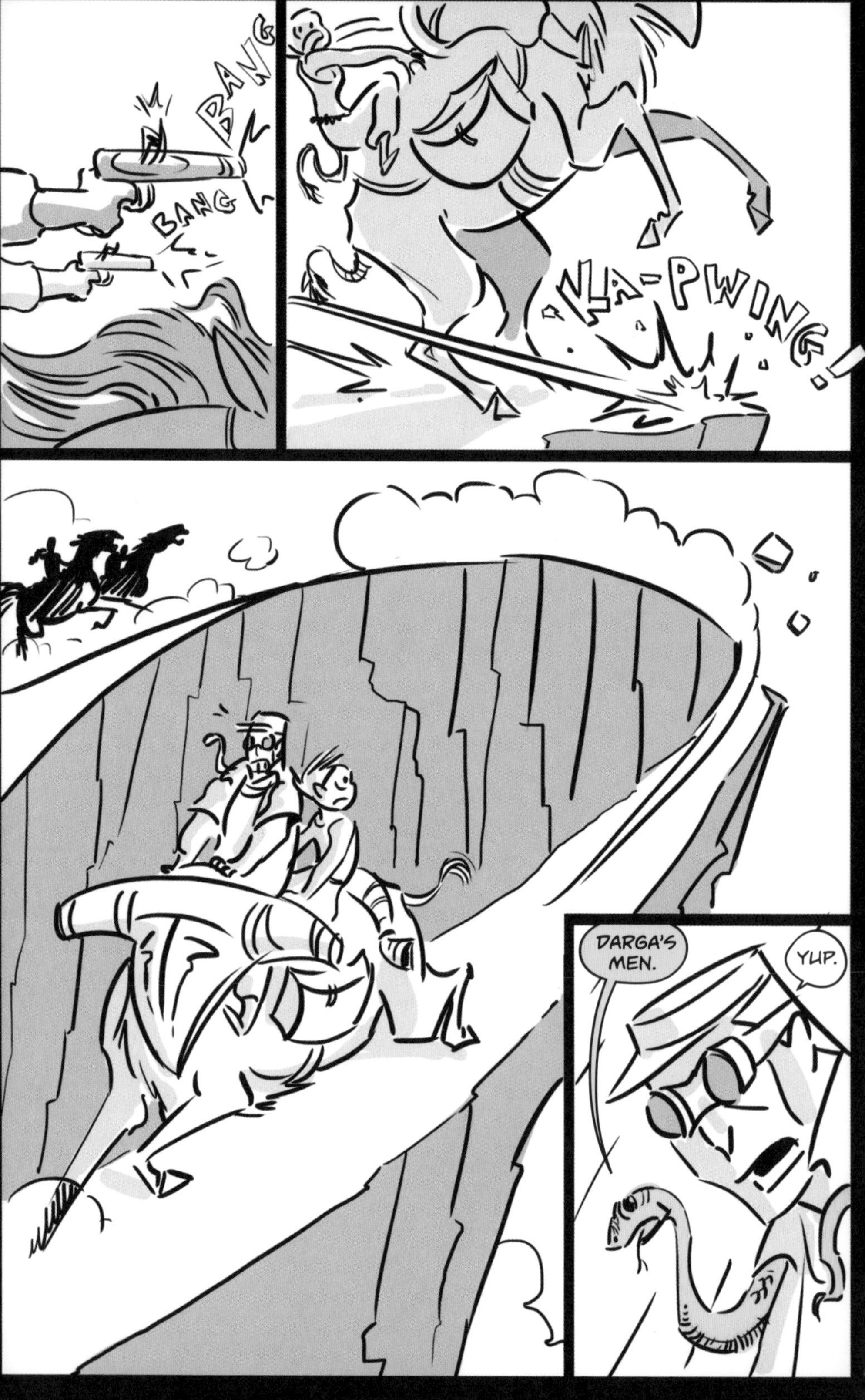
BANG
BANG
KLA-PWING!
DARGA'S MEN.
YUP.

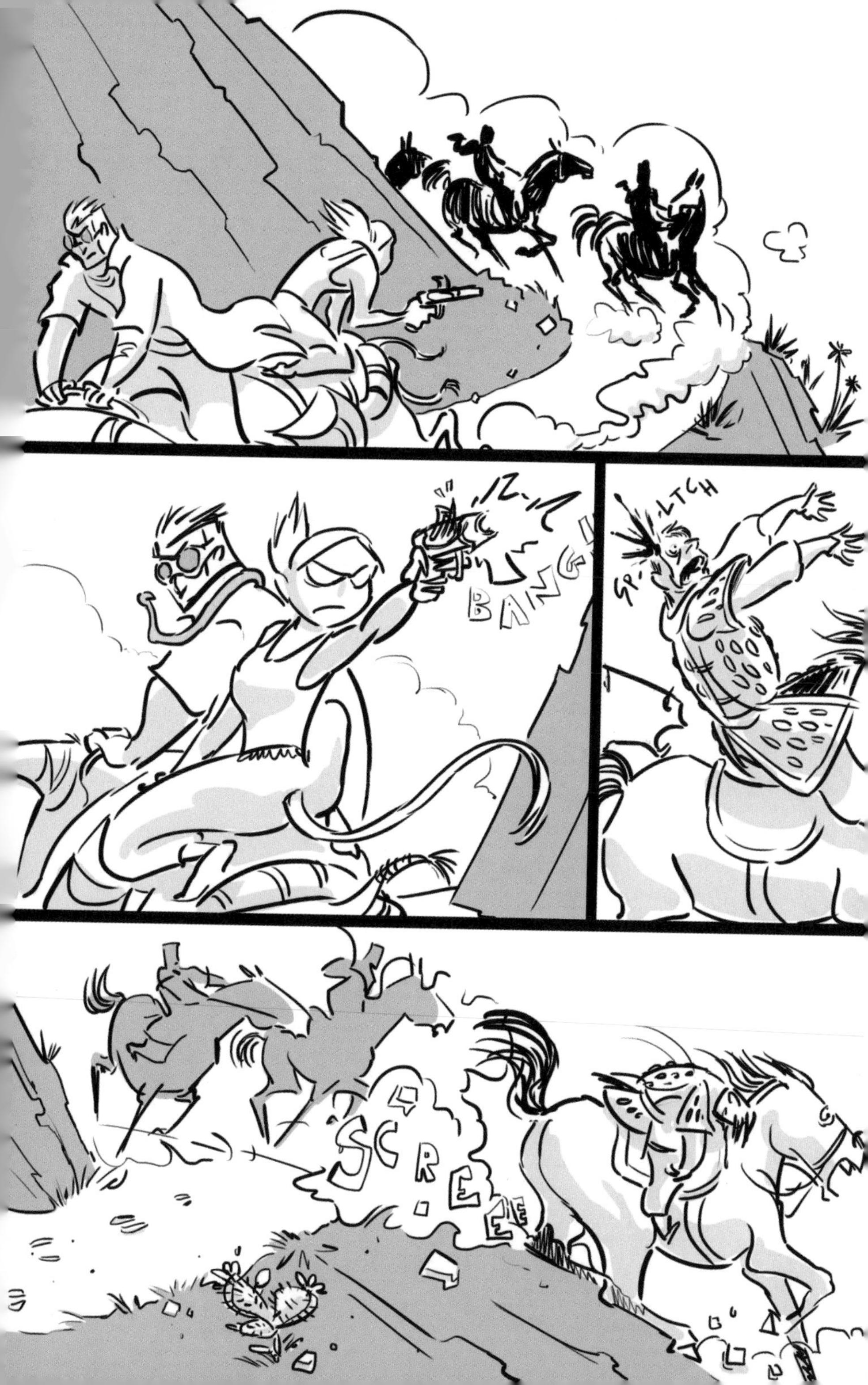
BANG!
SP-LTCH
SCREEE

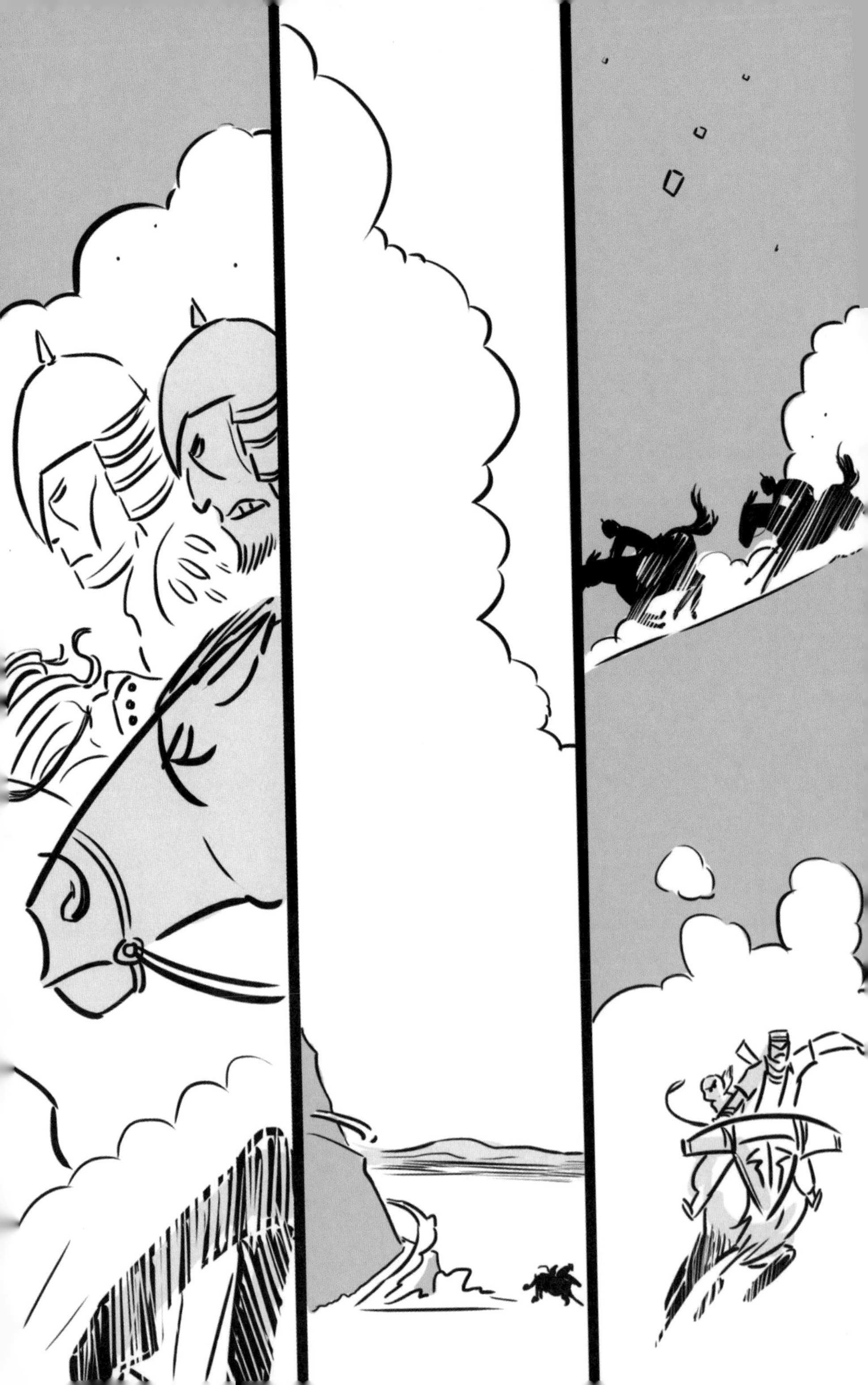

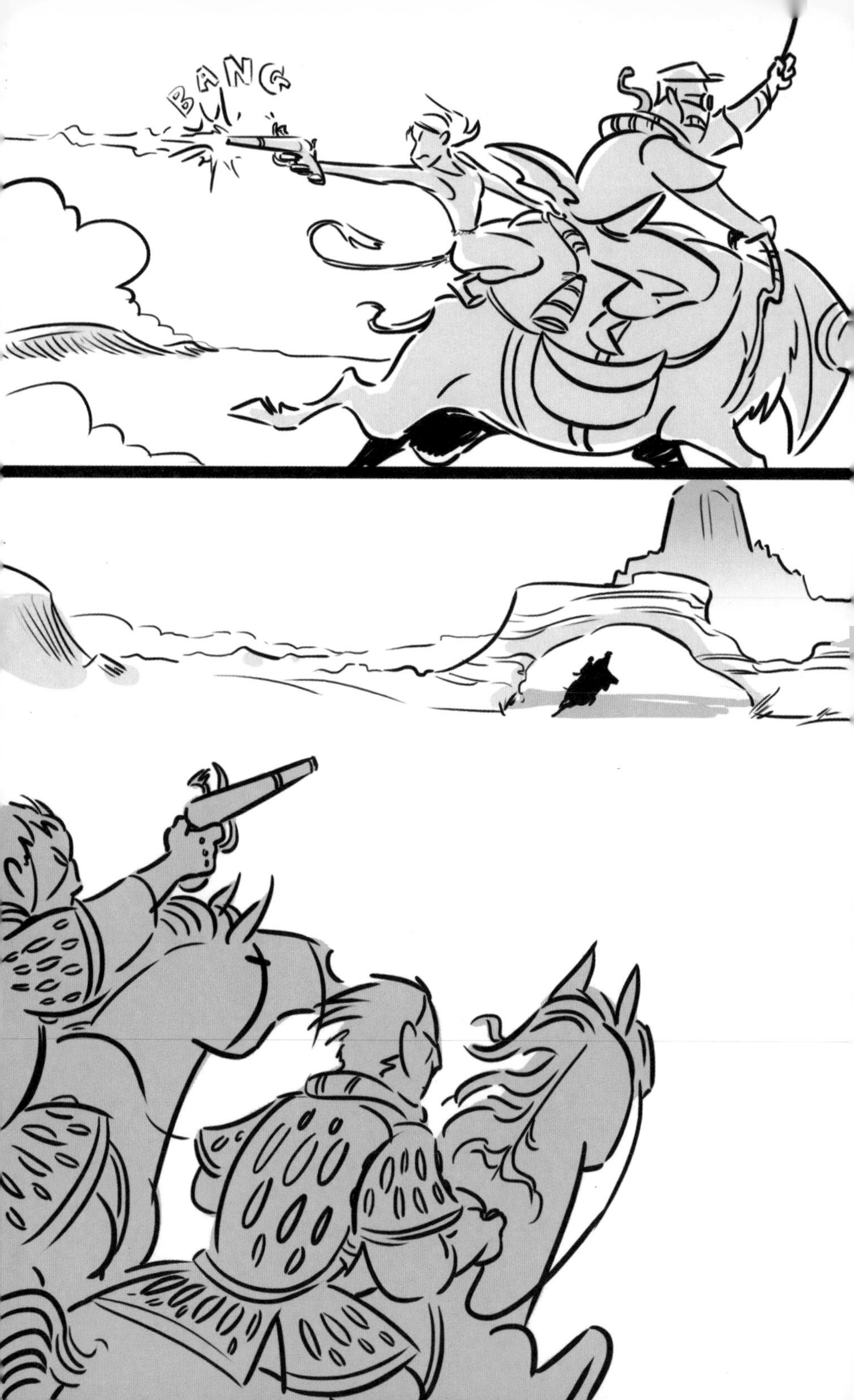
BANG

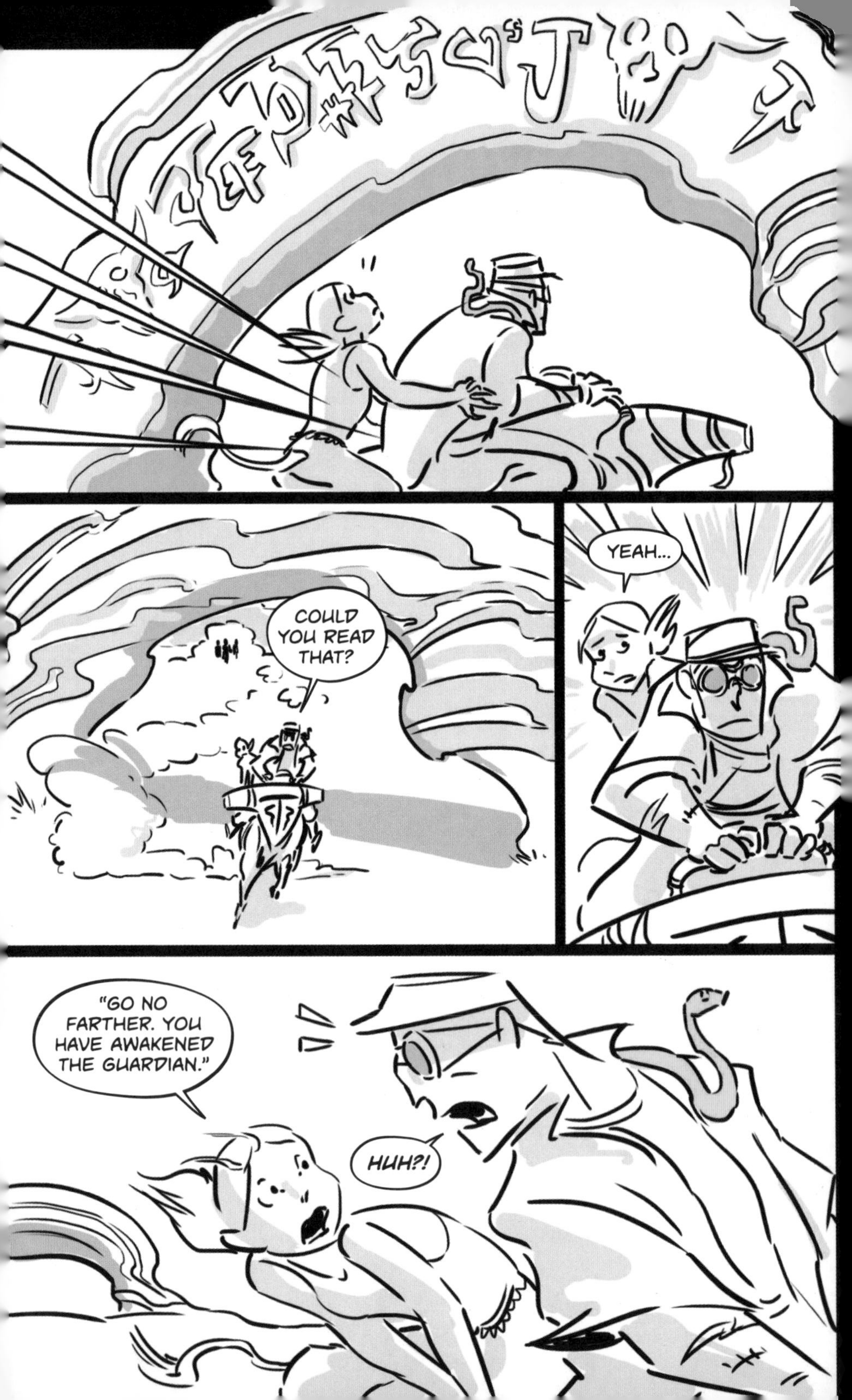
COULD YOU READ THAT?
YEAH...
"GO NO FARTHER. YOU HAVE AWAKENED THE GUARDIAN."
HUH?!

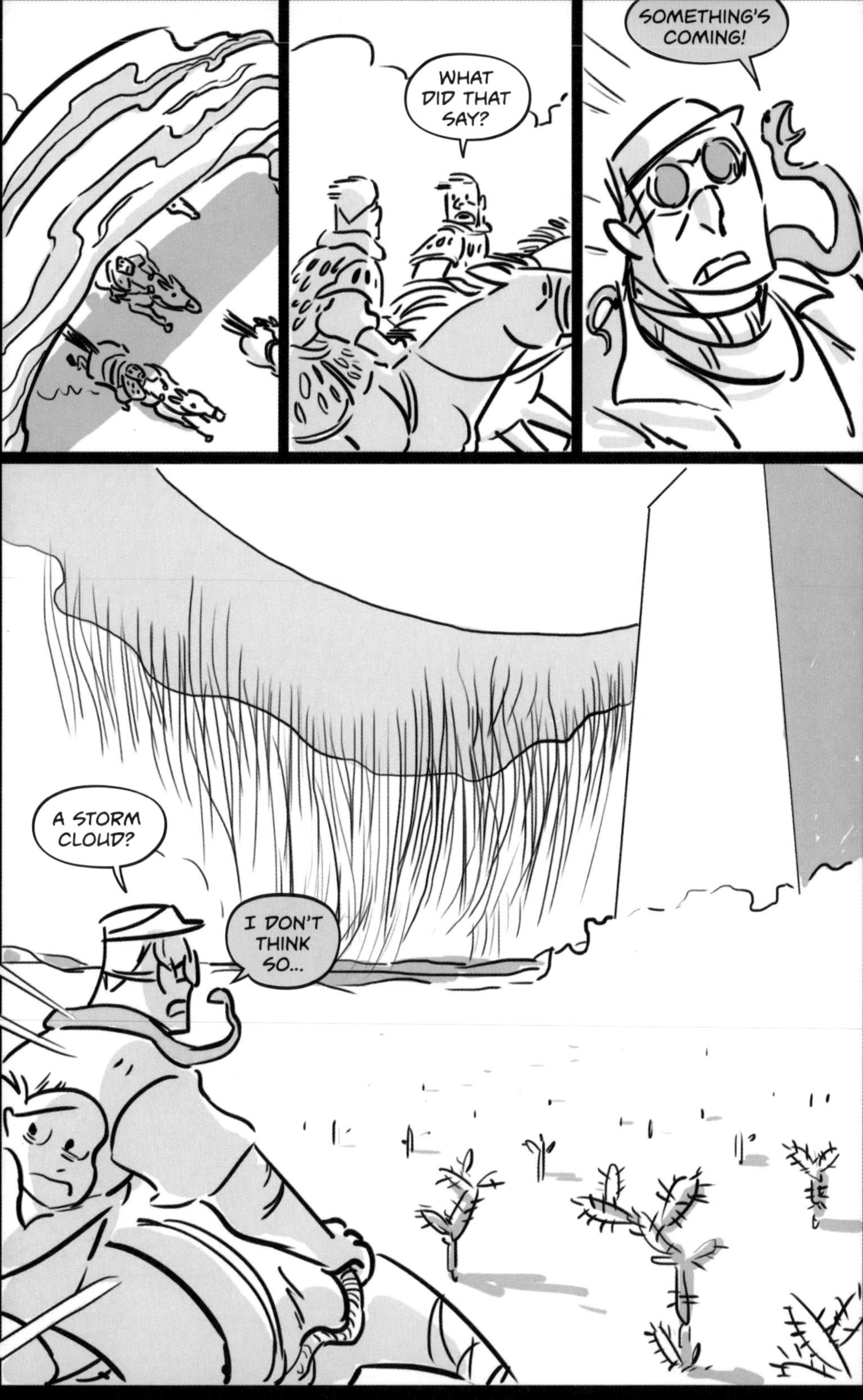
WHAT DID THAT SAY?
SOMETHING'S COMING!
A STORM CLOUD?
I DON'T THINK SO...

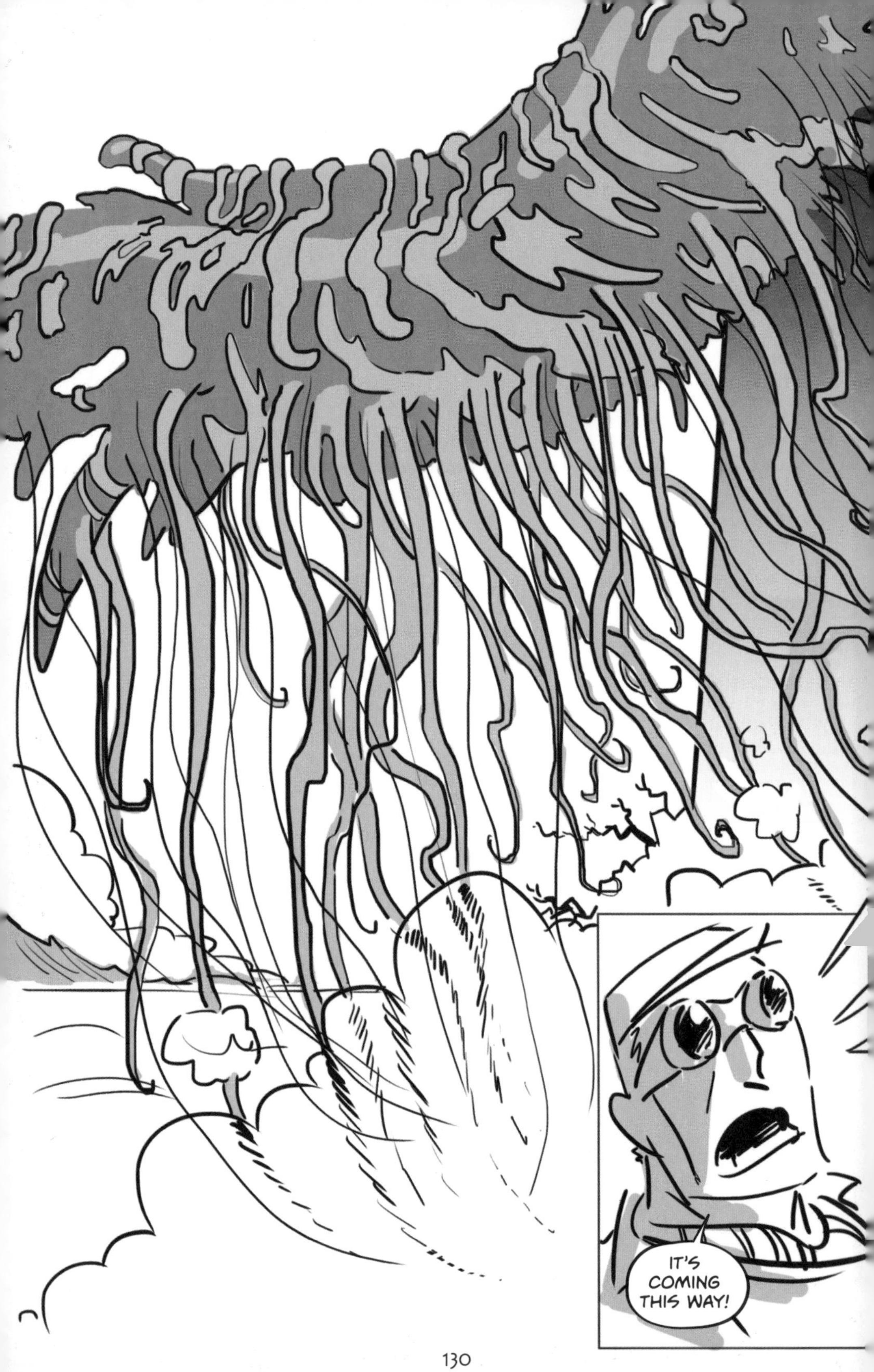
IT'S
COMING
THIS WAY!

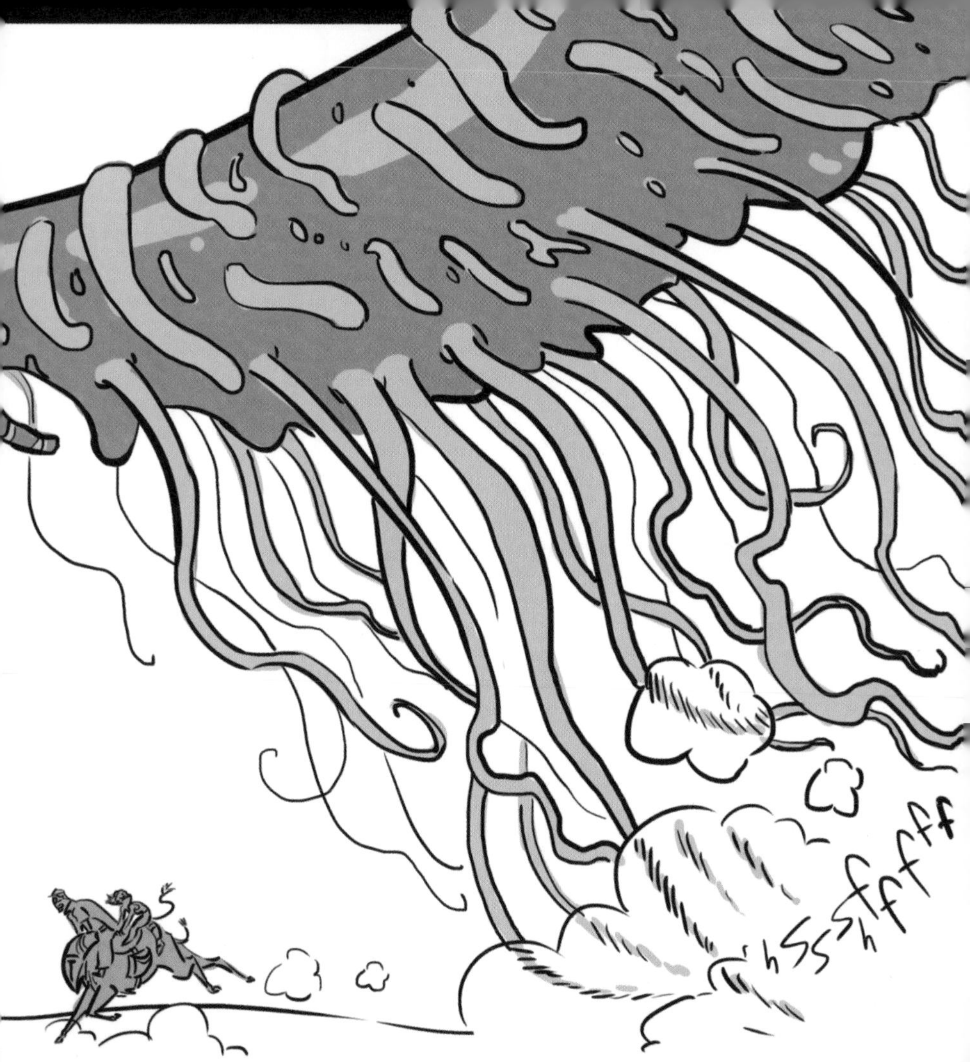
hSSShfffff

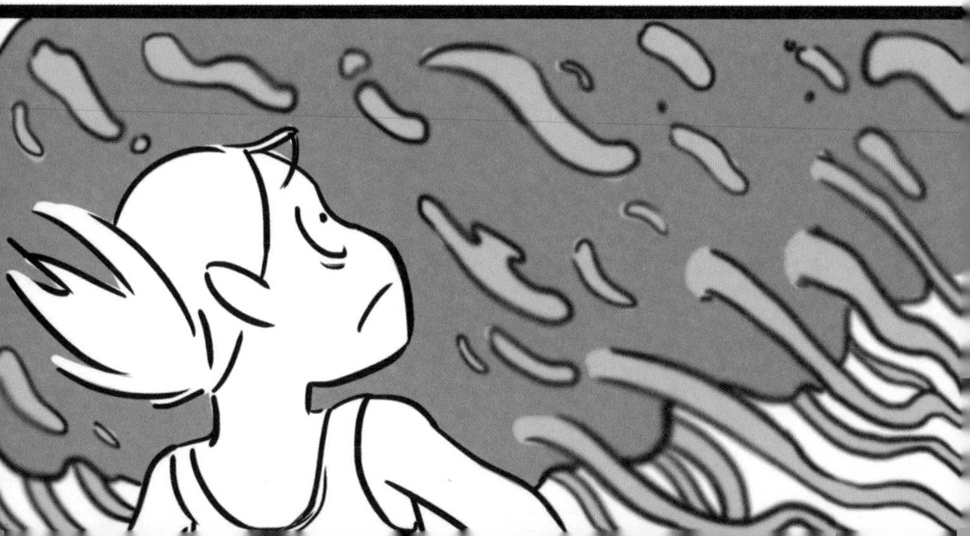

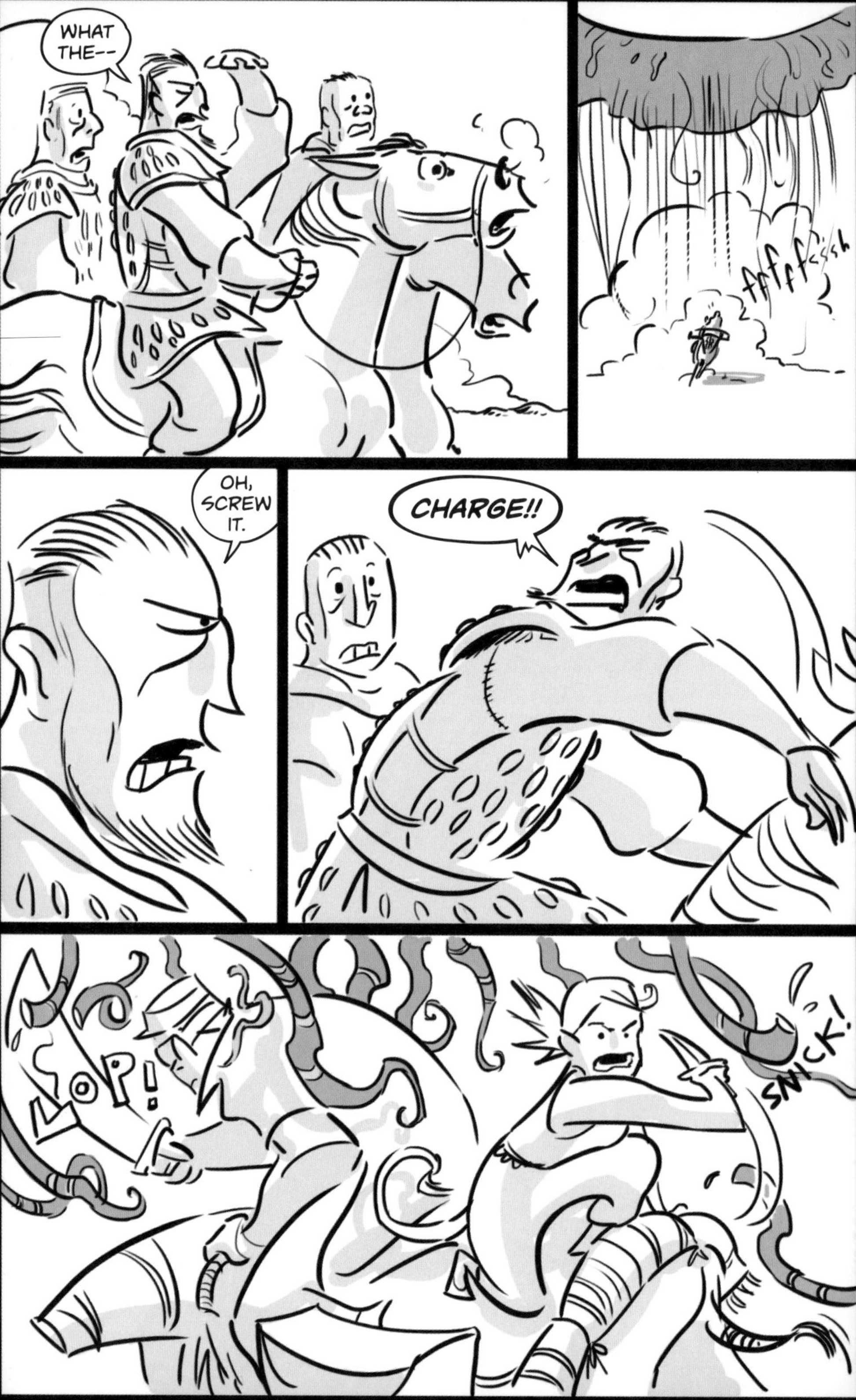
WHAT THE--
ffffffsssh
OH, SCREW IT.
CHARGE!!
LOP!
SNICK!

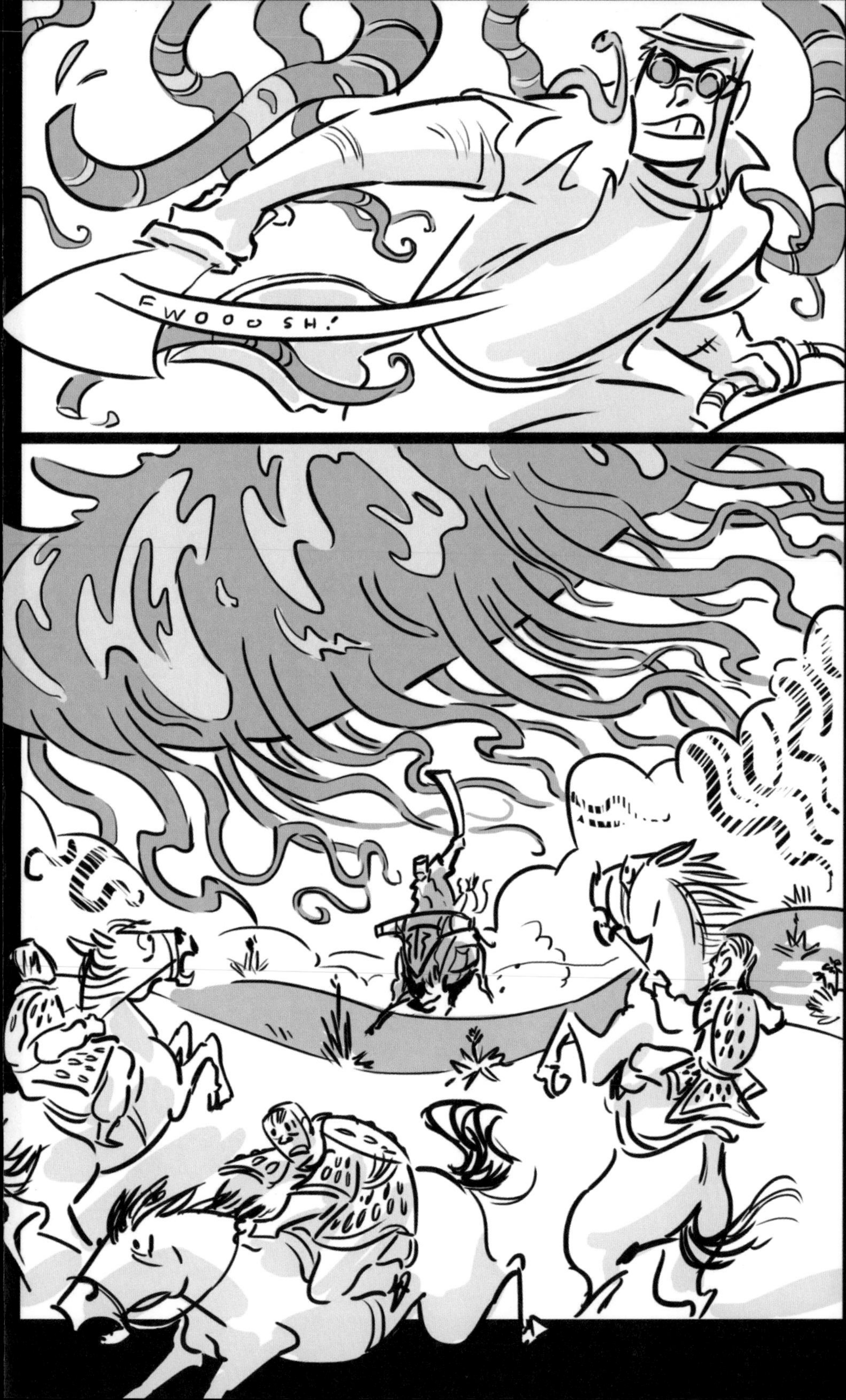
FWOOOSH!

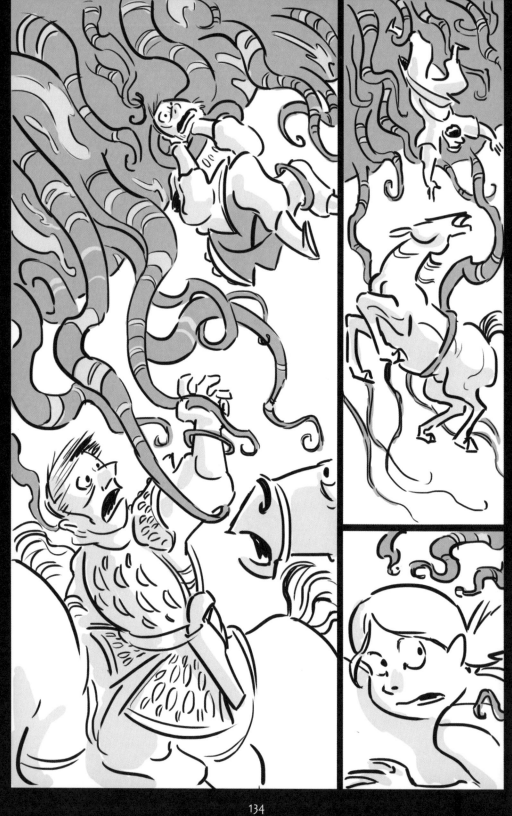

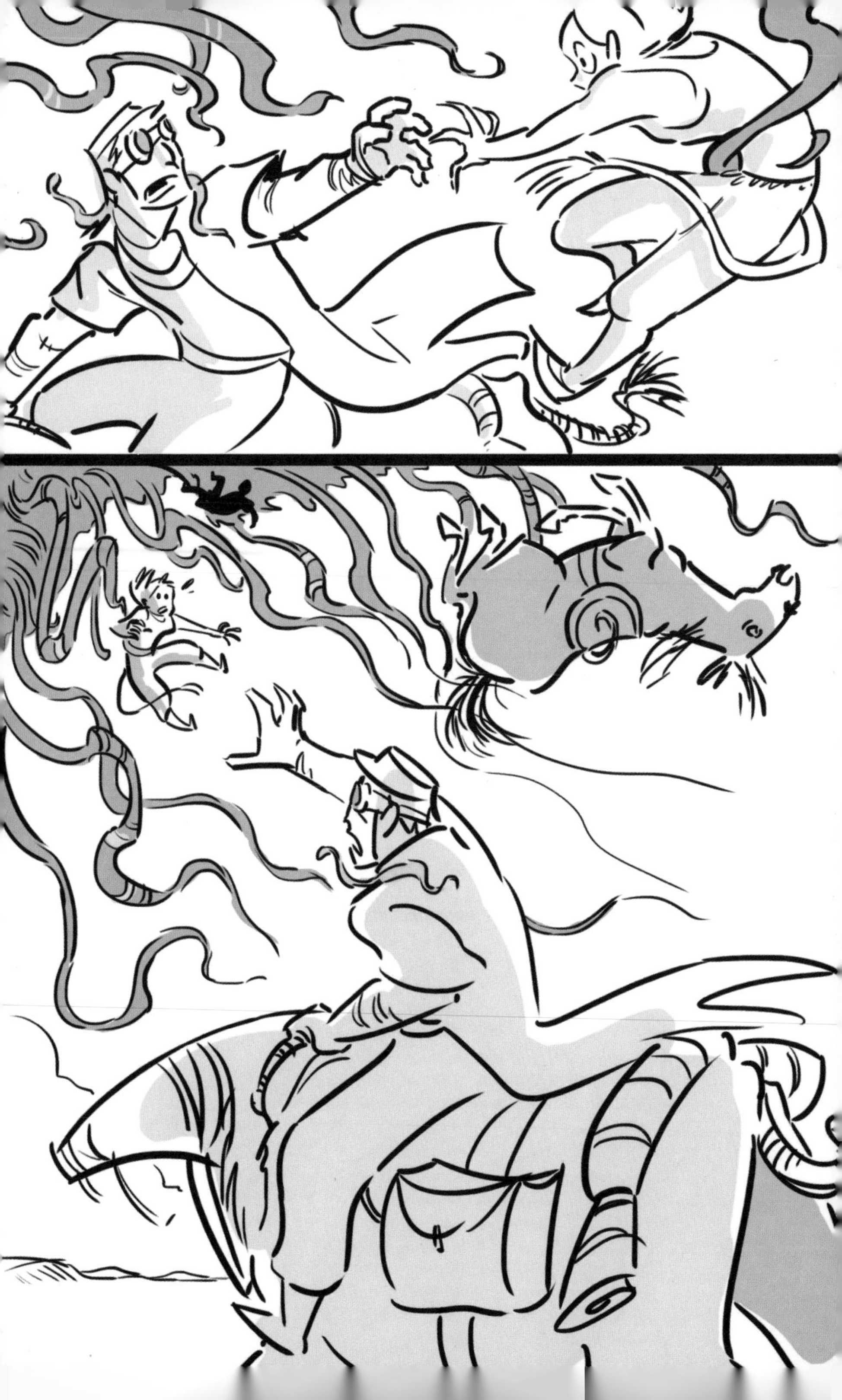

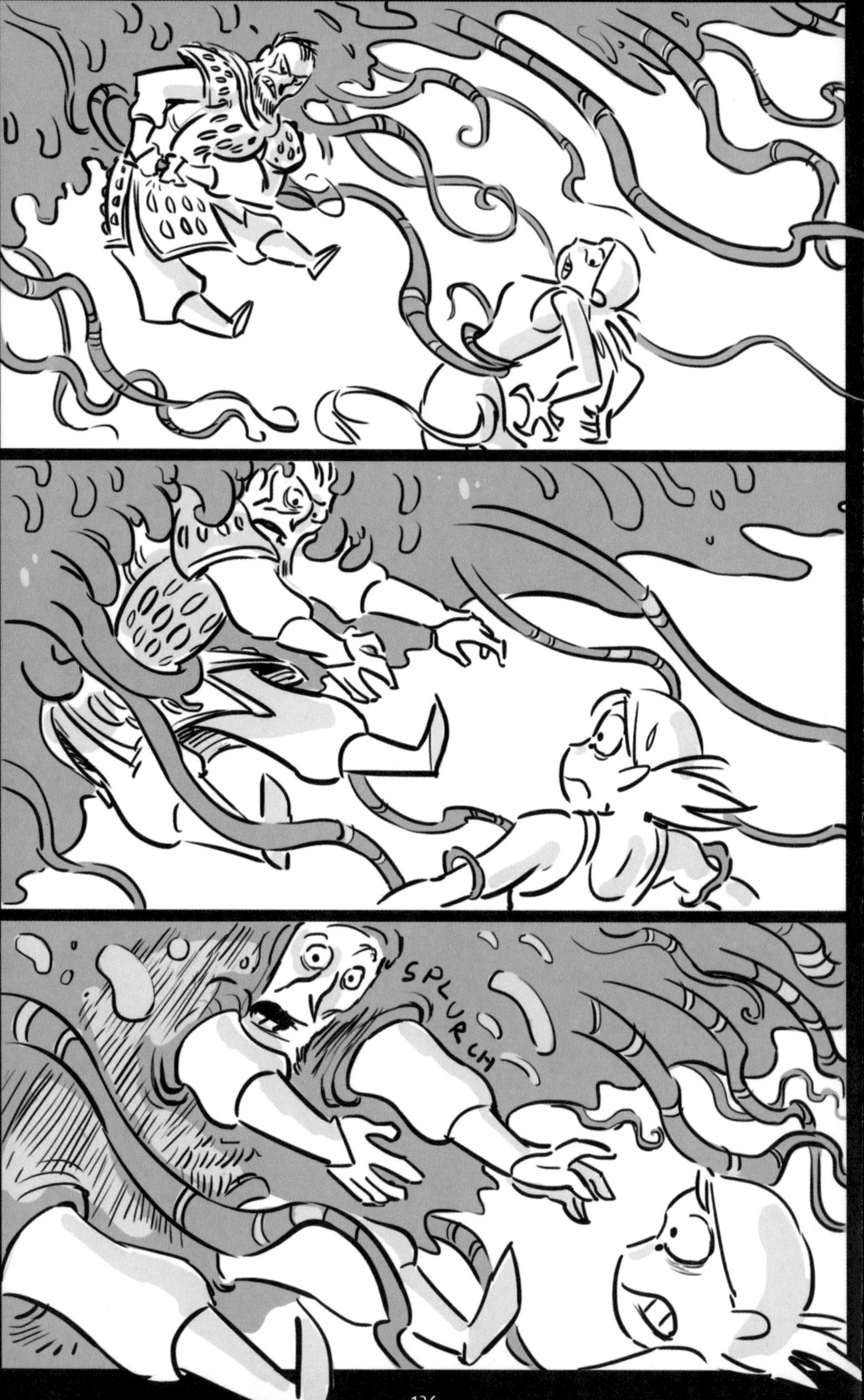
SPLURCH

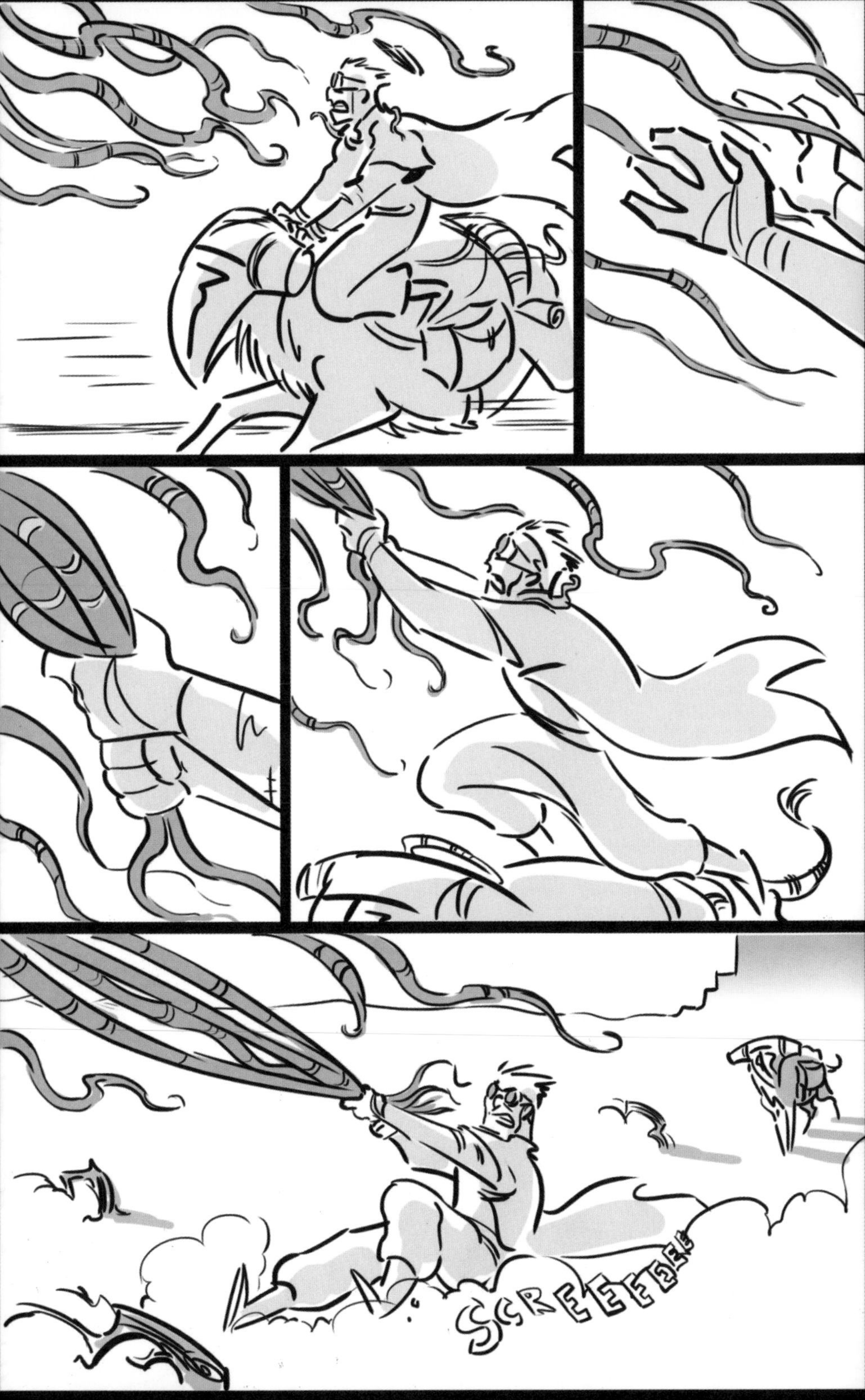
SCREEEEEE

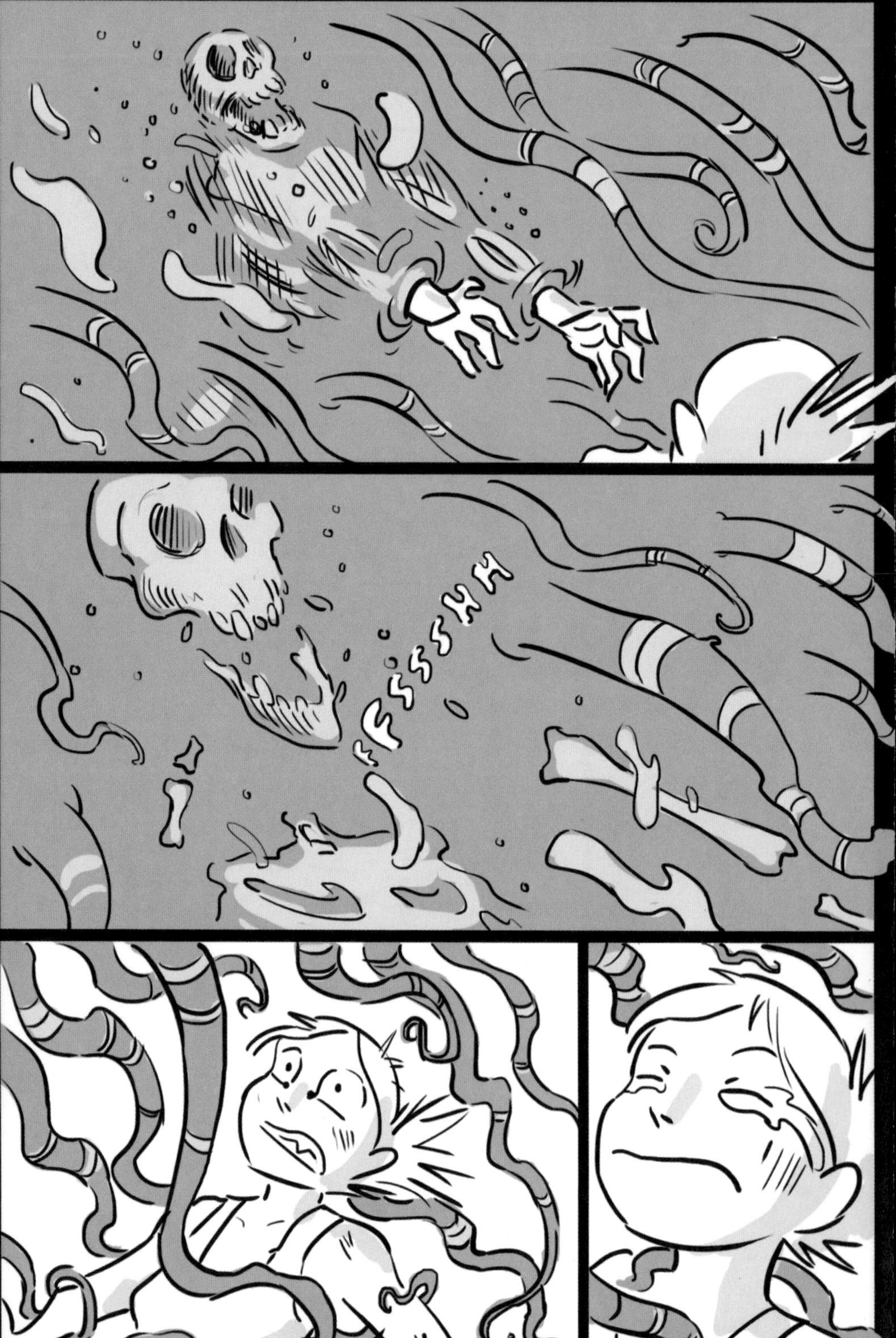
FSSSSHH

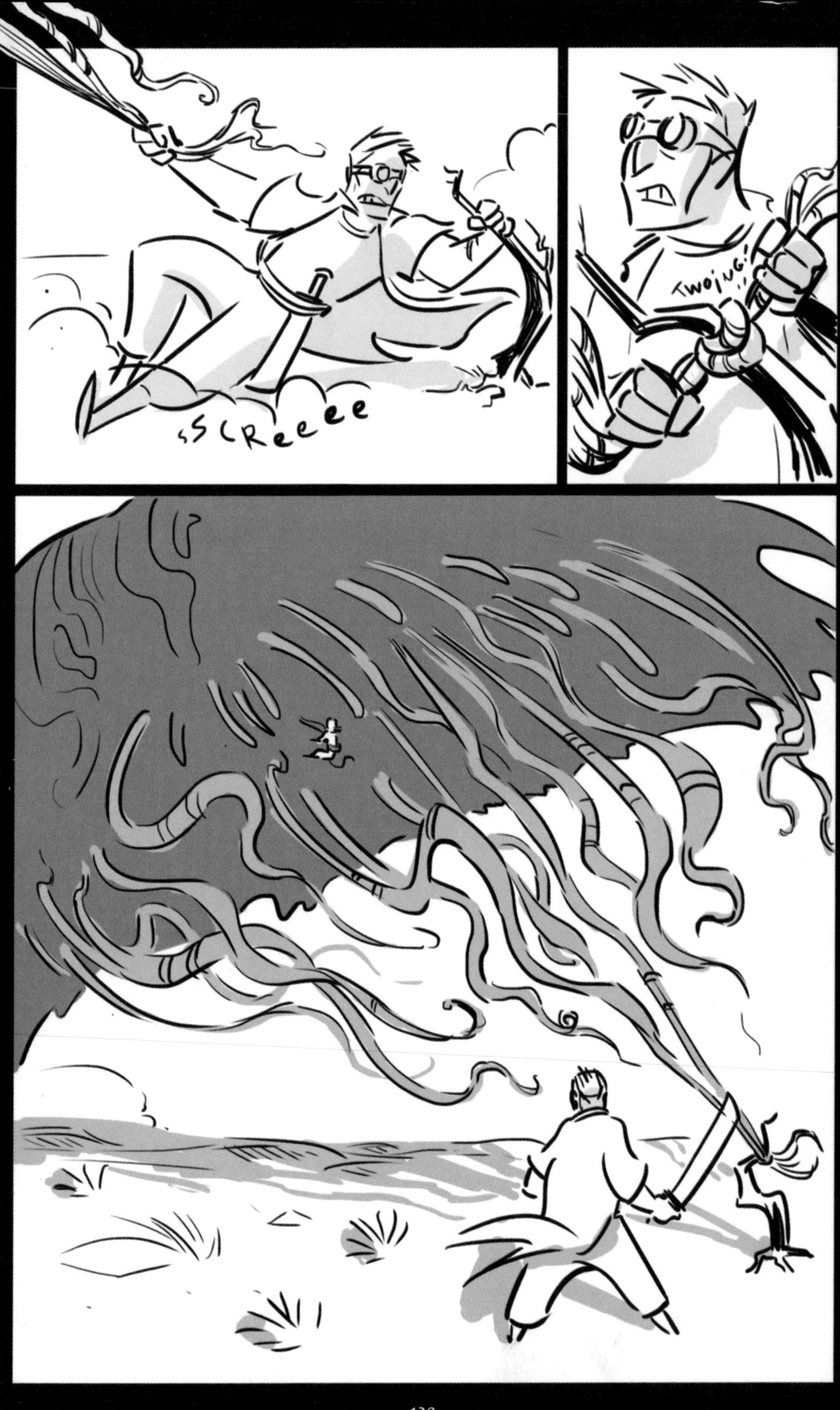

sSCReeee
TWOING!

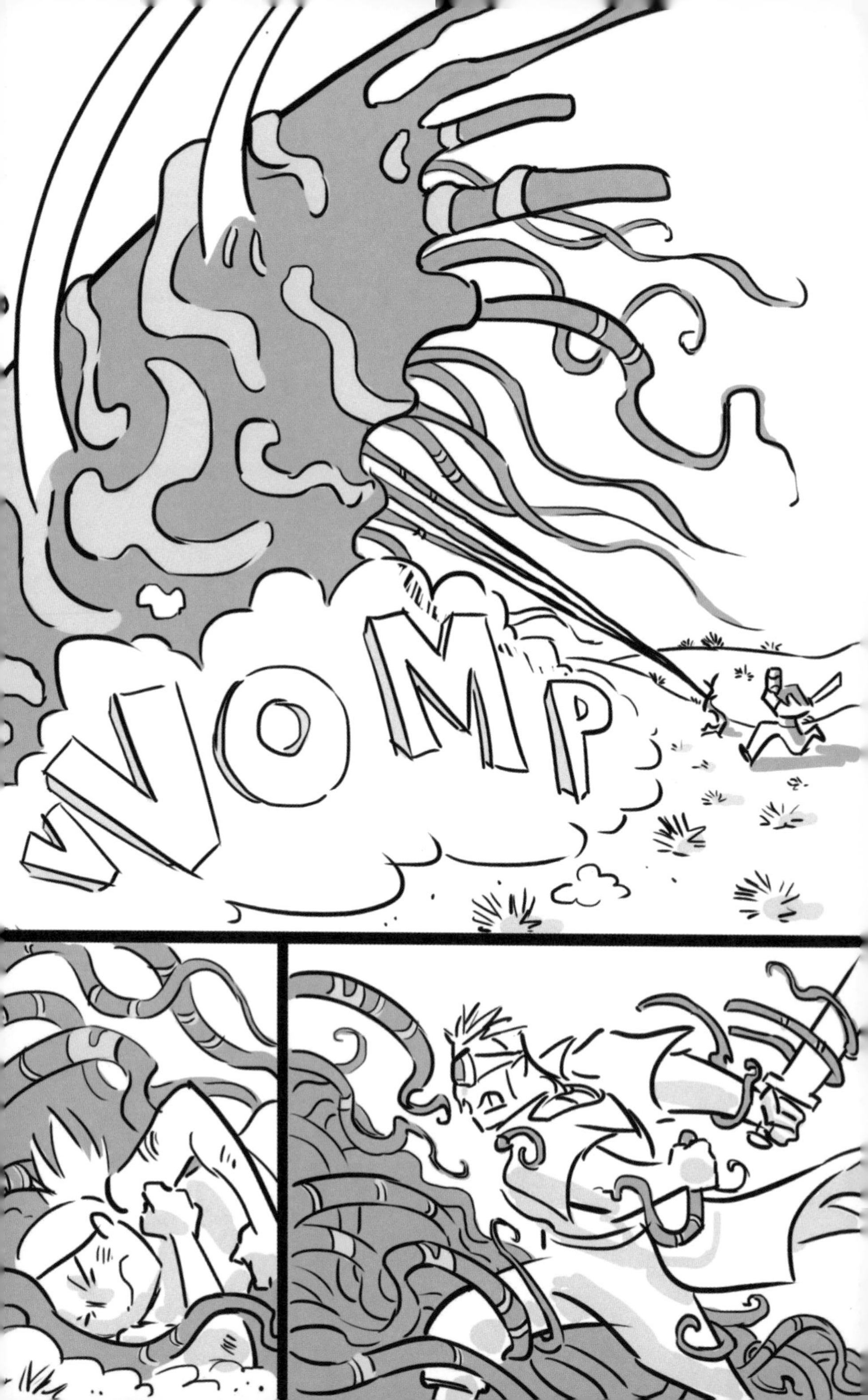
VVOMP

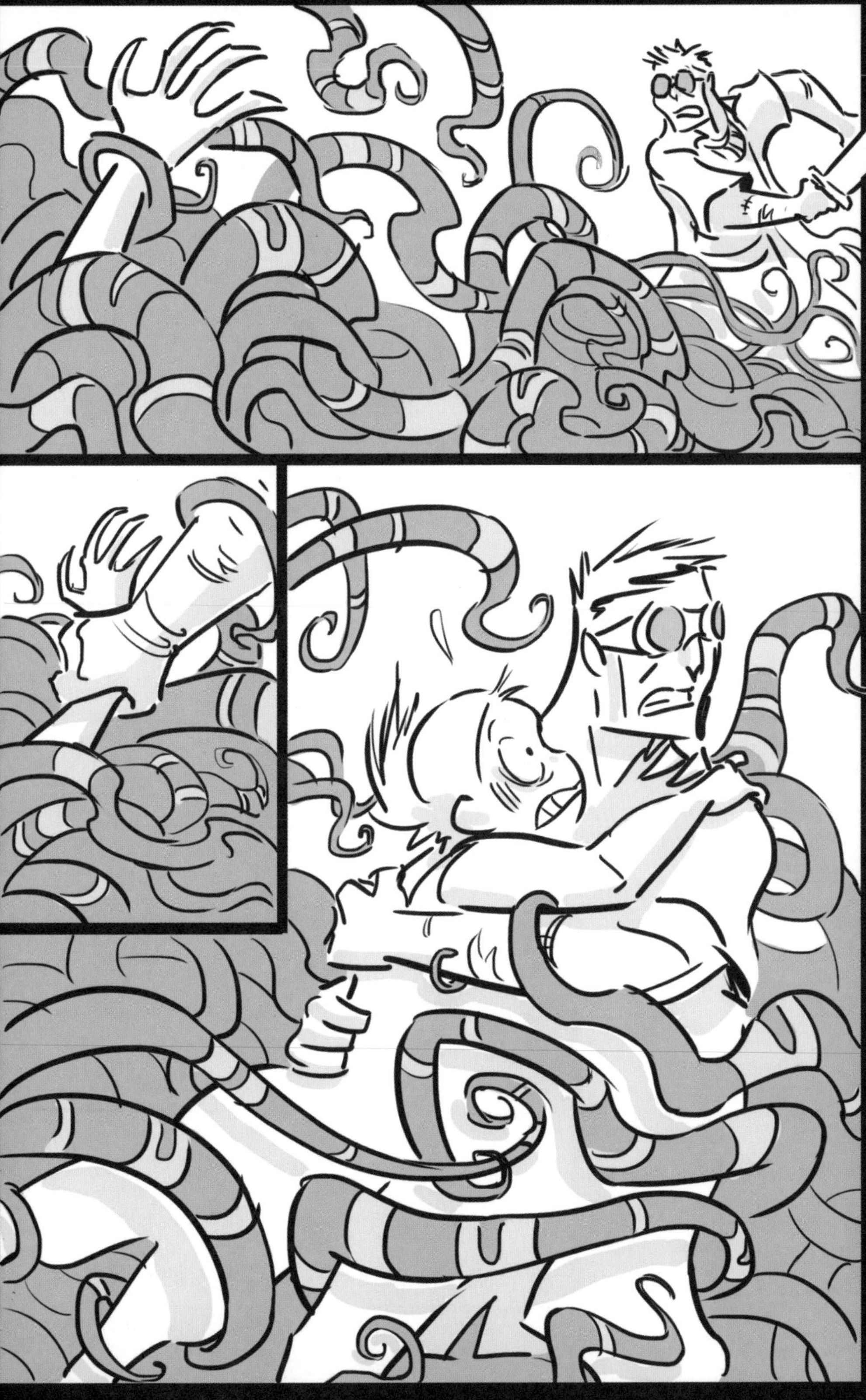

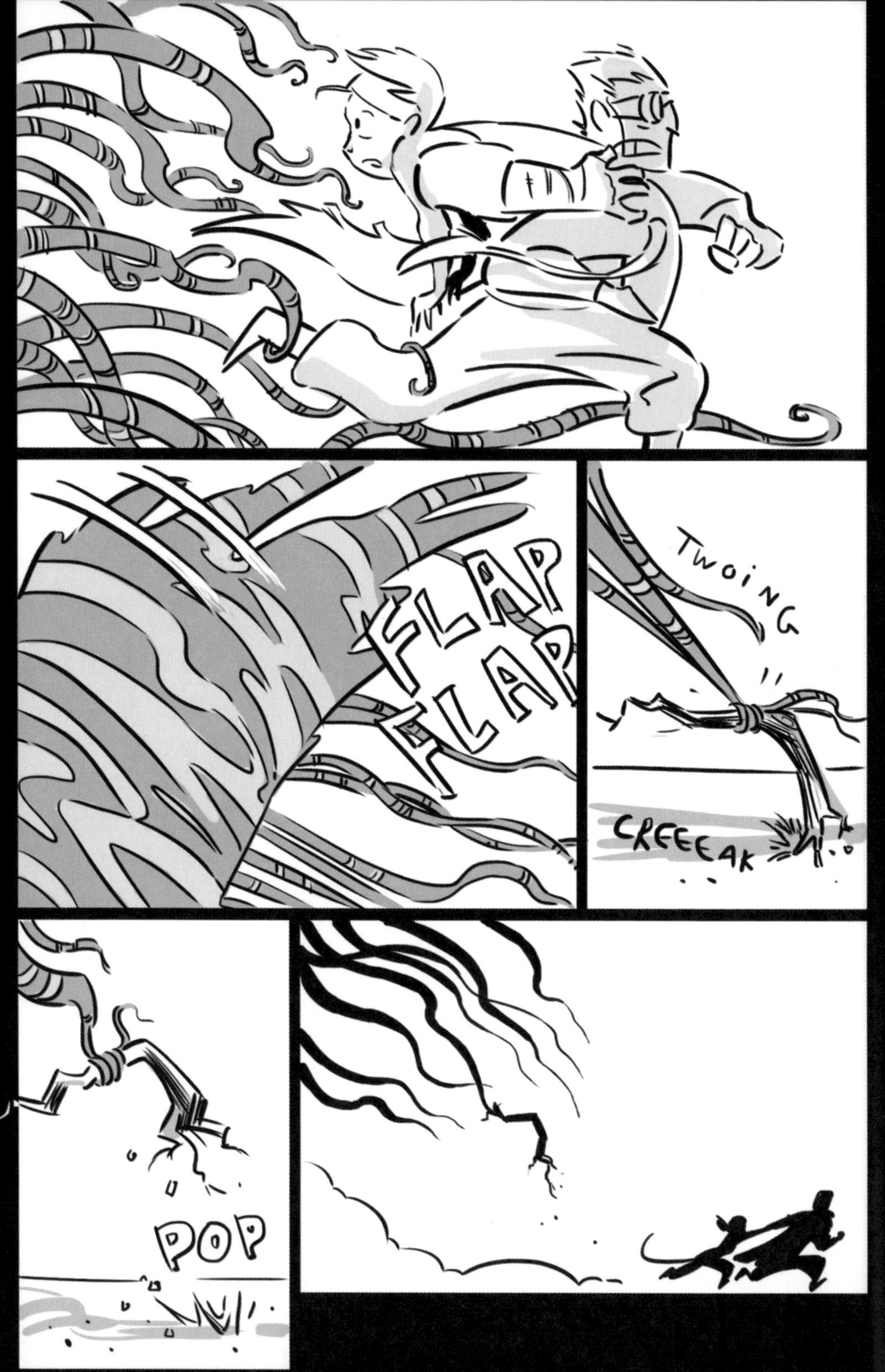
FLAP
FLAP
TWOING
CREEEAK
POP

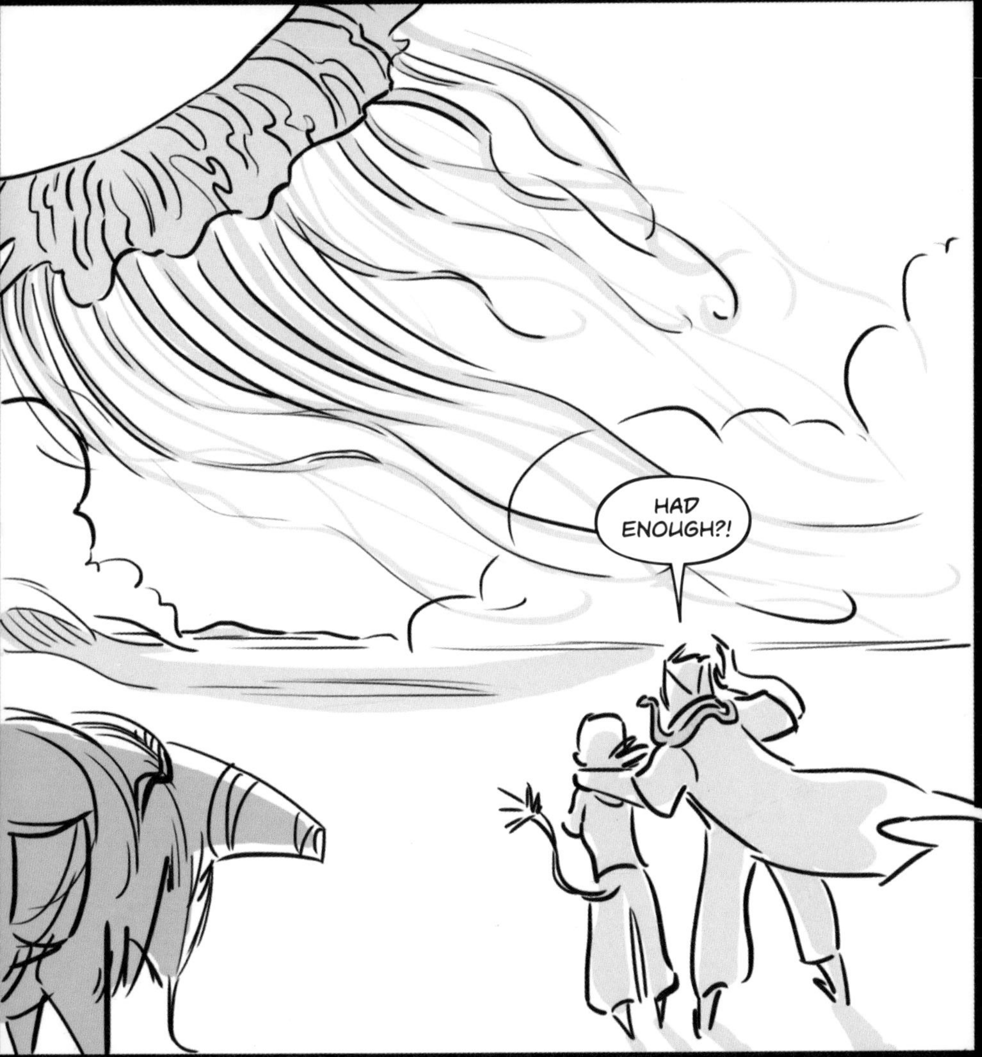
HAD ENOUGH?!

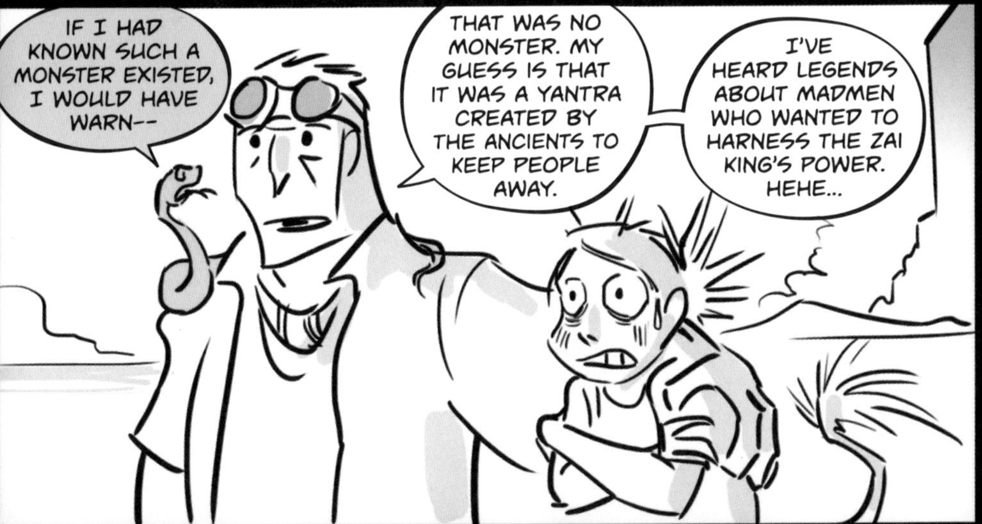
IF I HAD KNOWN SUCH A MONSTER EXISTED, I WOULD HAVE WARN--
THAT WAS NO MONSTER. MY GUESS IS THAT IT WAS A YANTRA CREATED BY THE ANCIENTS TO KEEP PEOPLE AWAY.
I'VE HEARD LEGENDS ABOUT MADMEN WHO WANTED TO HARNESS THE ZAI KING'S POWER. HEHE...

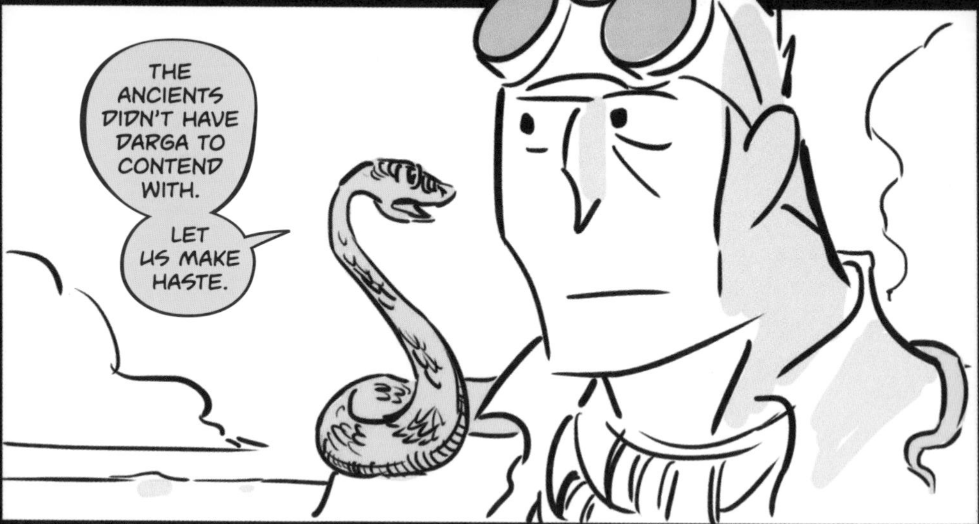
THE ANCIENTS DIDN'T HAVE DARGA TO CONTEND WITH.
LET US MAKE HASTE.

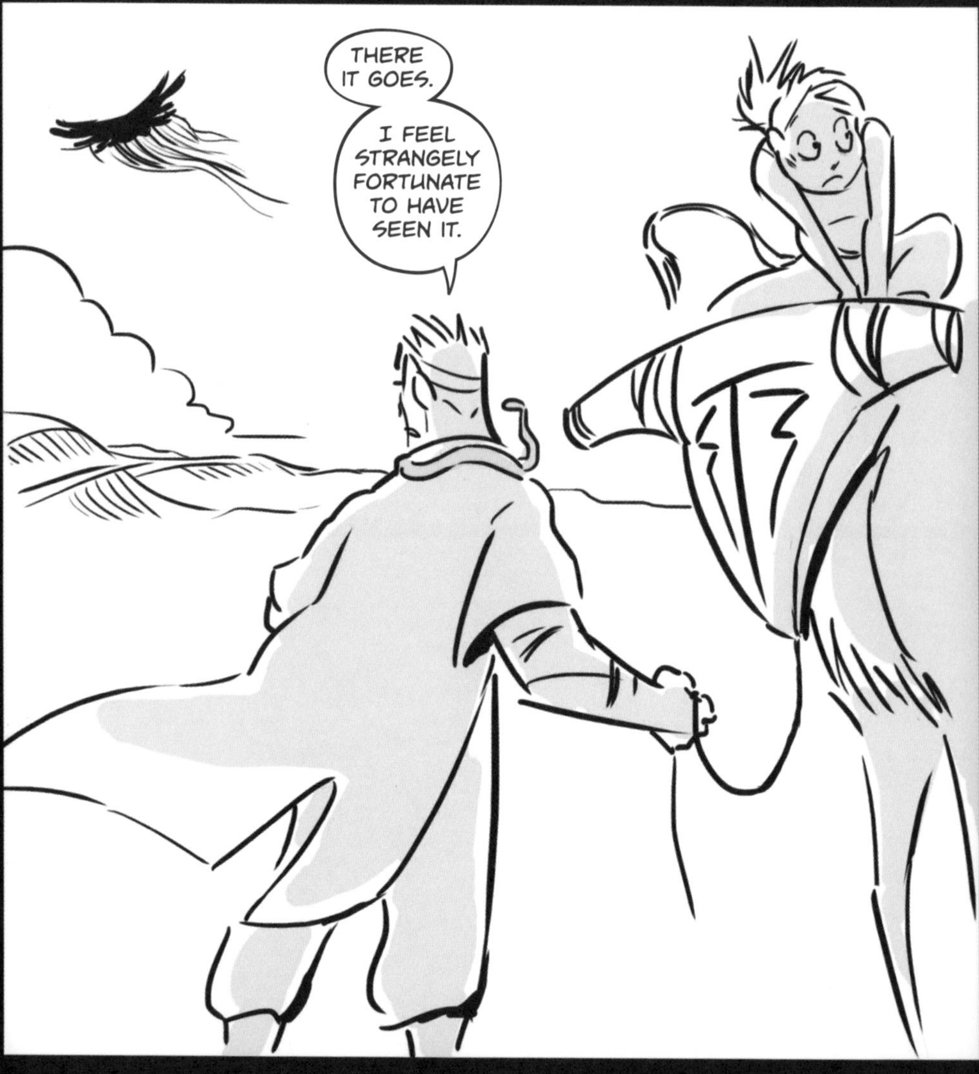
THERE IT GOES.
I FEEL STRANGELY FORTUNATE TO HAVE SEEN IT.

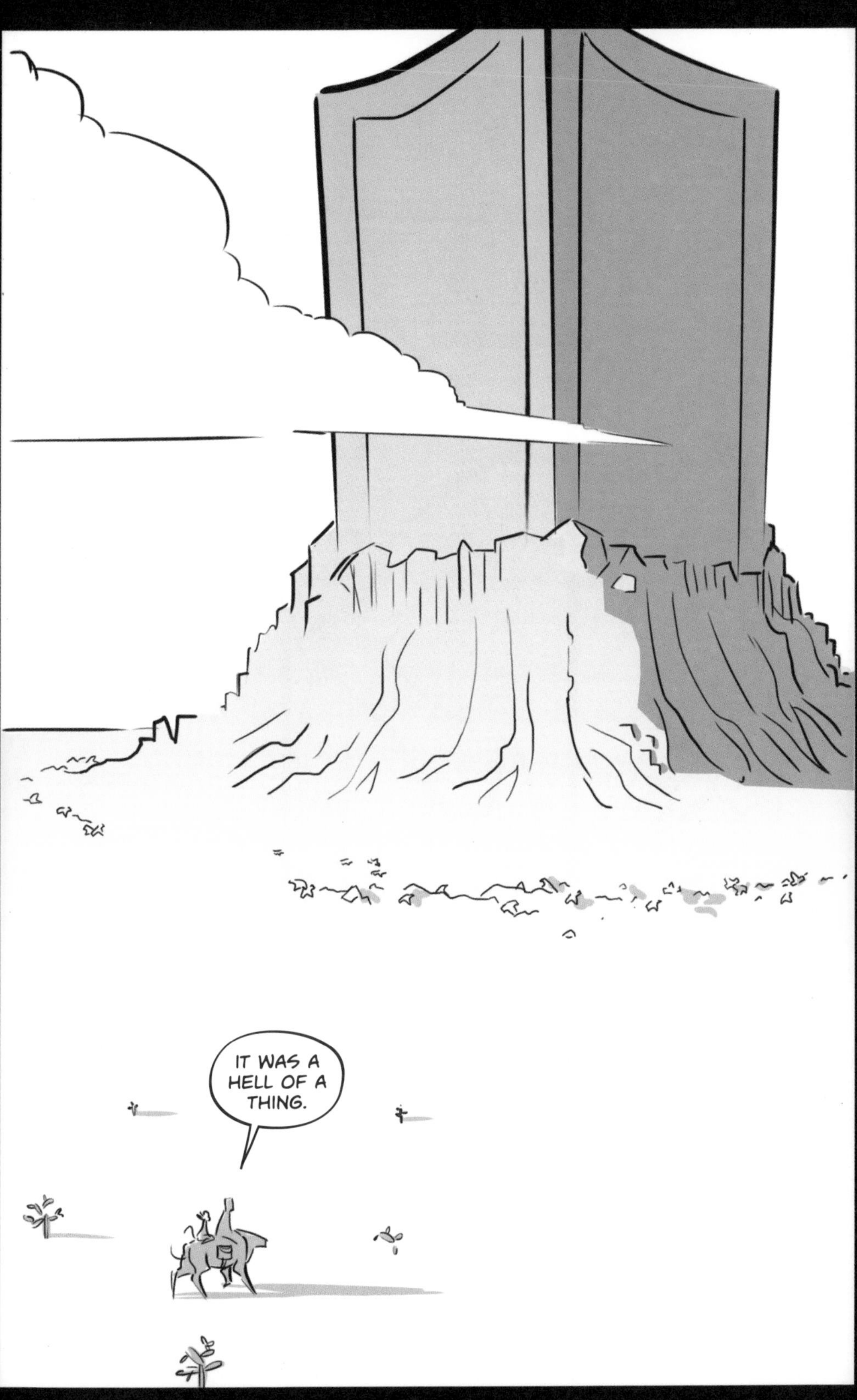
IT WAS A HELL OF A THING.

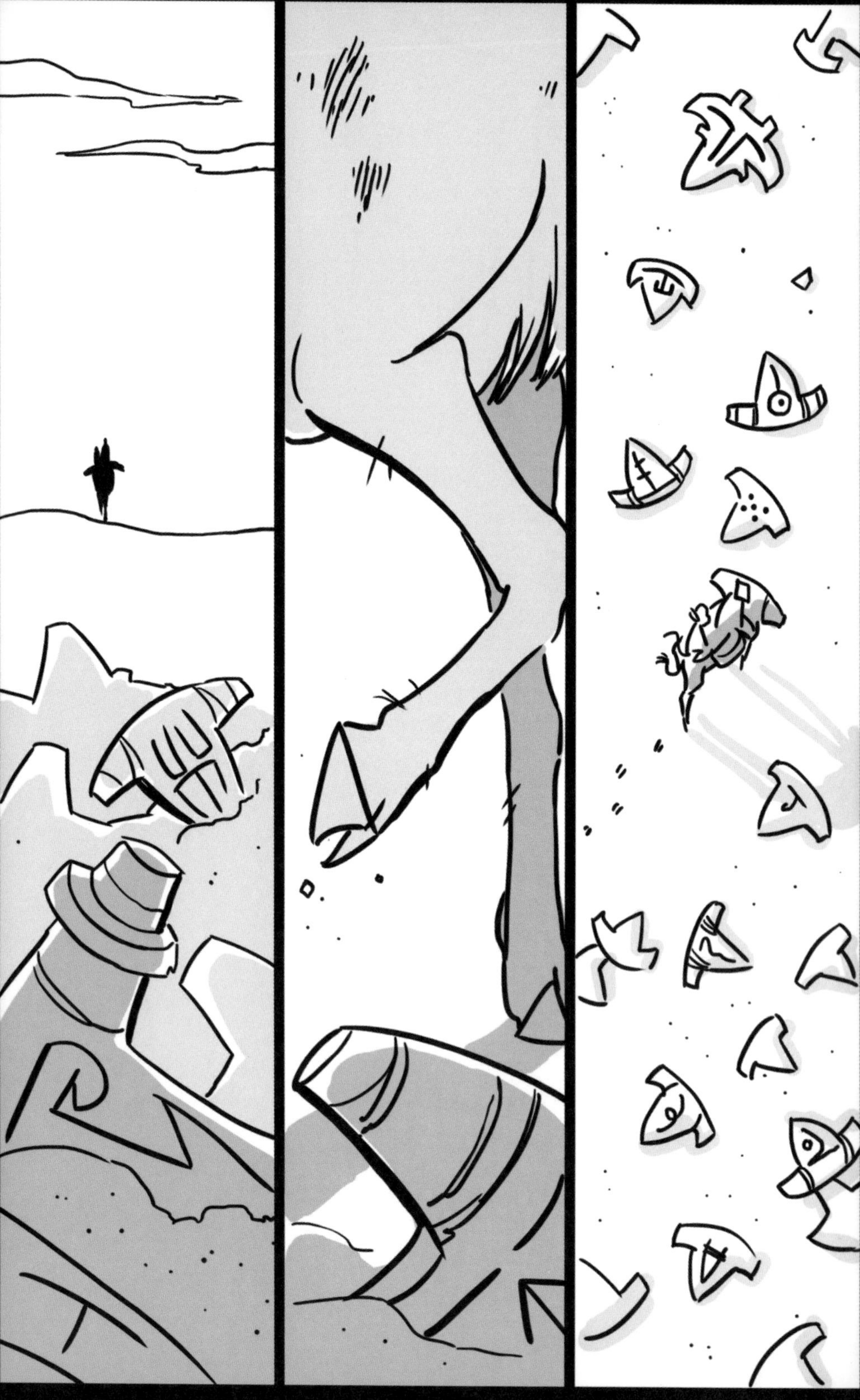

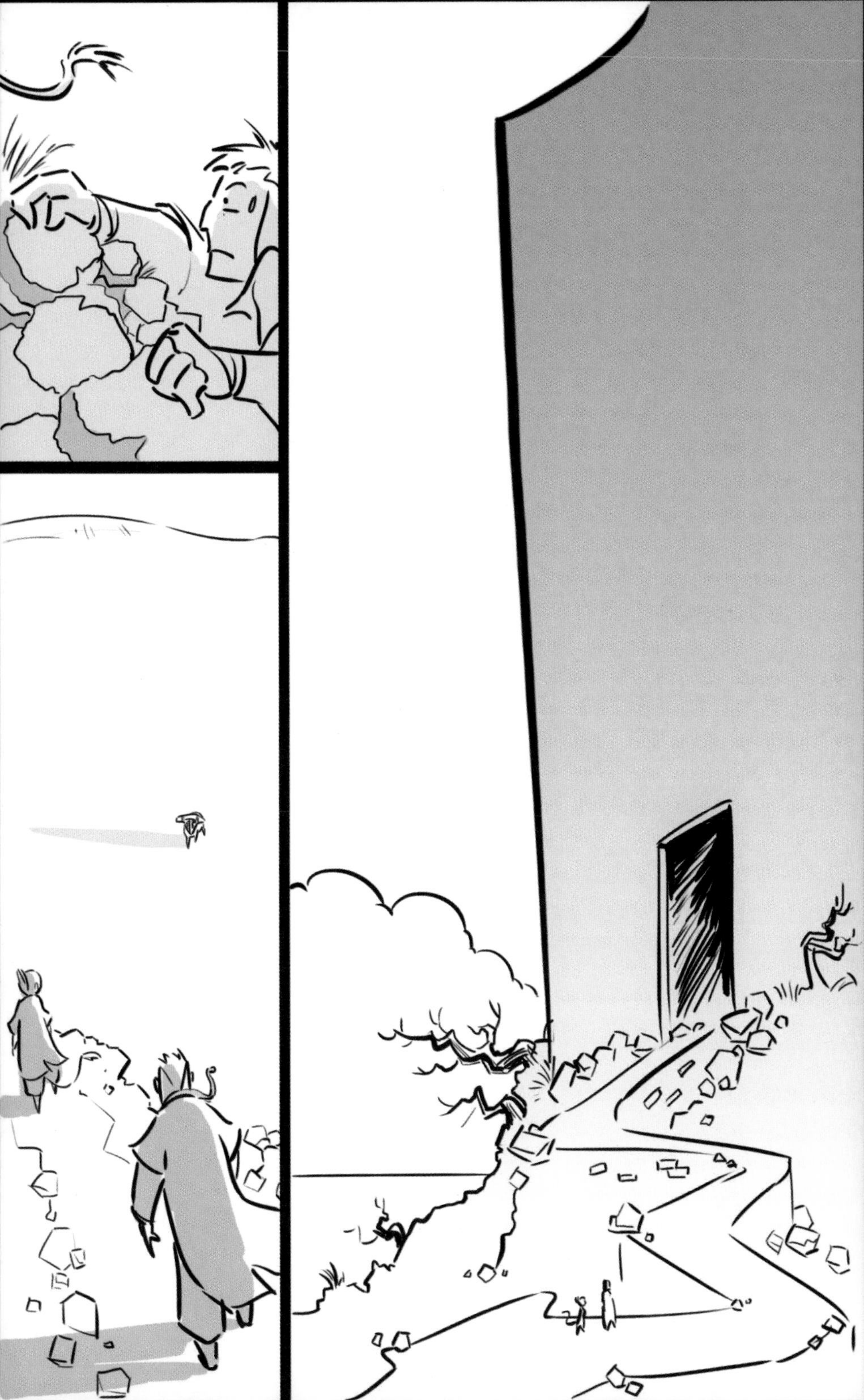

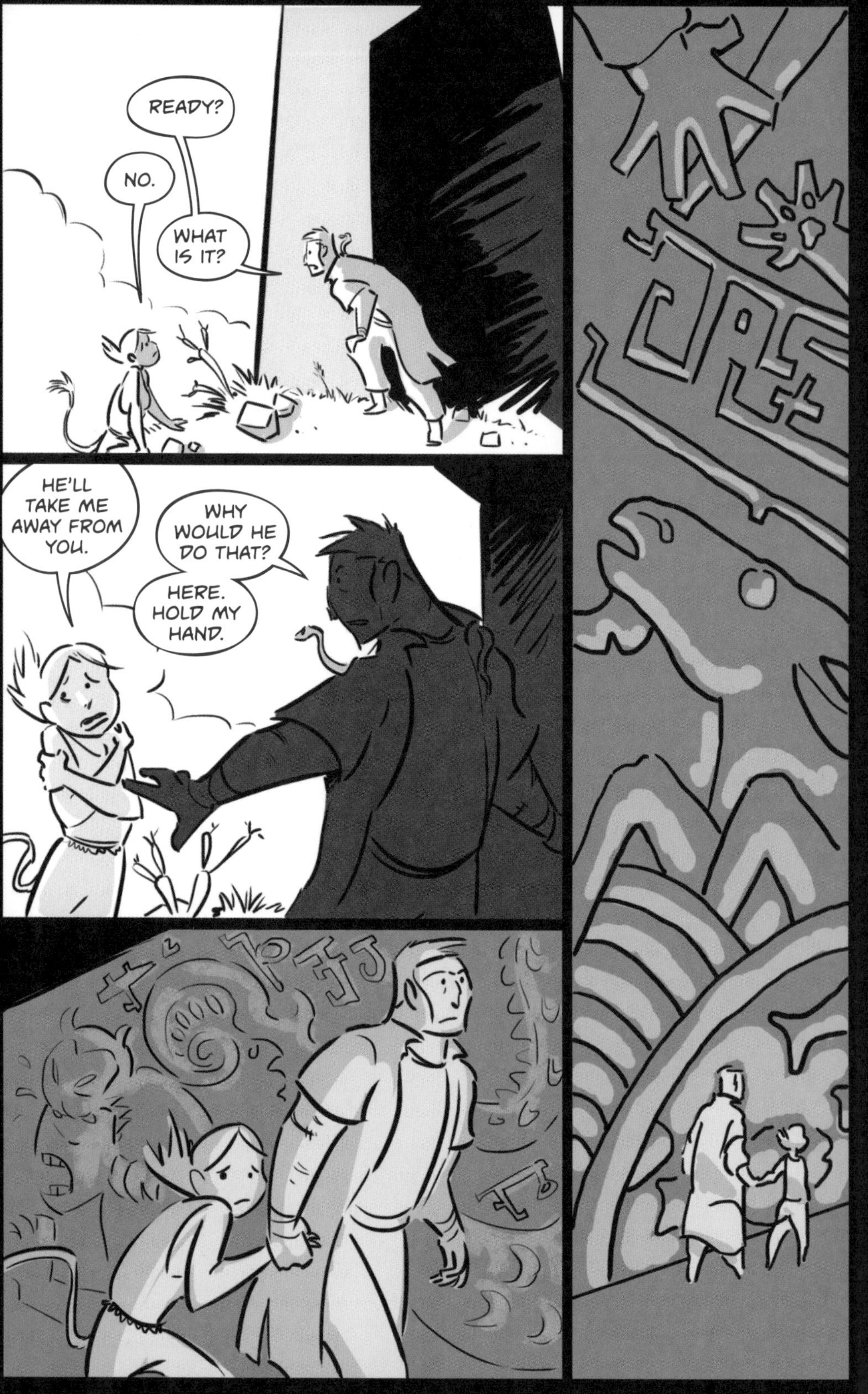

READY?
NO.
WHAT IS IT?
HE'LL TAKE ME AWAY FROM YOU.
WHY WOULD HE DO THAT?
HERE. HOLD MY HAND.

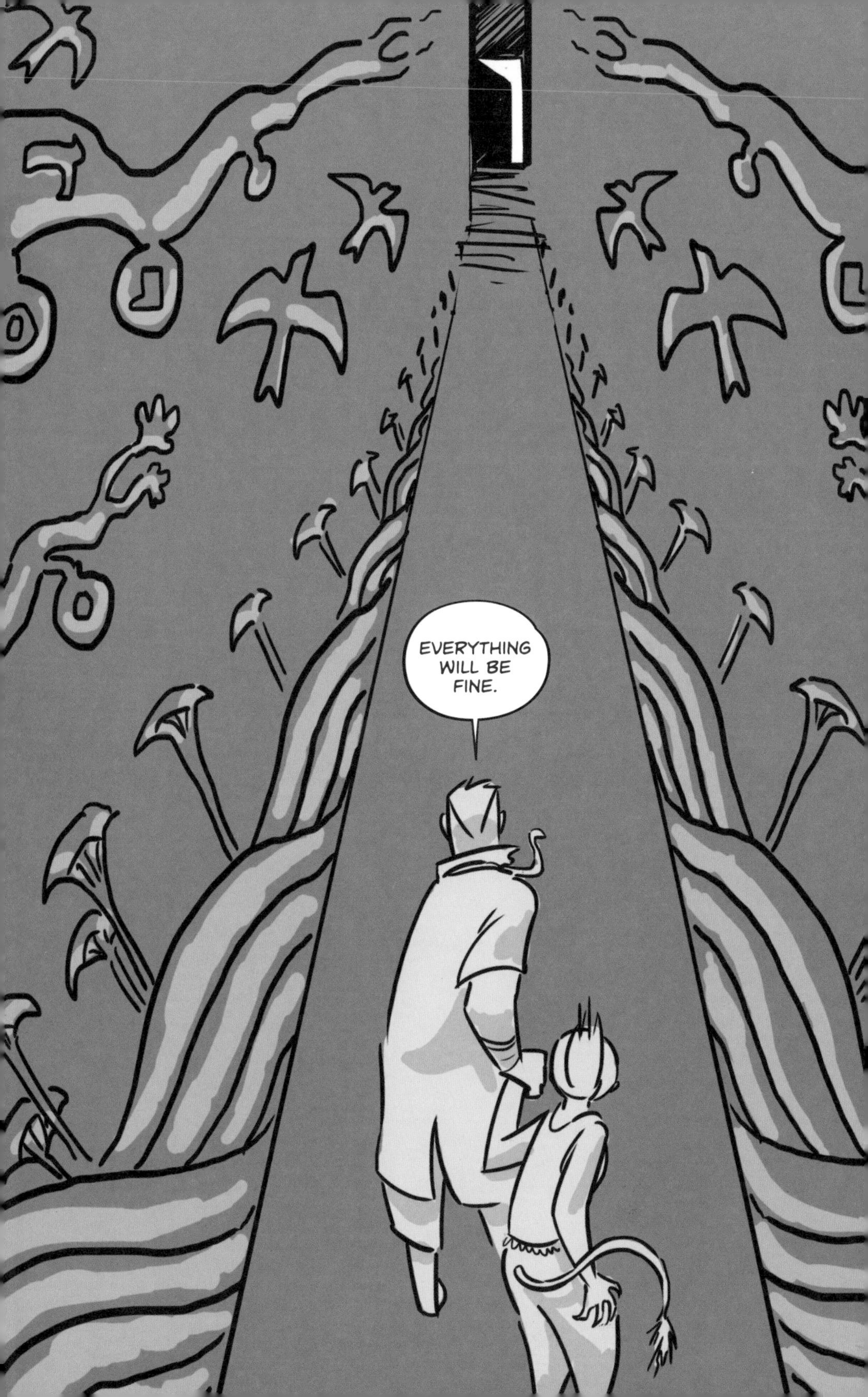
EVERYTHING WILL BE FINE.

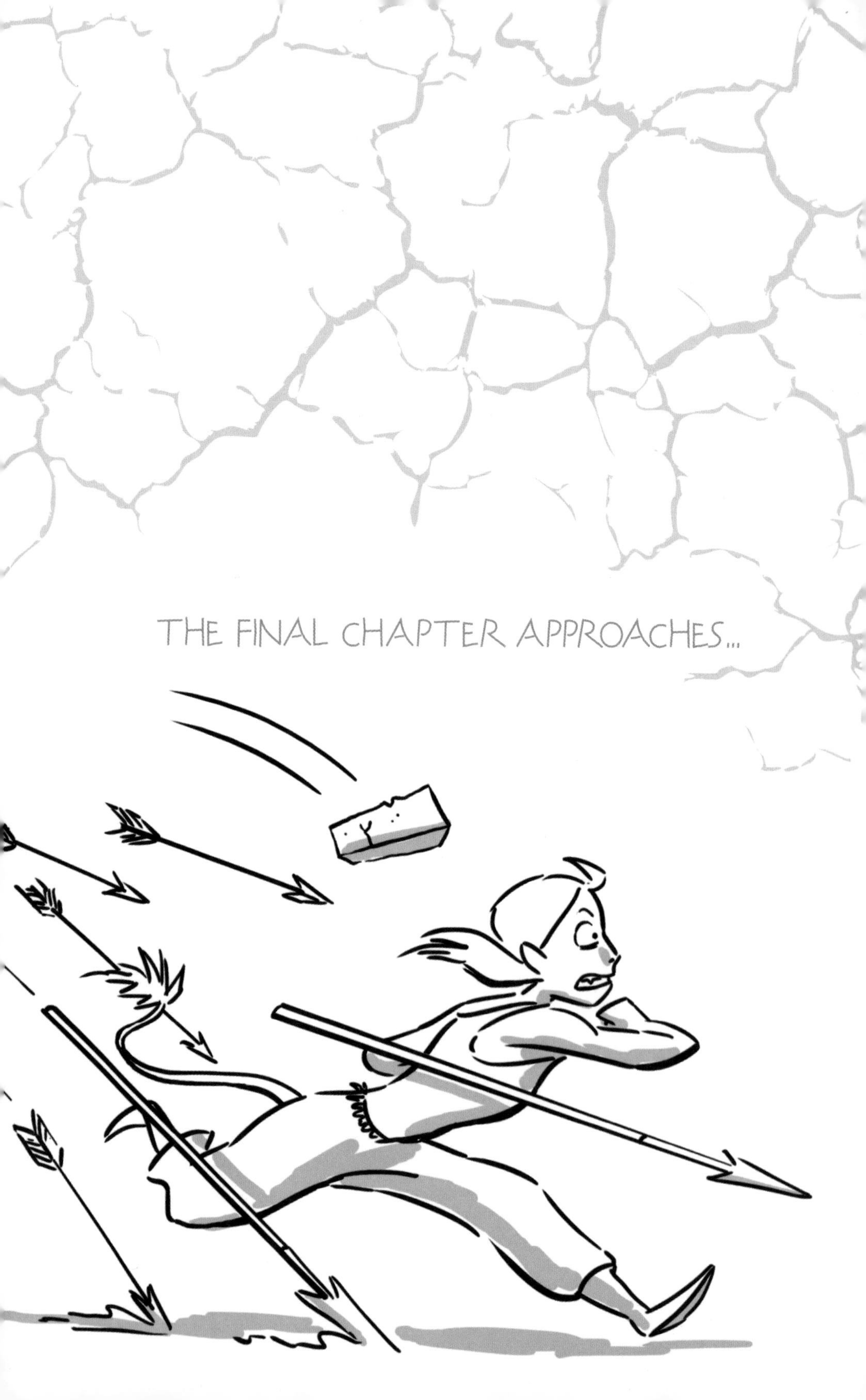
THE FINAL CHAPTER APPROACHES...

THE BROKEN WHEEL
COMING SOON...

# MORO ROGERS

MORO ROGERS LIVES IN EL SEGUNDO,
CA, WITH HER HUSBAND, JASON, AND
GOZER THE CAT.